THE
INNER
FIX

Be stronger, happier and braver

PERSIA LAWSON &
JOANNE BRADFORD

To you x

First published in Great Britain in 2016 by Yellow Kite
An imprint of Hodder & Stoughton
An Hachette UK company

1

A CIP catalogue record for this title is available from the British Library

Trade Paperback ISBN 978 1 473 62020 9
eBook ISBN 978 1 473 62021 6

Typeset in New Baskerville by Hewer Text UK Ltd, Edinburgh

Printed and bound by Clays Ltd, St Ives plc

Hodder & Stoughton policy is to use papers that are natural, renewable
and recyclable products and made from wood grown in sustainable
forests. The logging and manufacturing processes are expected to
conform to the environmental regulations of the country of origin.

Permission for Lyrics from *Give up and let it go* kindly granted by Francis Dunney

Hodder & Stoughton Ltd
Carmelite House
50 Victoria Embankment
London EC4Y 0DZ

www.hodder.co.uk

www.yellowkitebooks.co.uk

CONTENTS

JOIN THE ADDICTIVE DAUGHTER
COMMUNITY ONLINE

We've put together some free resources for you to use alongside this book. Join us online and go deeper with *The Inner Fix* work:

Download Our Free Meditations

Throughout the second section of this book, we share our own meditations that will guide and support your journey towards healing. These can be downloaded for free at www.theinnerfix.com

Listen to *The Inner Fix* Spotify Soundtrack

We've created a playlist for you to listen to as you work through *The Inner Fix*. Check it out over at www.theinnerfix.com

Access Videos, Interviews, Programmes, Articles and Community Over at www.addictivedaughter.com

We're always creating more resources and helpful tools to inspire and challenge ourselves and our community. Make sure you sign up at www.addictivedaughter.com to hear about our latest events, workshops and programmes.

Head to www.theinnerfix.com and use #InnerFix on social media to join in – we look forward to seeing you there.

Love,
Persia & Joey
xx

INTRODUCTION

'Life always waits for some crisis to occur before
revealing itself at its most brilliant.'

Eleven Minutes, Paulo Coelho

I n our respective bedrooms, we both have a slightly different
version of the same painting hanging on the wall. It shows a
middle-aged man carrying his young daughter in his arms.
She looks exhausted, dejected, broken, he – strong, steadfast,
benevolent; he is her last hope.

The painting is called *The Prodigal Daughter*, and was created
by our artist friend, Charlie Mackesy. Charlie painted it some
years ago for a friend of his who was going through a dark time
in her life. It was his way of trying to show her that she was not
alone, and that she was loved.

The image was inspired by the well-known parable of the
lost son, from the New Testament. If you aren't familiar with
the story, it begins with the younger of two sons asking his
father to give him his share of the estate on which they live. The
father agrees and divides the property. When the younger son

receives his money, he packs his belongings and leaves his father's house to travel across faraway lands.

While away, the son squanders all of his inheritance on living a wild and immoral life, until one day famine hits the country and he has no money left to live off. He doesn't go back home, assuming his father will have disowned him because of his shameful behaviour.

Instead, the son goes to work feeding pigs, but is given no food to eat and soon finds himself starving and desperate. Having hit rock bottom, he decides that his last resort is now his only option, so he swallows his pride and returns to his father's estate.

As he approaches the house, his father sees him from a long way off and runs to greet him with open arms, much to the son's surprise; the last thing he was expecting was for his father to actually be *happy* to see him, considering his wrongdoings. Yet, the father is so overjoyed that his youngest son has returned to him at last, that he calls for his servants to prepare the most exquisite of feasts to celebrate.

This story has become profoundly significant to us over the last few years. It mirrors our own personal experience of losing our way to a series of self-sabotaging and destructive choices, and slowly finding our way back to ourselves. In our lowest moments, it reminded us that no matter how far off the track we may have strayed, there was always the hope of a happier future. But, in order to get there, we first had to admit that we needed help, just like the son from the story.

Like us, you may have already undergone (or be in the midst of) your own personal crisis or 'dark night of the soul'; most humans inevitably experience one sooner or later. Whether you lost your way as a result of grief, heartbreak, substance abuse, depression, anxiety or anything else, it doesn't really matter; we believe there is a solution. This book is our attempt to demonstrate how it works.

We first met in our early twenties at drama school – a fragile and challenging period for the both of us due to the extremely competitive nature of the environment, and the physical and emotional demands it placed on its students.

Our friendship grew stronger when we graduated and were thrust out into the scary, uncertain world of work (or lack of, in our case), and we soon became each other's most supportive wing-woman.

While we shared a common predisposition to alcohol and unhealthy relationships with the opposite sex, we were very different people at our core. One of us strongly identified herself as a 'Sailor' character type – an extrovert who loved adventure, spontaneity and freedom, but also struggled with commitment, reliability and selfishness. The other was more of a 'Farmer' – an introvert who valued loyalty, stability and routine, but also had a tendency to control and micromanage the circumstances and people around her in order to feel safe.

The Sailor had had a painful and dysfunctional upbringing, as her parents were active drug addicts until her mid-teens. Yet, she was also raised with spirituality and religion as a normal part of life. The Farmer had enjoyed a more stable, happy childhood, and while faith in a religious sense was never explored at home, her parents had encouraged her to live by a set of moral and ethical principles.

Yet, despite having different personalities and life experiences, there was an unspoken bond of understanding between us, and by our mid-twenties we found ourselves in very similar places. It was a time when both of us were at the pinnacle of our unhappiness, and feeling more lost and alone than ever.

We'd grown up watching our parents' generation battling with their own issues – affairs, divorces, addictions, financial struggles and nervous breakdowns – often referred to as a 'mid-life crisis'. However, due to the rapid increase in the pace of modern life, it was no longer just the older ones struggling through a mental and emotional crisis of identity – it was us, too.

Like many of our friends, we'd been frantically devoting all our time and energy towards making our external lives look as good as we wanted them to feel. Was it any wonder, when the world around us fetishised the outer notions of beauty, fame and fortune, valuing such attributes far more than internal ones such as kindness, honesty and compassion? Not only that, but the growing impact of social media was beginning to make it incredibly difficult to keep up appearances.

Every day, we were being bombarded with the same message: that our worth was determined by our perceived value in the social marketplace. Followers and fans were our equity, and having more of them meant we were winning. Soon, we found ourselves meticulously curating every aspect of our lives – both on and offline – in a desperate bid to fit in. However, even when we successfully managed to make things look good on the outside, we still ended up feeling duped somehow, because this superficial validation failed to make up for our very real sense of emptiness.

Along with our peers, we did not grow up in an environment that encouraged us to express our pain in healthy ways. Britain, in particular, has a long-standing reputation for maintaining a 'stiff upper lip' in trying times – a reserved, stoical attitude when it comes to dealing with difficult emotions.

Any child who is not provided a healthy framework within which to process their pain is naturally going to develop all sorts of neuroses and insecurities as they attempt to transition into adulthood. Couple this with the added social pressures that insist on perfection and success above all else, and the premature arrival of a life crisis is not only probable, it is inevitable.

Feeling an enormous sense of urgency to 'make it' in both work and love before we were deemed too old and irrelevant, we desperately clung to relationships way past their sell-by dates, and, scrabbling to create a name for ourselves in the acting industry, we longed to have some form of significance in a world that was growing louder and more frightening by the minute.

We became increasingly anxious that we'd never have the success that we were assured would equate to happiness (or, if we did manage to get it, we feared we'd lose it). With every decision that we made, we panicked that the key to our fulfilment lay in one of the many options we hadn't chosen. We were depressed that others seemed to manifest the outer stamps of abundance – the relationship, the career, the money – so much more effortlessly than we could ever hope to. This in turn bred resentment and jealousy (which often disguised itself as sarcasm and superiority).

With mounting invitations to engagement parties and baby showers, it felt as though time was starting to run out. We knew that, on the one hand, we were hard-working, intelligent girls who were extremely fortunate in comparison to much of the world. Yet, we found ourselves on the brink of an existential crisis, wondering what the point of trying so hard was, if we were only going to die anyway.

We didn't really want to (or know how to) talk about our problems, so instead we numbed ourselves to the reality of them via the predictable refuges of sex, drink, drugs and shopping, clutching at fleeting moments of joy, which left as fast as they came.

We wished away our weekdays in eager anticipation of the weekend, our next holiday and a summer of festivals. These certainly did a great job of distracting us from how afraid and depressed we were feeling. But this solution was only ever temporary, because ultimately the things we were using to perk ourselves up were the very things that were bringing us down.

As soon as the sun came up and the party was over, we'd be chucked back into our realities, significantly poorer, our bodies and minds drained and depleted through excessive drink or drugs consumption, our souls a little saddened by the fact that we had no choice but to sit in our misery once more. So, we'd start eagerly planning and looking forward to the next time we could escape.

Soon, our gradual demise became a self-fulfilling prophecy; we were self-destructive because we felt bad about ourselves, and we felt bad about ourselves because we were self-destructive.

We were *just about* holding our lives together, however unmanageable they were starting to become. We were more or less making ends meet through sporadic acting work and our part-time jobs – even though the latter was making us miserable. We may have constantly struggled with our skin, weight and body image, but we didn't have full-blown eating disorders and, although we were consuming relatively high levels of intoxicating substances on a regular basis, we weren't physically addicted, so rehab wasn't a viable option. Essentially, *we weren't quite bad enough* to warrant any kind of intervention to force us to take action and change, so we just stayed stuck.

It didn't escape us that perhaps we were looking for a solution to our problems in all the wrong places. Not even *we* were naive enough to think that the answers we were searching for lay at the bottom of a bottle of wine or in the arms of a new lover. But, even when we did attempt to look for help from the magazine columns and other media we were consuming at the time, we were constantly told the same thing: that to be happier and build a better future for ourselves, we needed to start making better choices – do more exercise, cut out the junk food, get eight hours' sleep and end relationships that were bad for us. Which is, of course, exactly right. But what they failed to acknowledge is that it's very difficult to make better choices when you're a mess on the inside.

And that brings us to the message of this book – the solution that we'd been unconsciously seeking for decades: 'Focus on the insides, and the outsides will take care of themselves.'

What we didn't know when this advice was first given to us, is that it was to set in motion a chain of parallel events, experiences and much-needed life lessons, which began by us both independently exploring a healthier way of living through Twelve Step programmes.

A Twelve Step programme is a set of spiritual principles that provide a practical approach to dealing with problems such as alcoholism, drug, food, work and love addiction, and many more.

Alcoholics Anonymous (AA) was the first Twelve Step fellowship, and was founded in Ohio, America in 1935 by Bill Wilson and Dr Bob Smith. The original Twelve Steps were published in the 1939 book *Alcoholics Anonymous: The Story of How More Than One Hundred Men Have Recovered from Alcoholism.* This method was then adjusted and formed the basis for many other Twelve Step fellowships (of which there are currently over 200 different types worldwide).

These fellowships all share the same basic belief: that addiction of any kind – whether it's substance based, or more linked to codependency within relationships – is a kind of spiritual disease, a *dis-ease* of the soul. This results from acting out self-destructive patterns that get progressively worse over time, if not confronted. The solution, according to the Twelve Steps, must therefore be spiritual in nature, also.

Although we'd had very different upbringings, we found that the Twelve Step philosophy resonated with both of us in a profound way. After all, contrary to what the world around us had led us to believe, we weren't in crisis because we didn't have the career, the relationship or the body we desired – even celebrities at the height of their fame and success seemed to be falling apart in front of our eyes. We were in crisis because our obsession with attaining these outer things had left us emotionally and spiritually bankrupt.

Having dipped our toes into the world of self-help, it was not all that surprising that we both became drawn to and began relationships with two sober addicts who were in Twelve Step fellowships themselves.

However, in mid-2012, both boyfriends dumped us on the very same day. When we learned of our similar fates, we realised that we ultimately had two choices: go back to our old ways, or continue to forge ahead along this new spiritual path that we'd begun treading.

Armed with each other for mutual support (and the sense that the bizarre timing of our break-ups had to be more than a mere coincidence . . .) we opted for the latter. We decided to use all the addictive energy we'd previously directed towards obsessing over our relationships, to healing our insides through the tools and practices that are set out in this book.

Although the first few months of living in this new way were very challenging, before too long our entire outlook on the world (and ourselves) had changed almost beyond recognition. For the first time, we felt truly good about who we were, and where we were going.

This internal transformation was mirrored on the outside, too. We looked much healthier, found ourselves reconnecting to our creativity, and eventually began attracting attention from men who were much more emotionally available than our previous romantic partners had been.

After experiencing the extraordinary benefits of this new way of life, we felt inspired to share what we'd learned with the friends around us who also tended to gravitate towards drama and chaos. One thing led to another, and three months after our respective break-ups, Addictive Daughter was born with the intention of making the basic spiritual concepts and tools – that had helped us accessible, engaging and relevant to those that might not come into contact with them otherwise.

Today, we still experience our fair share of problems; life is still life, unpredictable and confusing at times. Being human, we *do* still make mistakes and revisit old patterns of self-destructive behaviour occasionally. The difference is that now we have a vast range of tools to help us manoeuvre our way through the lows so much faster. When we choose to use these tools, life begins to flow again, and when we don't, unsurprisingly, we find ourselves stuck once more. These tools are all of ours for the taking, but it's up to each of us individually to pick them up and put them into practice.

How This Book Works

Our goal with this book is not to tell you the specific details of how you should live your life – whether you should go teetotal, end a stressful relationship, or what exact diet and exercise plan you should take up. Our intention is to give you the opportunity to get to know yourself, to explore what you want out of life – and how you might go about making that happen in a way that works for you.

This book is divided into three parts, which each have five chapters for you to work through at your own pace. In order for the narrative and nature of the work to make sense, we would encourage you to read through this book chronologically first time around. You may want to revisit certain chapters in isolation at a later date.

The first section is all about becoming aware of your negative habits and patterns, and what lies beneath them.

The second will introduce you to the spiritual principles and tools that will help you begin the process of healing. These spiritual principles are predominantly (but not exclusively) based on Twelve Step philosophy.

The third part will guide you to take big action in all areas of your life, inspiring you to become the best possible version of yourself, inside and out.

Each chapter incorporates a relevant story from both of our lives, as well as insights and practical exercises to keep you moving forward. We've chosen to focus on some of the more extreme examples from our past in order to make the various chapter themes clearer. Our narratives may be far more, or far less, extreme than your own, but we urge you to look out for the similarities, not the differences. For example, you might not have had multiple one-night stands, blacked out from drinking too much or grown up around drug addiction, but you may relate to the feelings of loneliness, fear and resentment associated with these experiences. In other words, focus more on the emotions and thought patterns that speak to you, and less on the specific circumstances and situations.

Perhaps you're holding this book in your hands, eager to find another way, knowing for sure that your own stopped working some time ago. If that's the case, then you'll likely work through all the exercises first time round and see big change, fast – as we did.

Or, maybe, you've come to this book intrigued, but cynical, and not sure that you have all that much to inwardly examine. You might read through the chapters and develop some aware-ness about yourself, but are not quite ready to do all the written and practical exercises straight away – that's fine, too; this book may have come into your possession simply to plant a seed.

Whichever camp you fall into, our hope is that the coming chapters will at least cast some light on those areas that have so far been kept in the dark corners of your unawareness.

Don't be fooled, though. While the solutions in this book work, they are not a magic pill or a 'quick fix'. You're about to embark on a journey, a way of life. It's simple, but it's not easy, because it's so different from what most of us are used to. In fact, you could do the work in this book several times over, each time going in at a much deeper level.

Our main advice is just to *begin*. There's never going to be the perfect time to start this process, and you're not ever going to feel completely 'ready'. There will always be a reason to put it off until tomorrow and justify staying in your rut, because it's easier in the short term. Don't wait for your ducks to all be lined up in a neat little row; *start where you are*.

What You Need

We recommend getting yourself a journal that's big enough to write a fair amount in, but small enough to carry around with you. One of the main tasks in this book is regular writing exer-cises and we have found that these are most effective when hand-written. However, if a phone or tablet is more convenient for you, feel free to use that instead.

As well as answering the questions in each chapter, we encourage you to try and journal daily to keep a running document of your progress. Perhaps commit to writing two or three pages every morning while you work through this book, just noting down how you're feeling or what you're struggling with that day.

Another useful thing to do that will enhance your experience is to create a space for yourself where you can meditate, read, journal and have some quiet time – whether it's in your bedroom, or in a quiet corner of your living room or office. Make this space as comfortable and cosy as you can – use candles, cushions, pictures and anything else that helps you feel calm and relax.

Self-Care

If you find yourself in the midst of a life crisis of sorts, it's likely that you've been burning the candle at both ends when it comes to unhealthy habits. We'll be looking at this in more depth in the third section of the book. In the meantime, start to become aware of those habits and make it your intention to look after yourself as well as you can as you work through the chapters.

You'll probably find that a lot of feelings are going to come up that may be painful. In order to be able to face them head on – instead of numbing your pain with addictive vices – you need to be taking good care of yourself.

Make an effort to eat as healthily as possible and do some exercise throughout the week, as well as getting around seven to eight hours of sleep. Also, set the intention to do one loving thing for yourself each day, whether it's taking a bath, booking yourself a hair appointment, or getting an early night – whatever works for you.

A Final Note

The Chinese word for crisis is made up of two characters – one signifying 'danger' and the other 'opportunity'. As anyone who has successfully made it through their own 'dark night of the soul' will tell you, the only way out is through; sweeping things under the carpet and hoping that they disappear simply doesn't work.

Our twenties and thirties are the launch pad to the rest of our lives; the decisions we make in them *will* dramatically impact where we are in ten years' time. Doing this work now provides you with the opportunity to make some much-needed changes that your future self will thank you for.

Whatever difficulties any of us may have experienced over the years, we're ultimately all accountable for the choices we go on to make, and if we want to heal and improve our lives, the responsibility to do so lies solely with us.

Finally, you may perhaps feel that working through a book like this in order to make yourself feel better is both self-indulgent or narcissistic. Several of our life-coaching clients have told us that this was one of the reasons they put off asking for help for so long. We want to assure you that, in fact, the very opposite is true. You're of no service to the world when you're living from a place of unhappiness and self-destruction. You can't give what you don't have. If you really want to make a difference in the world, put your own oxygen mask on first, then you'll have far more energy and joy to share with others. As Shakespeare wrote, 'Self-love, my liege, is not so vile a sin, as self-neglecting.'

PART ONE

THE
PROBLEM

An old fable we love clearly demonstrates the idea of letting go of the things that hold us back. It describes how natives used to hunt monkeys in Indonesia. There are several different versions of the tale, but essentially the message is always the same: the key was to let the monkey catch herself.

The hunter would take a coconut and cut a small hole in the top of it, just big enough for a monkey to squeeze her little hand into. Then he would scoop out all the coconut-y goodness from inside and drop a pebble into the hole at the top. The hunter would place the coconut on the ground, and take cover in some nearby foliage, where he would wait for an unsuspecting monkey to wander into the trap.

The monkey would appear, pick up the coconut, shake it, and hear the pebble rattling around inside. She would peer into the hole: *I want that pebble*, the monkey would think. Then, as predicted, she would squeeze her little hand into the hole, and close her fist around the pebble.

The hunter knew that the monkey would never be able to get her hand out of the small hole as long as she clutched on to the pebble. Even when the huntsman came out to capture and kill the creature – who could not escape up a tree as long as she had the coconut stuck to her hand – it would never occur to the monkey that all she had to do to liberate herself, was to simply let go of the pebble.

The first part of this book focuses on what that pebble represents for you. Divided into five chapters – fear, control, shame, denial and resentment – we explore how each of these manifest in our thoughts, beliefs and actions, rippling outwards, creating waves through every area of our lives.

The concept of self-examination in order to identify one's shortcomings is nothing new in the world of spirituality. In Buddhism, it's mandatory for monks to confess any wrongdoing to their superiors, while confession is a well-known requirement in the Roman Catholic faith. The Twelve Step approach also encourages this identification of 'character defects', where an individual lists their mistakes and past hurts, before sharing and discussing them with someone they trust, who has worked through the Twelve Steps themselves.

It's important not to discard and minimise what has hurt us in the past. Often, by comparing our suffering to others we know, we feel that our own pales in comparison. Or, because our painful situation has now blown over, we believe it shouldn't affect us any longer. However, if something was traumatic at the time, it will keep coming up until it's properly processed. And if it isn't worked through, it will continue to affect us adversely.

In Greek tragedy, the noun 'hamartia' is used to describe a protagonist's tragic flaw, which leads to their ultimate destruction. This flaw ensures that the character's plot culminates in the reversal from good fortune to eventual downfall.

In many instances, we witness a character's hamartia play out as pride or inflated ego – in being too proud to ask for help, admitting they may be wrong, or shunning that quiet, knowing voice of their soul. In exactly the same way, *we* also have character defects, often manifesting as a particular area of struggle that shows up *time and time again* for us.

In whatever way this outer struggle may present itself, whether it's attracting dysfunctional lovers, drinking too much, shopping, always being broke, pornography, disordered eating, being addicted to drama, people-pleasing or anything in between, it's actually all one and the same. Our *external* realities and the way we experience life are a consequence of our *internal* thoughts.

Our individual ability to make positive decisions is in direct proportion to how mentally and emotionally healthy we are, as we act in accordance with our belief system. When we're in a state of crisis, it's inevitable that our belief system is going to be negative and self-defeating if we are not internally healthy, and so too will our actions be.

This is where our ego often starts to whisper . . . *Oh, I'm not that bad, I'll grow up and grow out of these habits,* or even, *This is just the way I am – there's no changing it now.* Since our thoughts inform our choices, habits and wider reality, without intervention, things slowly and insidiously grow more extreme. That, we can almost guarantee.

At this point, we ask only that you keep an open mind. The reality is that investigating the more negative parts of self that you may not yet be aware of, are perhaps reluctant to own (or doubt you're able to change), takes courage. Part one of the book is going to invite you to take a look at your innermost thought processes: the internal blocks that are keeping you stuck.

We are the way we are because of our history. Each of us has wreckage from our past to clear, and, in order to do that, awareness is key. Only then can we move towards a place of acceptance and, further, begin to take the action to work through it. It's no good trying to quit external behaviours until we understand, on a very personal level, the *why* behind the things we do. Acknowledging our weaker spots or failings is not intended to make us feel bad or guilty; it's actually about setting ourselves free.

Don't expect to acquire all the answers in this section, since its primary aim is for self-reflection. Working through these chapters is about understanding yourself more fully, in preparation for the solution laid out in the following two sections of this book.

Our hope for you is that you decide to approach these topics bravely, with a willingness to discover things previously unseen. Some of part one will undoubtedly feel heavy, and you may well experience overwhelm and a reluctance to continue. Our advice is to *keep on* anyway, especially when you feel resistance.

CHAPTER I

FEAR

Persia

'No one ever told me that grief felt so like fear.'

A Grief Observed, C.S. Lewis

It's the week before Christmas, and I'm stood on the stage at the front of my primary school's local church in south-west London, about to start singing the 'Once in Royal David's City' solo. This is a real achievement, as not only is it the most highly revered role in Lake Hill School's annual carol service, but I've somehow managed to win it over my best friend Salena, who's pipped me to the post every single year since we can both remember.

Salena and I have always been competitive with each other – probably because we've more or less been brought up as sisters. Her parents own the stables where I ride on the weekends, and spending so much time together inevitably means that, as much as we love one another, we also can't stand each other. Maybe it's because we're so similar – feisty, bossy and used to being top dog in social situations. However, with her long, thick hair and big brown eyes, I've always been secretly afraid that she's much prettier than I am. This is why I'm so happy that it's me standing front and centre stage today, not her.

As I wait for the piano cue from our singing teacher, Mrs Rooney, I glance towards the back of the church, certain that I'll see my parents slip in any moment now, flustered and out of breath from rushing to make my performance on time.

The doors remain closed for the rest of the service.

When it's over, and I've said goodbye to my friends and teachers, I leave the church and take my big red Sony Walkman out of my rucksack. Placing the earphones over the top of my bobble hat, I press play and begin the five-minute walk to my family's terraced house through the grizzly mid-December afternoon. 'A Little Fall of Rain' from my *Les Misérables* cassette begins to play.

As I arrive outside my front door, I brace myself, anxious as to what scene might lie the other side of it. I put my key in the lock, turning up the volume on my Walkman as I do so. I open the door to find that all the lights are off. Creeping up the stairs, I glance into the living room on the first floor to see my mum asleep on the sofa. The TV is blaring, but I don't hear what's on because of Jean Valjean's voice booming through my headphones.

Dad appears to be out, and my big sister and baby brother don't seem to be here, either. I let out a sigh of relief and quietly make my way up to my room.

While my life may look like that of your average suburban nine-year-old, the reality is that my parents are high-functioning drug addicts. I don't really understand what that means at this time. I just know that something feels very, very wrong at my home – and I think some of it might be my fault.

Mum and Dad met on a houseboat in Amsterdam when he was nineteen, and she in her early twenties. Both kindred spirits that had run away from their own troubled upbringings, they were each looking for an escape – and the hedonistic backdrop of 1980s Amsterdam was it.

Mum was a headstrong punk model with multicoloured hair and a bulldog named Too Bad, and a kitten called Cliché and Dad a mischievous young traveller who'd got mixed up in selling drugs after falling in with the wrong crowd.

She first realised she was in love with Dad when, on returning to their friend's houseboat after a three-day bender to discover the cat's food bowl was crawling with maggots, Dad picked it up and disposed of both bowl and surrounding maggots like it was no big deal. Mum said she'd never met anyone so manly before, and within a few months, they'd opened their own punk clothes shop in the heart of Amsterdam.

Falling pregnant with my sister, they swiftly returned to London, got married and moved into their first flat, while Mum worked various part-time jobs and Dad began forging himself a career in property. Eighteen months after the birth of my sister, I showed up.

No stranger to risk-taking, Dad soon started his ascent up the property ladder, despite having only one O level to his name. But, just as Dad's career is progressing, so too is both my parents' substance abuse. Mum's also going through chemo after contracting hepatitis C from a blood transfusion, so spends much of her time asleep in the living room.

In the words of Oscar Wilde's Lady Bracknell, 'To lose one parent . . . may be regarded as a misfortune; to lose both looks like carelessness'. Having two parents so unavailable does feel unfortunate, and it does feel like a loss – a profound one; I miss them both terribly.

For much of my early childhood, I've been confused as to why I feel so afraid of being at home, where there is an ever-present feeling of tension in the air. It's as though we're all living inside a pot of boiling water, and the pressure could blow the lid off at any moment.

My parents never really say it out loud, but I know that I'm not supposed to tell anyone what's going on behind closed doors, and I rarely ever invite friends over. Life here feels like one big secret, shrouded in uncertainty and sadness. Although I'm never neglected physically, the emotional abandonment my siblings and I undergo feels just as painful as if we were.

So, for the past couple of years I've spent the majority of my time at Salena's parents' stables and home, leaving my sister Evie to bear the brunt of looking after our baby brother, Toby. This makes me feel really guilty, but it's the lesser of two evils and I don't know what else to do.

Evie's the rebellious sister with the huge heart, I the achiever – selfish, but successful. While Evie puts everyone else before herself, my first instinct is always self-preservation.

I seek refuge from the frequent fights in the house in any way I can, scrupulously crafting my very own fantasy land to drown out the pain of my real one. The moment I hear so much as a raised voice, out comes the Sony Walkman and *Les Misérables*. In my short little life span, I've become an expert at hiding and isolating whenever I feel unsafe.

A born perfectionist, I also spend an abnormal amount of time studying for tests and exams – often until the early hours of the morning. It's not uncommon for my bedroom walls to be plastered from top to bottom with Post-it Notes, mind-maps and diagrams – much like the bulletin board for evidence in a detective's office.

Studying at least brings me some much-needed validation: the year after I win the 'Once in Royal David's City' solo, I stay up all night revising for weeks and get 100 per cent in my history exam on the Normans, an achievement I go on to mirror some years later when I come joint top in the country in my English Literature GCSE while my dad's in rehab. But, the recognition and praise I garner from my parents as a result is always short-lived, and they soon retreat back into their own fantasy land.

Rowdy parties have become quite commonplace in our home. My sister and I know all the words to Haddaway's 'What Is Love' – mainly because everyone's too drunk to change the CD, so it just plays the same few tracks again and again.

Recently, I've got very addicted to telling lies to Salena and the rest of my school friends – stupid ones, like I've appeared in *Joseph and the Amazing Technicolor Dreamcoat* in the West End and I have a boyfriend in Ireland. I want my friends to feel as jealous of me as I do of them.

Although I am a wallflower at home, desperate to be invisible amidst the chaos, outside of it I'm a full-blown drama queen and attention seeker. I thrust myself onto any stage that will have me, determined to be the best at every pursuit I try my hand at. I constantly measure my accomplishments up against those of my peers; when I 'win', this satisfies my ego's need to feel superior, but when I don't, my biggest fear is confirmed: that I'm neither good enough, nor loveable.

I'm bad, I'm bad, I'm bad, my subconscious tells me whenever things are rough at home and Evie steps up, and I check out. Pretty soon, this becomes a self-fulfilling prophecy and I start to behave very badly towards those I love the most.

Joey

'We can easily forgive a child who is afraid of the dark; the
real tragedy of life is when men are afraid of the light.'
Plato

'SHE'S AN ANGEL, BUT SHE SINS SOMETIMES, DRESSED
IN WHITE, GETS DRUNK ON RED WINE . . .'

We sing at the top of our lungs on the ride home from
school. Kristen and I know every beat and every word of every
song from the *Alisha Rules the World* album and we belt it out
in her white Volvo 440, with windows down and manual
sunroof ajar.

Kristen looks just like me. She is fair and freckly, with blue-
green eyes and blonde-flecked hair. In my mind, she is the
epitome of cool. She's my go-to advice source when conflict
arises with classmates (which is often – I'm a strong-willed kid).
I love that she always knows exactly what to say and I soak it all
up, word for word, ready to relay it to the offending party the
following day at school.

I am seven and Kristen, nineteen. That would make her an
extremely young mother if I were her own. I haven't really
thought this through – and clearly neither have any of my classmates – who've totally bought into the story that Kristen is my
mum. After all, she's the face at the school gates every day, the
one who feeds me, washes and irons my stuff, the one I share
all my school-day sagas with. It doesn't feel like *so* much of a lie
but, of course, if we're being black and white about it, it isn't
strictly true either. I actually have a wonderful mum and dad of
my own, who love me very much. Kristen is my full-time nanny;

my two-year-old sister and I have had several nannies and child-minders over the years, since both my parents work demanding jobs that often require travel.

My dad was born and raised in Zimbabwe, only moving to England after he graduated from university in South Africa to escape the pressures of apartheid and seek a new life across the ocean. He is one of the most relaxed people you'll ever meet ('So relaxed he's practically horizontal', Mum often says), yet when he loses it, he *really* loses it. When Dad goes from mellow to monster, you really don't want to be on the receiving end of it. We both possess a fiery stubbornness that, thankfully, only surfaces once in a blue moon. Mum, on the other hand, is far less Zen when it comes to day-to-day living. Always frantically busy, she's the hard worker and eternal worrier of the family, never managing to sit down, and yet somehow always available to anyone in need of her support. She's an unusual mixture of ruthlessly determined and nurturing, and in years to come I will grow to be very like her in my desire to control and fix other people (generally for their greater good, in our defence).

Both my parents came from humble beginnings, Dad as the only child of his parents out in Africa, where, as my grandma likes to reminisce, they 'used to sell their clothes in order to eat'. Meanwhile Mum, who was raised by working-class parents near Manchester, was awarded an academic scholarship at her local grammar school and hustled her way to success, eventually leaving university with top grades. Both my parents arduously climbed the corporate ladder over the years at the same company, paving the way for the comfortable family life they envisioned.

Before meeting Dad, Mum was in an on-off relationship with a man only ever referred to these days as 'John Smith' (she's always refused to reveal his true identity, lest I search for him on the internet). John Smith was a typical loveable rogue – a heavy boozer, pothead and womaniser – who early on had given Mum a torn but handsome photograph of himself in a white suit. She spent several chaotic years with John Smith, but knew he was no good for her, once pleading with a close girl-friend over a glass of red, '*Never* let me marry that man'. In hindsight, that would've proved difficult, since John Smith was married to someone else all along – the picture he'd given her was in fact half of his wedding photograph, ripped down the middle.

On a holiday abroad with a group of mutual friends from work, Mum and Dad's worlds collided and, although both in rela-tionships at the time, Dad promptly dumped his current squeeze and Mum ended things with John Smith for good. My parents have been the best of friends and happily married ever since.

Anyway, back to me. My favourite film, to date, is *Harriet the Spy*. In it, the lead character, Harriet, is also very attached to her nanny, Ole Golly. The story touches me at my core. I see myself in Harriet – particularly as, like me, she's a girl who finds comfort in the structure and certainty of things. She refuses to eat anything but tomato sandwiches. I get this – not her taste in sandwiches so much, but her yearning for the familiar.

> **Harriet M. Welsch:** How long have you known me, Golly?
> **Ole Golly:** Since you were born. That's 11 years and 12,000 tomato sandwiches ago.
> **Harriet M. Welsch:** And you'll never leave me, right?
> **Ole Golly:** Well I won't *leave you* leave you, but one day you'll be old enough and . . . well, old enough to take care of yourself and when that day comes you won't need me around anymore. But *that* day is not *today.*

I relate to Harriet to such an extent that I've appointed myself as chief spy of my own village, where I live in the north of England, and I take my neighbourhood-watch duties *very* seriously. Through practice, I've become a highly skilled tree-climber and often break into neighbours' gardens to eavesdrop on their conversations. Dad has helped me to construct a spy belt (just like Harriet's) and I too have my own spy book. In it, *I write down everything I see.*

My upbringing is stable and full of love, and yet, I am an intense and sometimes angry child. I prefer to keep my bedroom curtains closed during the daytime and, much to Mum's dismay, my wardrobe is comprised of almost entirely black clothing. I fixate on things often, things that I feel empathetic towards. When I do, my head's consumed with little else.

'Really Jo, you're getting *obsessive* now, please stop,' Mum will plead.

But it's just the way my mind works; some things take a strong hold of my headspace. On a lighter note, I'm currently devoted to all things Forever Friends, which is reflected strongly in my choice of bedroom decor; everything is on theme. Forever Friends bedcover, pillows, curtains, photo frames, wall art and pyjamas – my room's like a museum for it. My fascinations and compulsions manifest in many ways. Not long ago, Kristen and I made homemade chocolate liqueurs for Father's Day and, finding them moreish, I sat by the fridge where they were on trays cooling and ate my way through the entire lot. Not surprisingly, she refused to help me make another batch.

Sitting on the ledge of my bedroom window, I clasp my half of the Forever Friends heart necklace that Kristen gave me as a gift some months ago. She has the other half of the heart but

I notice she doesn't wear hers nearly as much as I do mine. Dad *hates* me sitting up here. I've often asked him whether, if I fell from the windowsill by accident, I would die. He thinks not. I'm not so sure though, from up here the hard stone of the patio below looks menacing. I suppose today is the day we'll find out.

The worst bit in *Harriet the Spy* is when Ole Golly decides to leave Harriet. Last night, Mum broke the news that Kristen is doing an Ole Golly on me. As usual, Kristen picked me up from school today and I've retreated up to my room in silence, leaving her downstairs in the kitchen with my baby sister. While I am aware that even having a nanny puts my family in a very privileged light, when you take a step back, what you're left with is a little girl who grows attached to people who sooner or later disappear.

Harriet M. Welsch: Are you gonna go be some other kid's nanny now?

Ole Golly: And love them more than you? Never. Remember in my life, in this world, there will always only be one Harriet.

I lean as far as I can out of my window without losing balance, surveying the ground beneath me. Do I count to three? Close my eyes? I definitely want to be found with this necklace in my hand – that way Mum and Kristen will know the cause of my agony. I pull myself back on the ledge slightly and interlace the chain more firmly between my fingers. No chance of it separating from me now. I shuffle forwards again, my heart pounding loudly in my chest. With my eyes closed, I begin to count silently in my head, *One, two . . . three . . .* I'm still here. Five, I'll go on five. *Four*, I squeeze my eyes tight . . . *fi—*

'JO?' Kristen yells from the bottom of the stairs. 'TEA'S READY.'

I must have been holding my breath, as my chest's bursting. I exhale heavily and open my eyes. I am actually quite hungry . . . I cautiously swivel my legs round back into my room, hop down from the window ledge, and head to the kitchen for dinner.

You

'We are more often frightened than hurt; and we suffer more from imagination than from reality.'
Seneca

From an early age, most of us are encouraged to become self-reliant, guided by the notion that self-will is needed for survival. By this point in our lives, however, many of us will have discovered that there's a limit to the personal power we've come to depend upon. Most likely, experience will have shown us by now that we don't *always* get to dictate how life unfolds, and that can be a frightening realisation.

Growing up, a lot of us will have experienced dysfunction in the family home or at school, anything from divorce, addiction, bullying to abuse, loss or abandonment. There are others of us who've had relatively smooth childhoods, but have faced challenges during our teens and early adult years. By this point, life will probably have thrown a few curveballs our way: we failed to land that dream job we believed was meant for us, our 'one' did not love us in return, or a friend was tragically taken away, far too young.

Whatever path we've walked so far, the fact is that, the majority of us will have developed coping mechanisms to protect those places inside of us that have been hurt in the past. What else are we expected to do when the world has proved itself to be unpredictable? When our belief is that things are *not* going to be OK? Unsurprisingly, we turn to the behaviours we know best, whether that be running away, clinging on tighter, manipulating, hiding, denying, lying, threatening, blaming or playing the victim – anything to help us cope and protect ourselves from more pain.

When these behaviours are left unchecked, we often find ourselves in a state of dis-ease and look to quick fixes to settle the anxiety we feel. We may make rash decisions, and use the temporary plasters of alcohol, drugs, sex, shopping and the like to distract ourselves from our discomfort. The more we anaesthetise in this way, the more we rely on these things to make us feel anything at all, finding ourselves trapped in a cycle of fear and destructive behaviour. What we sometimes neglect to consider is whether our coping strategies are *serving* us or whether they are taking us to new, darker depths.

The fear thoughts residing in our heads are often the result of our 'ego' running riot. In the fields of self-help and spirituality, the term 'ego' is frequently used to describe our sense of personal identity and self-worth. Every person's ego is different, and although the ego tends to be associated with being overbearing, prideful and self-important, it actually possesses the extreme opposite qualities in equal measure: it is also shy, lacking in confidence and full of self-pity. Our ego loves to add fuel to fear thoughts, drowning out the voice of reason that all of us have access to deep down.

The majority of what we fear *hasn't actually happened yet.* Something similar may have happened in the past, prompting us to feel afraid that it might happen again, but what we currently feel fear over has usually not yet occurred. When we are living in fear that it will, we're not living in the present. Almost all fear is a result of focusing on the future – of anticipating outcomes ahead of time.

When we stop and examine what evidence there is to justify our fears, we tend to struggle to identify anything palpable at all. There is a well-known acronym that sums this up perfectly: False Evidence Appearing Real. We may feel convinced that our lover is going to betray us, even when there are no hard facts to suggest that this will be the case. Ironically, the more we behave *as if* it were true, the less healthy our relationship becomes – potentially making our fear a self-fulfilling prophecy.

The fear we experience tends to be the consequence of deeply engrained primary fears from our past, which are triggered by something in our present. The most important thing to identify, therefore, is *why* we're feeling afraid, and to understand this we must look to the root of our fears. Our past is a powerful tool in understanding our current struggles, and can help us to identify what's keeping us stuck.

This chapter requires you to look closely at the thoughts you're choosing. In facing your fears and what thoughts you are entertaining, you get to refocus and consciously choose again, in order to experience different results.

The exercises below will help you to recognise the root of your personal fears and develop your awareness around what triggers fear within you. In becoming skilful in using your mind, you can expect to become less anxious, and instead: clearer, happier and better connected to both yourself and the people around you.

EXERCISES

In your journal:

1) List the most painful/frightening/significant things that happened during your childhood and early years.

2) Draw out a grid in your journal and write down your biggest fears. The aim is to make the connection between where you think each stems from and what can trigger that particular fear in you today. You may want to leave space below your grid, to add to it any other fears you identify as you work through the book.

FEAR	CAUSE	TRIGGER
1. *People not liking me/ sensing that I'm being pushed out.*	*Getting bullied at school. Being excluded in the playground and not being invited to birthday parties, etc.*	*When my work colleagues forget to invite me to lunch.*
2.		

3) What things outside of yourself do you reach for to feel better? e.g. Compulsive shopping to distract myself, drinking heavily to numb my heartbreak.

CHAPTER 2

CONTROL

Joey

'He who controls others may be powerful, but he
who has mastered himself is mightier still.'

Lao Tzu

'm feeling euphoric. Fourteen years old and here I am, in the
middle of the dance floor at the local nightclub in town. I
haven't acquired a fake ID (yet) but tonight I manage to slip
through the net by walking in with an older-looking crowd.
The interior is all red cheap leather sofas, wall-to-wall mirrors
and disco balls reflecting light from every angle. This is my first
experience of being able to walk up to a bar and order whatever I want and, aware I might not get another opportunity for
quite some time, I'm taking full advantage.

Tonight is one of many nights to come where I may seem
coherent, but I'm actually fairly far gone. I don't display signs
of extreme inebriation – I'm perhaps louder and slightly more
outrageous than usual, but I blend in with ease among the
other swaying bodies on the dance floor. There's no doubt that

I'm the youngest in here by a mile. Liberation. I'm a child in an adults' world and it feels new and exciting. Creating 'shit mixes' with school friends and glugging away from plastic bottles outside our local memorial hall teen disco is now dead and gone, a thing of the past.

Hours later, the club lights go up and we spill out onto the street outside, police officers and taxis everywhere doing their part to keep the order. My plans to stay with a trusted older friend fall through last minute and we get separated, but spontaneously I'm offered a couch with someone she knows instead. I accept the offer and head back with the group, all in their late twenties, to a nearby house. We continue drinking into the morning, and as the others eventually retreat to their rooms, I pass out alone on the sofa downstairs.

Some time later, I'm aware of a body sliding down awkwardly behind me. Musty breath warms the back of my neck and though I wonder momentarily who it might be, I don't turn around to find out. Evasiveness seems like the easier option, and as a hand creeps round my waist I instinctively scrunch myself into a foetal position before slipping back into unconsciousness.

I'm suddenly jolted awake by motion and open my eyes to see a staircase moving clunkily below me. Groggy from the drink and sleep I'm roused from, it takes me a minute to figure out that I'm hanging upside down, over a man's shoulders; I'm being carried upstairs in a fireman's lift hold. The minutes or hours that follow, on a bed I don't recognise, feel as if I witness them through the lens of a camera, where the shutter opens before closing into blackness for a while. There's a clear flash of him straddling my face, as he tries to push himself into my mouth but I keep it firmly shut and twist my face into the pillow. I'd always thought that if I was ever in a scenario like this, I would raise my voice. But I don't make a sound.

When I come to, he is standing by the window, wearing only a white t-shirt covering the top half of his body. My jeans and underwear are on the floor nearby, and I'm unsure of exactly what's taken place.

'Do you know how old I am?' I decide to ask.

I tell the man in front of me (who I later find out is twenty-eight and engaged to be married) that I'm fourteen. He comes to sit near me on the bed and, concerned, puts it down to a misunderstanding. One, he suggests, that it might be better we both forget.

I share this experience with no one for several years and, instead, resolve that where intimacy is concerned I'll make sure that I'm the one in control from now on. It strikes me that the best way of doing this is to be the initiator, always a step ahead of the other person. If I can lead and be the uninhibited driving force behind my romantic interactions, then I can avoid being vulnerable again.

Throughout my teenage years, this decision will get me quite a reputation for being the outwardly confident, 'forward' one in high school. I remember a boy telling me that his mother had expressed reservations about the two of us dating, concerned that I'd 'chew him up and spit him out', as she put it. Although hurt by this comment at the time, looking back, it turns out she had a point.

Even in my friendships, the need to feel in control was a strong theme for me; my default was to overpower the other person and their views because it made me feel safe. Not one for accepting the differing opinions of others or allowing situations to unfold naturally, I preferred to manipulate the outcomes into being what I believed they *ought* to be.

As the years rolled on, I discovered an absolute favourite pastime of mine: the pursuit of 'fixing' boyfriends. The type of guys I ended up with rarely had it together, but that was fine, since I was drawn more to the potential that I saw in (or bestowed *upon*) them anyway. I found myself attracting self-professed 'bad boys', constantly managing to get myself into dysfunctional relationships with people who showed little sign of being reliable fixtures in my life. Not one to be deterred by this, I'd then try every trick in the book to make them stay. My tendency, in both romance and friendships, was to be repelled by anything reliable (to me, that equated to boring) and to fervently pursue the impossible, determined to win them round.

I met my first long-term boyfriend, Trey, at the age of fifteen, a handsome, semi-professional footballer from Moss Side in Manchester. Trey also happened to be a full-time compulsive liar and cheat. I was perhaps naive in thinking that he would devote himself to me at the age of seventeen, when we only ever saw each other on weekends. However, we'd agreed on being mutually exclusive and so I had no reason to think otherwise. That was until three months into our relationship, when a stream of text messages on his phone led me to discover Kim, his Monday–Friday Manchester girl.

We broke up for ten agonising days, before I was swiftly won back by twelve red roses and an eternity ring (which we secretly agreed was actually a commitment to marry each other). Cue months of misery for both of us – as I cross-examined and obsessively checked up on Trey's every move, desperate to know with *absolute certainty* that he was, as he claimed to be, a changed man. I'd vet his text messages while he was in the shower and even kept tabs on the number of condoms kept in his bedside drawer. I felt justified in this; he'd given me ammunition to be suspicious, after all. And yet I carried this same neurosis into so many of my later relationships too, without any real legitimate reason.

Despite months of non-existent evidence to pin on Trey, I was wrought with anxiety and it actually came as a relief, much later that year, when I caught him texting a new girl under the kitchen table. I ended things between us, although not before manipulating him into telling me about any other girls he'd been involved with. I convinced him that if he was completely honest with me, we could wipe the slate clean and give the relationship one final try. This (somewhat controlling) tactic of mine worked:

Tash
Sarah-Louise
Nadia
Keisha
Claire
And a girl he fingered at a party but couldn't recall the name of.

Six girls. Tortured by this newly acquired information and clueless as to why he'd do this to the girl he was adamant he loved, I broke up with Trey for good. However, it was only a matter of months before I found myself with someone new; this time, a guy of volatile moods, who was a daily pot smoker and an enthusiast of coke and pills. Suffice to say, after much micromanaging on my part, that relationship didn't go too smoothly either.

I wouldn't come to recognise it for many years, but I had a real issue with just letting go. I feared that if I took my hands off the steering wheel, the circumstances of my life would drive miserably off-course, and that was to be prevented at all costs. Controlling brought me closer to the certainty I craved. For a time – and with certain people – it worked quite well.

Persia

> 'A man without self-control is like a city
> broken into and left without walls.'
> Proverbs 25:28

The bell signalling the end of the last period decides to ring just as two paramedics carry me through the school gates on a stretcher. As students begin to pour out of their lessons, I cringe and squeeze my eyes tightly shut, willing the ambulance doors shut before everyone rounds the corner and sees me lying here, vibrating uncontrollably.

It's a Wednesday afternoon in early May and I'm fourteen years old. During my Year Ten English lesson, my body started reacting violently to the twenty-five caffeine pills I took at lunchtime on the field opposite my school. I'd been dared to do this by a friend, and seeing as there was quite a large crowd gathered around us at the time (including the ex-boyfriend I'm desperate to win back), I gladly accepted the challenge.

This sort of reckless behaviour has become pretty commonplace for me now – especially around boys. Whether it's taking a packet of paracetamol and locking myself in the toilet at parties, or turning up to school with bandages around my arms (and sleeves rolled up), I like making a statement with my self-destructive tendencies.

The weekend just gone was no exception. I'd spent the bank holiday Sunday with Max – the guy I've been cheating on my boyfriend with for the last couple of months. The two couldn't be more polar opposite if they tried. My boyfriend Tom is intelligent, kind and loyal. Max – a dropout – is your typical bad boy: mysterious, arrogant and unpredictable. He has a reputation for stealing cars and dealing drugs, and I think he's been arrested more than once.

In years to come, I'll find myself jumping between these two types of men over and over again. One fulfils my need to feel safe and loved, the other my desire for danger and excitement. When I grow bored of the first, I'll sabotage it by diving straight into a relationship with the second. As soon as I'm inevitably burned by this one, I'll strap myself to the closest kind soul I can find to try and regain all my lost confidence.

Cheating on boyfriends is my release and I'm hooked. It's the world's best distraction and anaesthetiser, and I rarely even feel guilty about it now. It makes me feel cool and desirable, and stops me thinking about the fact that my dad's now in rehab – a real blow considering my mum's already been in twice. Most of all – just like with all the self-harming – it makes me feel in control of my life.

When I arrived at Max's house last Sunday, it felt strangely quiet – almost eerily so. Set on its own in the middle of the woods, there are no neighbours for miles, but usually there are dogs, chickens, peacocks and at least three young children constantly running between the field and house.

'Where is everyone?' I asked Max as we headed into the kitchen.

'Out,' he replied bluntly.

Max idolises Eminem – posters of whom fill his bedroom walls. I've spent many hours lying on his bed texting Tom, as Max swipes at the bloodied punch bag hanging from his ceiling, *The Marshall Mathers LP* playing in the background on repeat. The irony that he's slowly turning into Stan (the psychotic super-fan from Eminem's music video) isn't lost on me, but hasn't deterred me either.

Seeing as the house was empty, Max decided to steal one of his dad's bottles of gin. The drunker we got, the more skittish and irate Max became, and when he caught me texting Tom in the bathroom, he completely lost it.

The next few hours went by in a blur. We screamed at each other over the music, and I was consumed by an urge to provoke and taunt him, telling Max I loved Tom more than him, which caused him to collapse in a sobbing heap. When he regained control, he launched back into full-blown fury, chasing me around the house with a kitchen knife and threatening to kill me. Although part of me was terrified of him, I was secretly thrilled by the absurd, unnecessary drama of it all.

At some point I must've passed out, because I woke up on his bed half-dressed and covered in blood, my head thumping. Max was nowhere to be seen, so I called the local taxi service and cried for the entire thirty-minute car journey home.

As I was about to walk through my front door, a friend rang saying there was a big house party happening down the road. I promptly turned around and headed straight there, to find Tom smoking a joint in the front garden. When he saw me, he threw it on the ground and went inside. I knew instantly that someone had told him about Max and me.

By now, it must've been around midnight. Everyone was clearly wasted, and the boys had started to trash the place – first, just by throwing fags and half-empty beer cans on to the floor, then by ripping picture frames off the wall and smashing everything in sight with broken chair legs.

Something in me erupted, and I soon found myself joining in. Now that I'd lost both Tom and Max, I was desperate to gain back some form of control – even if it was just through breaking mirrors and kicking over plant pots.

Just as I was about to deal a heavy blow to one of the wardrobes in the main bedroom with a broken piece of banister, a hand grabbed my arm.

'I'll take that,' a male voice sniggered from behind me.

It was a policeman.

Luckily, I didn't get arrested, but the reputation I gain from that outburst stops me being invited to many house parties in the future, the absolute worst fate imaginable for a social butterfly like me.

My caffeine overdose at school the week after the party has unfortunately resulted in a week-long stay at our local hospital. My mum must be pretty shocked by this turn of events – I've been keeping up appearances to my family for so long that I've got it all together, when in reality that couldn't be further from the truth.

Totally deflated that both Tom and Max fail to visit me in hospital, I cry myself to sleep most nights. I tell myself it's about the boys, because that hurts much less than the truth.

Every now and then, I pick up the card my dad recently wrote me from rehab, which stands on the bedside table next to me:

Hi Persia,

I hope all is well with you. I am so sorry if me being in here when you are trying to concentrate on your exams is distracting you. However, I am doing well and working hard to make myself better.

I love you so much. You are my shining star. If you keep to your path you will achieve great things. In here, they teach us that this is a programme of action and nothing will change unless we take action. You do take action, and things happen.

You being strong and revising hard is one of the very positive things in my life and I am so proud to have a daughter who is not only intelligent, but a talented actor and singer.

If you are not too busy maybe you could write to me? So, when do the exams start? You are so determined to succeed. I will always be there to support you in whatever you choose to do.

Coming in here was so good for me because it has given me time to reflect on all the good things I have in my life today. I was so caught up in the pursuit of more, I could not see and appreciate what I already had.

I am so sorry I drove you drunk, the other week, it was unforgiveable. I was out of control, but I'm working hard to change. I'm finding the real me – not the loud, silly me I let everyone see.

Just keep being you Persia. You put a lot into your life, so you will get a lot out of it. I love you so much. I can feel your strength helping me get well.

Love always,
Dada xxxxxxx

You

'It is our attitude toward events, not events
themselves, which we can control.'
Epictetus

The source of a lot of anxiety in life comes from our attempts
to control the uncontrollable. We do it, quite simply, because
we think we know best; that if the world got on board with our
way of thinking, everyone would be better off. It's as if, 'all the
world's a stage, and all the men and women merely players',
and we have taken it upon ourselves to direct the whole production. How frustrating it is when actors enter and exit at the
wrong time, deviate from the script and worse, *dare* to challenge our artistic vision. If the artists and crew would only do as
we tell them, the play could be a raving success.

While our desire to control may be a tough habit to crack,
it'll break *us* if we don't choose to break *it*. Many of us insist
that life must go as we dictate, and we find reality problematic
when that doesn't happen. Although feeling in control of
things may bring us a temporary wave of peace, the irony is that
in chasing it, we often become stressed, angry, despairing,
manipulative, resentful and self-pitying.

Holding on to the belief that we're solely in control of
outcomes is not a sustainable way of life; in fact, it's an *insane*
way of life. The expectations and responsibilities that come
attached to this belief are enough to lead most people towards
a breakdown. We may be able to control the little things for a
time, but sooner or later, life will inevitably bring us something
far greater than we could ever handle alone.

Why do some struggle so much more with control than others? Maybe we were raised by caregivers who displayed a lack of responsibility and, therefore, we were forced to take charge and manage on our own. In the same situation, others might not have known how to rectify the problem, so became expert at creating the *illusion* of control instead – perhaps by attaining top grades at school or hiding behind a 'perfect' image, in order to prevent people from discovering what was really going on.

Others of us, having been raised by a controlling parent, find ourselves copying the behaviours that we grew up around. The controlling figure in our lives may have been so extreme that we've built our own control mechanism to defend against it – as a means of self-preservation. There are also some of us who, having had a negative experience in the past, vowed never to allow ourselves to be in so vulnerable a position again. And so, in an attempt to protect ourselves, we try to micromanage and manipulate the relationships and situations most dear to us.

Perfectionism and obsessive compulsive disorder are both rooted in a desire to feel more in control. Those of us in possession of these traits may have been known to place unhealthy emphasis on rituals, keep our space immaculate or show reluctance in delegating to others. More generally, those of us with controlling tendencies tend to display black-and-white thinking and a lack of flexibility, since deviating from our way of doing things causes us anxiety.

There's a marked difference in expressing our feelings honestly to another person, and using our words to exert control over them. This is easily identifiable by how attached we are to the outcome. If we are dependent on the other person responding in a particular way: that's control. When people do respond in a way that isn't to our preference, we often feel that they're against us, when they're simply making a different choice to our own. Our efforts to control can be so subtle that we may not even realise we're doing it. It can also be the underhand manipulation or pulling of someone's strings in order to get our own way.

As a result of growing up within our own family dynamic, each of us will have a dominant way of behaving in order to get what we want from other people. This idea is explored in James Redfield's book *The Celestine Prophecy*, where he describes these learned behaviours as 'control dramas' – the four types of behaviour a person exhibits when the stakes in a situation are high. Firstly, there's the 'Intimidator'. This person forces us to pay attention to them, usually by making us feel fearful as a result of their threatening words, actions or energy. Secondly, there's the 'Interrogator', who, through their persistent questioning, makes us feel conscious about the way we're being perceived and leaves us feeling judged. Following on from these two aggressive control dramas are two more passive approaches. There's the 'Aloof' energy: this person behaves mysteriously and is difficult to read, often retreating in an attempt to draw us in further, as we try to figure them out. The fourth drama is the 'Poor Me' and this person plays the victim, making us feel guilty, leaving us defending ourselves against the feeling that we're not doing enough for them.

Whether we're aware of it or not, we will all have used (and been on the receiving end of) control dramas at some point. As fully rounded human beings, it's likely that we've inhabited all four, though we will each have our dominant choice – the control drama we call upon most often.

Relations between two people are much like a dance: it doesn't flow if both partners are always hell-bent on leading.

Conflict arises when we're constantly working to dominate each other using whatever means we believe will get us what we want. The trick is to become conscious of how we (and the people in our lives) use control dramas, in order to break the cycle and become healthier in our interactions.

Exercising control in a positive way can bring structure and productivity, helping to soothe our day-to-day anxieties. A need for excessive control, however, can be detrimental and have the exact opposite effect. It's about figuring out the role control plays in our individual lives and understanding how we use it.

Time and time again, experience shows us that excessive control isn't the answer, and yet we continue chasing it, hoping for a different result next time round. By any other definition, this is an addiction: addiction to control. The middle section of this book is going to guide you towards living a solution based on what *is*, rather than what *should* be.

First, however, we must look at how we've been exerting our self-will in order to control the world around us, so that we can approach life from a new perspective.

EXERCISES

1) Growing up, who was in control at home? What control drama was dominantly used – Intimidator, Interrogator, Aloof or Poor Me? E.g. Stepdad = Interrogator, Mum = Aloof.

2) List the five people you are closest to and what their dominant control dramas are. (You may see parallels with your parents here – knowing this helps to understand what energy you tend to be drawn towards in others.)

3) Think of a situation when the stakes were high (a situation that was very important to you). Can you identify which control drama you used to get your power back?

4) Which people or situations are you most attached to and why do you try to exert control over them? In your journal, draw out and fill in the grid below.

PERSON/SITUATION	WHAT I WANT TO CONTROL	WHY I TRY TO CONTROL IT
1. *My boyfriend going on nights out with his friends, without me.*	*Him talking to other girls/finding someone he likes more/realising that it would be more fun to be single.*	*I don't want us to break up.*
2.		

CHAPTER 3

SHAME

Persia

'We are only as sick as the secrets we keep.'

Anonymous

Open suitcases and piles of clothes lay strewn across my bedroom floor. Before I start getting ready for my second night at my new job, I'm finishing off packing up the little central London flat I've lived in on my own for the last two years. Next week, I'm moving to north London with Joey – a girl from drama school I became close to when staying with a mutual actor friend in New York last year.

I'm going to miss this place. In typical acting-student fashion, my friends and I have spent countless nights sat on the floor drinking red wine, discussing the meaning of life according to Shakespeare, while intermittingly snorting lines of cheap coke off the glass coffee table.

Considering my parents' penchant for narcotics, other than the odd spliff with boyfriends, I successfully managed to bypass harder drugs in my teens and at uni – I knew I'd probably like them too much.

That was, until last year, when I found myself being offered cocaine at an actor's party in Chelsea. I wasn't that fussed about experiencing the drug itself, but I was massively up for impressing the good-looking boy that handed it to me. Unfortunately, me talking at double my already very accelerated rate of speech failed to attract his attention. It did, however, succeed in making coke become my go-to party favour – despite being the last drug that an egocentric narcissist like me needs in their system.

Ironically, my parents have both been clean for well over five years now. It still baffles me how much our family life has changed in that time. Friends and boyfriends are regularly welcomed into our home to the smell of fresh muffins hot out of the oven. The house is always immaculate, and both parents show up to every production I'm in without fail. We no longer just look like the perfect family from the outside, we actually *feel* like it behind closed doors, too.

And yet, my own life's more of a shambles than ever.

I once read somewhere that Jerry Hall's mantra growing up had been 'Yes, but more'; *God*, I feel that. In the time that Mum and Dad have been sober, I've found myself becoming increasingly drawn to wanting *more*. More sex, more drink, more drugs, more attention, more drama. I have an insatiable appetite these days. I don't know how to sit with the normality of my new nuclear family, so I actively seek out the chaos I'm more familiar with via other avenues – mainly relationships. No other high can top the experience of falling in love; I'm completely addicted to it.

In many ways, it looks like I've got it made: this summer alone I'm going to a friend's wedding in the US, to Shanghai for six weeks on an acting job, to play the title character in a production of *The Taming of the Shrew* and to Moscow to visit my Russian actor boyfriend (who also happens to be the son of a KGB general – as well as an alcoholic). I started dating him when I was acting in Russia last year, despite having a loving and devoted boyfriend at home.

Consistency and routine has always bored me. I proudly own the fact that I'm a Sailor personality type like my father – always seeking spontaneous new adventures in far and distant lands. But, where he eventually managed to settle down properly with Mum once they got sober, I have no desire to stay in any one place (or relationship) long enough to have to risk real commitment or intimacy.

Ever the oversharer, I boast and joke about my conquests to friends to get a laugh, and pride myself on being the life and soul of every party, certain that I'm doing a grand job of convincing everyone that my exhibitionism is a result of being so very free and liberated.

Although my life may look full and exciting to those who don't know me well, in reality everything's starting to crumble under the strain of my escalating self-destructive tendencies. The lies I'm telling to my family and long-distance boyfriend are now too complex for even me to remember. By the end of this year, my bank account will be in an even worse state than when I was a student, as the acting work dries up and my partying habits do the opposite.

I often find myself wandering around Shoreditch at three in the morning after my friends have all gone home, looking for someone to kiss to take my mind off how lonely I am. If I haven't ended up in a new lover's arms before dawn, my night has been a failure. And even if I have, the morsels of affection I get never feel enough to satisfy this relentless need to feel wanted.

Although my ego appears to have ballooned, my self-worth has disintegrated into nothingness, which is why it's maybe not all that surprising that, six weeks ago, I found myself starting a new job as a 'hostess' in a gentleman's club in Mayfair. I told myself I needed the quick cash to fund my jam-packed summer, but really I just wanted something to fill the hours and provide me with more fuel to fan the flames of self-sabotage.

Though I originally hated the fact I felt I was betraying my own feminist morals, I quickly became addicted to the rush of earning lots of money up front – simply by flirting with men to get them to buy the most expensive bottle of champagne possible.

I spent most of my evenings in the Mayfair club feeling humiliated. Whenever a new customer came into the room, me and the other five girls working had to dance in the middle of the deserted club to the song 'Linger' by The Cranberries (always an odd choice, I thought), as the men decided which one they wanted to talk to. I dreaded and craved being picked in equal measure: if I was singled out, I felt dirty and ashamed, and if I wasn't, I felt like a failure.

Last week, my cash payment was about £200 short. When I spoke to my manager, she denied knowing anything about it, and said I shouldn't expect to see the balance any time soon.

A few of the other girls were also down on their payment too, and decided to try working at a Soho club instead. To my surprise (and delight), they invited me to join them. Last night was my first shift.

This place is a far cry from the one in Mayfair – which now seems tasteful in comparison. It's in a dingy, smoky underground basement down an alleyway. The floor's littered with fag butts and smells of stale beer, and silver trays of coke are passed around openly, as strippers do shows on rotation in the middle of the cramped space.

When I arrived yesterday, I felt totally out of my depth, and so gladly accepted the free coke and champagne on offer. After a painfully slow first hour stood on the edge of the room watching the strip shows, the Cuban manager Luis sat me next to a very large, ageing red-haired American man.

From the get-go, this man was only ever kind and respectful towards me, and spent the majority of the evening asking me questions about myself. I think he was lonely, too.

As the early hours of the morning drew near, I noticed a subtle shift in the energy of the room, which was slowly emptying. Two of the older hostesses had been eyeing up the American for some time now, observing him buying me bottle after bottle of champagne, and slipping me fifties under the table – 'For making me feel so welcome,' he'd said.

By this point, he was very, very drunk. Seizing their opportunity, the two women sauntered over to our table, and draped themselves over his lap. One shoved her cleavage into his face, while the other undid his trousers with one hand and prized notes out of his breast pocket with the other, whispering obscenities into his ear.

Just as I was attempting to quietly slip away from the table unnoticed, the American spotted me and called out my name. The woman with the cleavage yanked me back down onto my chair, while the other took my hand and placed it over hers on top of the American's crotch, shoving a handful of fifties down my top as she did so.

Twenty minutes later, I stumbled up the stairs of the basement and out into the morning sunshine, having promised the manager I'd be back this evening.

I haven't told Joey about last night yet. Even though she's seen me in some truly shameful situations before, the fact I accepted money is just one step too far – even for me.

Joey

'It is the false shame of fools to try to conceal
wounds that have not healed.'
Horace

Stephen, his disability chaperone Carl, golden retriever Essie and I are sitting in a pub. I have spent the last few days with them – Stephen and I as vocalists for a music project were working on. Stephen is registered blind and, now in his thirties, works as a performer. He's happily married to a beautiful woman – he's just shown me a picture of her on his phone. I can't get my head around the fact that he's never actually *seen* her.

During the long rehearsal days, we've had a lot of time to talk. He shares the experience of unexpectedly losing his eyesight in his early twenties, the gutting lack of support from his jack-the-lad mates at the time, and how he shut himself away from the world and slipped into a deep depression for years. As someone in my early twenties myself, I can't imagine how I'd deal with suddenly having my sight taken from me. Although I haven't known Stephen long, I feel a lot of respect for him and what he's overcome.

At the end of an intense few days of music rehearsals and the subsequent performance, the four of us decide to hit the town centre and throw ourselves a mini wrap party. Opting for the local Wetherspoon's, we settle down at a small round table with low-slung stools and crack open our first bottle of wine.

Although Stephen and I have great rapport, there is absolutely no chemistry or flirting between us. For one, he can't *see* me. Secondly, although I can appreciate he's a handsome man, I don't fancy him at all. And most significantly, he's married – for that reason alone I wouldn't think about going there.

Ever since my first long-term relationship with Trey, I've been adamant that I will *never* be a cheat – my experience with him engrained in me an unshakable value about fidelity. I swore at the age of almost sixteen that I'd never play around like that – whether it be in a relationship of my own or with someone who was spoken for.

Although I'm all for enjoying the freedom that comes with being single, I am fiercely loyal – almost *too* loyal, if that's possible – when in a relationship. I'm a Farmer type, I like to put my roots down, and long for consistency in a partner. Persia – a drama school friend I've grown close to over the last year – is the antithesis to this, which is probably why we get on so well. Chalk and cheese, and all that.

Wetherspoon's is growing more out of focus and, five or so bottles later, I must assume total blackout, as I've absolutely no memory of the end of the evening or getting back to the hotel. Although I have vague flashbacks of drinking with Stephen at the hotel bar, I can recall little else.

I open my eyes, some time later, to make out the shapes of a dimly lit hotel room. It's at this point that Stephen slowly comes into focus: he's on top of me and we seem to be having sex.

I instantly become hysterical as Stephen, bewildered by my sudden reaction, jumps away from me across the bed. The noise must disturb Carl next door, who has an adjoining room with Stephen – whose room, it turns out, we're currently in. Slowly, the adjoining door opens to reveal a silhouette of Carl, naked, and Essie the dog standing side by side in the doorway, looking in on us.

In time to come, this surreal memory will serve to remind me why alcohol and I are *not* a good mix. I'm not sure that any of us exchange further words, and somehow, I make it back to my own room. I'm awoken hours later by the morning light, and find myself curled up on top of the covers, in last night's clothes. Utter shame.

On the occasions that I've woken up with a handsome stranger – aside from the agony of exchanging minimal texts the following day before they disappear off the radar – I've dealt with giving my body to someone I don't know quite well. I've justified it by telling myself that I'm a twenty-something, and pretty much everyone's doing it – many far more extreme than I. But this? This is not the person I am at all, it's as if alcohol skews my morals completely.

As a teenager, my diary entries frequently alluded to my concern that the way I drank felt different to the way others did; I was aware even back then of the power it could have over me. At sixteen, my friend Elle and I got banned from any college event where alcohol was available, as punishment for escaping from our hotel and pulling an all-nighter on an art trip to Berlin. Although the consequences were justified, being publicly banned from social events felt humiliating. Of course, I was solely responsible for my escalating drinking career (which was already lengthy, having discovered alcopops at the age of twelve). However, taking on the identity as the 'unruly one' growing up didn't do much for my self-esteem and, consequently, the decisions I was making.

In the same way that my school chemistry teacher used to taunt me with the nickname 'Slow Jo', (I was diagnosed with dyslexia in high school and periodic tables *really* weren't my thing), I internalised the label and didn't consider myself to be intelligent.

Similarly, when a girl in the year above accused me of being a 'slag', it only served to fuel the fire. It was frustrating that people formed opinions without really knowing me, yet at the same time my ongoing actions did serve to reinforce the judgements they made.

I once read an article about binge-drinking, describing the way in which alcohol generally leads men to fight and women to other people's beds: 'Men do things to other people, women have things done to them.' My stomach turned, since the words spoke so specifically to my own experiences over the years. I felt confused as to why it kept happening, and yet it kept happening.

Lying on the bed, I realise I have absolutely no idea how last night came to be. I'm starting to feel I have no idea who I become when I drink, full stop. It is me, but it's not me.

I reach down and pull my phone out of my bag to see what time it is: it's mid-morning. I'm at risk of missing my train back to London if I don't move now. Throwing everything into my suitcase, I head towards the door. Coming down the corridor, I see Carl ahead of me. He nods awkwardly, keeps his eyes to the carpet and shuffles past towards the lift. Stephen follows soon behind with Essie at his ankles, and now we stand face to face. I speak before he has a chance to:

'I want you to forget whatever happened last night,' is what tumbles out. 'You don't deserve to have this ruin your marriage – please, please don't feel bad about it. Just forget it happened and get on with your life.'

My own shame is not enough; I want to take on his, too.

We step into the lift alongside Carl, all of our eyes fixed firmly on our shoes, as we make our way down to reception. I walk with them, pretty much in silence, to the train station, before saying goodbye. Giving Essie an affectionate pat, I wander off to find my platform.

After an episode like this, I withdraw into what I like to refer to as my 'shame bubble'. I will abstain from drinking completely – usually for two to three weeks – until the shock has worn off and then, tentatively, I'll pick up another drink. Sooner or later a similar drama occurs, and the cycle begins again.

The thing about shame is that it doesn't like to be shared; it much prefers being quietly swept under the carpet. Unlike Persia, I don't tend to make light of what happens. Being a control freak, I find the repercussions of my drinking mortifying and keep them very much to myself.

Along with some of my other more reckless friends, there've been numerous occasions where I was obviously hammered, or made it clear I wasn't interested but the guy has pushed his luck anyway. Often he's just as drunk and not thinking straight either. The blurred lines of consent where intoxication is involved is something that many of us are familiar with.

The thing is, because it's not a man jumping out of the bushes when you're innocently on your way home from work, you let it go. You were drunk. You were high. You may even have led them on.

You take a shower and shove it to the deepest darkest recesses of your mind, because usually you know them and can't even entertain the alternative course of action.

Alcohol has been aiding my efforts in being forward with the opposite sex since the age of fourteen. At this point the irony is still lost on me that what began as a ploy to feel more in control, has now become the complete opposite pretty much a decade on.

You

> 'A man's past is not simply a dead history . . . it is a still
> quivering part of himself, bringing shudders and bitter
> flavours and the tinglings of a merited shame.'
> *Middlemarch*, George Eliot

The majority of us are familiar with the word 'shame', and we've all encountered it at some time or other. Yet, the experience itself can be difficult to define. Shame and vulnerability researcher Brené Brown describes the difference between guilt and shame as: shame focusing on *self* and guilt focusing on *behaviour.*

Shame tells us that there's something fundamentally wrong with us, that we're worthless. It's the feeling that we are flawed, and is often the voice that persuades us that: we're not good enough, we're wrong to be feeling what we feel, our past mistakes mean we're a disgrace, or we shouldn't be struggling in the way that we are.

Whereas guilt is an adaptive state that enables us to learn from our mistakes and move on, shame acts as an obstacle to our growth. After all, we can work on adapting our behaviour, but we can't fundamentally erase who we are. Consequently, shame leaves us feeling trapped in a no-win situation.

Those who have grown up around dysfunction have a predisposition towards feeling shame; as a child, they may have been made to feel that the chaos going on around them was somehow their fault. They might, therefore, find it difficult to differentiate between what *is* and what *is not* their responsibility, accept blame, even when it isn't their place to, simply to avoid conflict.

Until we take a close look at our own relationship with shame, which we'll be doing in the exercises at the end of this chapter, it's not always easy to spot how it's played out in our lives so far. The behaviours that we find ourselves shrugging or laughing off and not giving a second thought to now, may later reveal themselves to being closely linked with shame and the distorted beliefs we've been holding about ourselves.

The toxic emotion of shame has strong links with depression, addiction, bullying and eating disorders. We feel bad, so we fix on a behaviour that brings us temporary relief, then we feel bad about what we have done – reinforcing the already low opinion we hold of ourselves. Most compulsive behaviours, for this reason, perpetuate our feelings of shame. Yet, it's not the *behaviour* but the *feeling of shame* itself that is most destructive, because while we're consumed by it we're unable to progress. We push down our feelings into a deep abyss and refuse to look at them. When we're in shame, our ability to connect honestly with others is limited, our self-esteem diminishes and our anxieties grow progressively worse.

Secrecy is also very much linked to shame. By believing that having problems is shameful, we bury our feelings, keeping our pain hidden from view and staying stuck. It feels counterintuitive to expose the darker parts of ourselves, but shame thrives in secrecy. When we get honest, we set ourselves free. By sharing our struggles, we begin to unlock shame's hold over us.

Although, for some of us, our experiences of shame are completely independent of anyone else, others may have experienced shame as a mechanism for control. We may have been shamed for wanting to give and receive love at home, as our parents were unable to participate in affection and rejected us, leaving us feeling unworthy of it.

Perhaps we were shamed by a school teacher for falling behind in class, and their tough approach in getting us up to speed left us believing we were stupid. Later in life, we may have had a friend who shamed us for finding a new relationship because she was still single, or a partner may have tried to shame us about how much money we earned, because they felt resentful that it was so much more or less than their own income.

Whether intentional or not, people around us often use shaming tactics to feel more powerful and in control and, as long as we allow it, the dysfunction is able to continue.

Even when we begin practising new, healthy behaviours, we may still need to contend with feelings of shame. Taking care of ourselves, communicating our feelings, having fun and finding success can induce shame – we may feel bad that we're leaving people behind. Alternatively, those around us may try to make us feel shame because they're threatened by the change they see as they watch our situation improve, while they continue to feel stuck.

In recognising how shame plays out in our lives, we're able to break the cycle and find the freedom to grow into who we wish to become. Nothing in life gets to define who we are. Once we recognise shame for what it is, it's down to us to decide.

EXERCISES

1) Write down any critical thoughts you frequently tell yourself,

e.g.
I'm worthless.

My feelings don't matter.

I'm not _____ enough.

2) In your journal, complete these sentences:

I feel shame about . . .

(This could be things you've done in the past, things you failed to do, things you believe about yourself or things people have said to you.)

When I feel shame, I tend to . . .

(numb my feelings with junk food, isolate myself from others, withhold information.)

The mistakes that I'm still beating myself up for are . . .

CHAPTER 4

DENIAL

Joey

'And that is how we are. By strength of will we cut off our inner intuitive knowledge from admitted consciousness. This causes a state of dread, or apprehension, which makes the blow ten times worse when it does fall.'

Lady Chatterley's Lover, D.H. Lawrence

It's a late summer's evening on Highbury Fields in London. Having spent the last few months stepping up the guilt tactics and sexual incentives to keep hold of Rory, he's finally mustered the strength to end it with me. The dumping takes place here, on a bench, where we now sit side by side as if perfect strangers. He attempts to side-hug me (not quite the romantic farewell you see in the movies), before standing up and walking away. He looks back one last time, before disappearing between the moving traffic on Upper Street and out of sight.

From pretty much the moment our lives collided some eight months ago now, Rory's focus has consistently been on making it big in the music industry, while my focus has consistently been on him. He is dark, bearded, the best lover I've had by a mile, and is completely emotionally unavailable to me. He spends almost every waking hour in his studio and mainly texts me out of the blue at 10.30 p.m. to invite me to join him before bed, and I've very much been dancing to his tune.

Because of this, I am currently broke – I'm working £6.25 per hour catering shifts (that's *before* tax) and the regularity of these late-night taxi rides from my flat in Crouch End to his place in Islington are a real drain on the bank balance. On top of my cab expenditure, I'm also way too generous towards him with money I don't *actually have*. Perhaps subliminally because I'm trying to buy myself more time with him, I'm not too sure. Still, seeing him is the highlight of my existence, so it's worth it.

Having graduated from a militantly structured drama school schedule almost a year ago, I'm currently taking a breather from healthy routine and find myself surfacing at 1 p.m. most days. I'm not a daily drinker by any means, but I seem to be losing a handle on my wine consumption more and more lately. This makes it near impossible to do anything but lie in a coma-like state under my duvet for at least half of the following day. Aside from this, my life mainly consists of reeling off letters to casting directors (who rarely reply) and waiting for my acting agent to ring with word of an audition.

Outwardly, my life may well look peachy; I'm twenty-two, reasonably attractive, have a great social circle, am a graduate of one of the UK's top drama schools, am represented by a decent acting agent, and live in a beautiful north London flat with three of my close actor friends. Inwardly, however, I'm rapidly losing my sense of purpose and fear I'm slipping into depression.

I've known I was going to become an actress since I was seven, but I'm beginning to feel like it might not happen. Until very recently, one of my close friends and flatmates, Olivia, hadn't been having much luck with acting, either. Olivia has a tendency to be particularly neurotic about being out of work, which really winds me up (probably, if I'm honest with myself, because I do too). Of course, I haven't told her this. And I definitely won't be sharing it with her now, since she recently announced that she's landed the leading role in a new global TV drama, and has subsequently moved out of our flat.

Persia has taken over her room, which has come as a relief to me. It's more comfortable to avoid the reality of my own dwindling career by being around someone in the same boat. During this period, Rory has proved to be the perfect distraction and, for that reason, I've not been making it easy for him to wriggle away.

Although I haven't admitted this to myself properly, deep down I've known all along that Rory doesn't mirror the intensity of my feelings. When I'm not physically with him, I grow sick – sick in the head, I mean. Secretly, I feel like I might be obsessed with him; I'm addicted to the hit he gives me. When we're together, it's like I've been connected to the mains supply – I feel alive, energised and fully functioning. But during the times we're apart (and I swear these periods have been getting lengthier and more frequent than when we first hooked up . . .), it's as if my power fades, and I shrink into an anxious wreck. I've lost a fair bit of weight over the past few months from the stress of it. Still, I'd much prefer to sit with all this than not have him in my life at all. I guess I've been hoping that time will make his heart grow fonder.

I've found myself planning social commitments with friends only around the times I know I *definitely won't* see Rory (because he has other plans). All other slots are kept available, just in case he should contact me and ask to hang out last-minute. Subsequently, having neglected my friendships and every other area of my life, the blow of our break-up hits me even harder.

Rory's actions have been hinting at the fact that he isn't ready for a relationship (or perhaps, more specifically, a relationship with *me*) for some time, but I've only seen what I wanted to see. To acknowledge that it was heading here would have been to admit defeat, and that's never been my style. Despite the reality that he's chosen not to be part of my life anymore, I refuse to accept what is. After all, one of us has to fight for it. I fixate on the few words of hope he feeds me before departing, of the possible rekindling – 'A few years from now, when we're both more sorted . . .' – I wrack my brains for ways of speeding up the process, to get him back to me sooner. I hate feeling out of control like this.

A couple of weeks on from our bench break-up, and I've barely heard from Rory at all. Tonight, Louis, my gay best friend from drama school, is over at the flat for dinner. Rory has (inevitably) dominated the topic of conversation so far, and while ladling soup into Louis's bowl, he gently touches my hand and locks eyes with me.

'Babe. You do know he's not coming back.'

If there's one thing I don't want to be around right now, it's friends who tell it like it is. *Get the fuck out of my kitchen,* I say inside my head, before adding a dribble of soup into my own bowl and abruptly changing the subject. Right now, I don't think I'm mentally strong enough to handle the possibility of us not getting back together.

Toying with the idea of jumping out of the window back when I was a child – to punish those I felt had 'done me wrong' – is, weirdly, a theme that's been rearing its head again recently. The other day, I was sitting on the platform of the London underground, consumed with self-pity, when it suddenly crossed my mind to jump in front of the next train. For me, extreme thoughts like this seem to come from a desire to dramatically impact the person who has caused me pain. I just want to do something that'll make them care.

Alone in the flat the next day, and with a heavier heart than ever, I realise my period is almost a week late. My ankles have been slightly swollen (something I'd put down to the summer heat) but suddenly connecting the two, it dawns on me. I've been given the one thing that's certain to bring Rory back and keep him close for life. I don't believe in God but I put my hands together and throw my head upwards, 'Thank you,' I whisper. It's the first time I've felt the warm glow of hope in weeks.

Within forty-five minutes, I'm back from the pharmacy armed with a pregnancy test. Heart beating in my throat and ears, I plonk myself on to the toilet seat and cast my eyes across the diagrams. I need to see the blue line with my own eyes before I tell Rory the news. My mind's racing at a million thoughts a minute: *How do I tell him, how will he respond, how shall we break it to our parents?*

The fact that Rory has explicitly said he doesn't *want* to be in a relationship anymore has failed to register with me. My level of denial is so strong that the idea of having a baby together signifies the possibility of repairing what's temporarily broken between us.

Before I even get a chance to pull down my underwear, I'm suddenly aware of a familiar trickling sensation. I whip down my pants, and sure enough, there it is: *a damned spot.* My only hope literally flushed out of me, staring back, angry and red on the gusset of my knickers. A wave of grief rises up and my chest feels like it might burst. Tears of I-don't-quite-know-what tumble down my cheeks, and on to my bare thighs below. I am completely alone.

Persia

'Over time, hidden truths morph in the dark soil
of deceit into something much worse.'
Between the Tides, Patti Callahan Henry

I'm twenty-five, and sat with my new boyfriend 'Tiger' and my dad at a comedy night in Fulham put on by Dad's friend from AA.

Tiger – who I've known for over a decade now – gained the nickname from some of our mutual friends because of his predilection for wearing a tiger outfit at music festivals (in addition to possessing a decorative array of self-made scars across his torso and arms – a result of teenage hormones mixing with too much ketamine).

It's the first time Dad and Tiger have met, so I'm feeling a little on edge. The compère has just announced the meat raffle, which will be won by whoever's had the worst year. Without the social lubrication of alcohol, the answers are all pretty tame – 'I lost three iPhones', 'I broke my big toe'.

Tiger slowly raises his hand and stands up.

'Yes?' says the compère.

Tiger takes a deep breath and proceeds.

'I got fired from my dream job at the Secret Garden Party festival and escorted off the premises in handcuffs. I lost all my worldly possessions and ended up living in a squat, then I got hooked on K and lost my mind. I became a raging alcoholic, and had my family and all my friends turn their backs on me. I became so delusional that I was convinced I was a prophet sent here to save humanity, and all I could think about was getting to the Dalai Lama to give him the message that would save life on earth as we know it. I ended up getting sectioned when I tried escaping the country, then found myself in rehab, where I had to come to terms with the fact that I'll have to suffer the rest of my life on this planet sober – all before my twenty-fifth birthday.

'Pow,' he says, slamming the table with his fist, 'you try swallowing that lot down in a twelve-month period, and tell me I don't deserve to win that meat.'

Out of the corner of my eye, I see Dad slowly beginning to raise his own hand. I shrink down into my seat, well aware that if anyone can top Tiger's story, it's probably my own father.

Clearly amused, the compère turns to Dad.

'So, think you can top that do ya? How has *your* year possibly been worse than *his*?'

Dad looks at Tiger with a sly grin, before turning back to the compère.

'He's going out with my daughter,' he replies.

Needless to say, Dad wins the meat raffle.

It was the weekend of the Royal Wedding in April 2011 when Tiger and I first got together. After a year living with Joey, I'd moved back to my parents' place for a few months to save some money, and had started singing in a band with an old friend from home.

On the bank holiday Sunday, we were playing at a pub gig with a couple of mine and Tiger's mutual friends – including his ex-girlfriend, Sophie. Though they'd broken up years before, Sophie had been a rock for him while he was in rehab, and it had resulted in a complicated relationship in which she was still in love with him, and he was taking advantage of her attention, simply because he could. (It rang a bell.)

After the gig, we all went back to Sophie's house around the corner, and sat at the kitchen table drinking £5 bottles of wine and snorting cocaine.

All of us, that is, except for Tiger, who sat opposite me sipping Coca-Cola from the can, and rearranging the plethora of peacock feathers that he'd stuck to the side of his trucker hat.

As everyone got drunker and louder, Tiger began to tell me about the sequence of events that had led him to rehab. Before I knew it, I'd launched into my own story of my recent exploration into spirituality.

It had all started about six months ago. The day before my dad and I were due to set off for a yoga retreat in Thailand, I was lying hungover (*quelle surprise*) in Salena's bed, when, for some reason, a book on her bedroom shelf caught my eye. I went over and picked it out. It was called *Women Who Love Too Much* by an American therapist called Robin Norwood.

Well, that sounds shit, I thought.

I opened the book to a random page somewhere near the middle, and my eyes were immediately drawn to one particular sentence: 'Daughters of drug addicts tend to inherit a genetic predisposition to developing their own addictions.'

Every single sentence on the page resonated with me on a profound level, and I knew with absolute certainty that I must read this book in its entirety.

'Knock yourself out, mate,' Salena said when I asked if I could borrow it. 'I was gonna give it to you for Christmas anyway.'

Had the book come into my orbit at any other time, I would've probably tossed it aside and no doubt continued eating, drinking and banging my way into oblivion. But, having no drink, drugs or men to distract me for the next few weeks while on this trip, I soon found myself absorbed in the book's message. On the final morning of the retreat, Dad and I were sat sipping honey, ginger and lemon tea on our porch.

'I haven't really known how to bring this up with you darling,' Dad said, 'but you haven't seemed in the greatest place since you left drama school. We're worried about you.'

I nodded solemnly, looking down into my tea.

'You've always been such a hard worker Pers,' he continued, 'it's so sad to see you heading down a bad road, because I know you could do anything you wanted if you put your mind to it. If you worked as hard on yourself as you used to at studying and acting, miracles will happen. I know they will. Take it from me, if you focus on your insides, the outsides will take care of themselves.'

That was the cue I'd been subconsciously waiting for. As soon as I returned home, I followed Robin Norwood's advice and started attending a Twelve Step meeting called Al-Anon – a spiritual fellowship which focuses on overcoming the destructive effects of living with an addict or alcoholic.

Over the next few months, I attended these meetings sporadically, realising that I had some serious inner work to do if I wanted to live the happy life I'd once envisaged for myself.

When I'd finished my story, I looked up at Tiger. Suddenly, I felt naked and exposed.

'Persia, I had no idea about your parents; I always thought you were a princess who had everything.'

A princess who had everything.

On the outside, I *had* always seemed to 'have everything' – good grades, boyfriends, a nice house. But, I'd never felt how I'd imagine someone who 'had everything' would feel – good about themselves.

As everyone carried on drinking and laughing around me, I looked down at the half-finished wrap in front of me, unsure whether or not to finish it.

'It's not working anymore, is it?' said Tiger.

'No,' I said, before handing the wrap to one of the other girls.

The following day, I found myself experiencing the most horrific anxiety and come down I'd ever had. Desperate, I rang Tiger, who told me to meet him in Richmond Park.

When I arrived at our meeting point, I spotted Tiger in the distance on a rainbow-coloured bike with tassels trailing off the handlebars and peacock feathers poking out of the basket on the front. When he reached me, he wrapped his arms around my waist and I sobbed into his shoulder.

As the afternoon progressed, we wandered through the park, talking about our past relationships. Just like me, Tiger had cheated on and lied to everyone he'd ever been out with, too.

Since starting Al-Anon, however, I seem to have developed a conscience. Where I was once totally numb to the consequences of my behaviour, I now feel actual guilt and shame; I can't hide from myself anymore.

'Fancy coming back to my parents' place for some grub?' Tiger asked after our walk.

It sounded innocent enough, so I agreed.

After we'd finished eating, Tiger invited me upstairs to listen to some music in his bedroom, which was covered with brightly coloured wall hangings of Ganesh, and various poems and trinkets from his travels in India. We spent the next few hours playing each other our favourite songs like two loved-up teenagers, and he shared more about the spiritual beliefs he'd cultivated while travelling.

It must've been at least eleven when Tiger jumped into his bed, opened the covers and gestured for me to get in to watch

Harold and Maude – his favourite film. I stood hesitantly by the bed, well aware that if I got in, I wouldn't be getting out.

I got in, and after the film had finished found myself having sober sex with someone new for the first time in my life.

The next day, I felt awful; I knew Sophie would be devastated. I made Tiger promise that it wouldn't happen again, and we both agreed not to tell anyone – there was no point in hurting Sophie unnecessarily.

Alas, my words and my resolve appeared to have fallen on deaf ears; several impromptu romantic gestures (on Tiger's part) later, as so often happens when people jump into bed together too prematurely, we now find ourselves in the lascivious throws of a new relationship that neither of us is anywhere near ready for. And I'm back to pretending that this is going to have a happy ending.

You

> 'We are slow to believe that which if
> believed would hurt our feelings.'
> Ovid

Denial is our unwillingness to acknowledge reality as it really is. Whether we're in denial over our problems, feelings or needs, over time we come to rely on this lack of honesty with ourselves in order to endure our circumstances. Denial makes our situation more tolerable; it becomes a way of life.

For some of us, the truth of our situations while growing up was too painful, and so we avoided it with the only option that offered us temporary sanity: burying our heads in the sand. We couldn't control what was happening at home, but we could save ourselves the shame and humiliation of others finding out by pretending that things were fine.

Whether we were indeed raised in a dysfunctional environment, or circumstances later in life simply became too hard to bear, it's often only on reflection that we're able to acknowledge that 'deep down, we knew it all along'. At the time, though, we may need to be dishonest with ourselves (and those around us) as a coping mechanism.

The problem is, telling lies quickly develops into a habit, and our web of deceit soon leads to life becoming unmanageable, as we lose sight of who we are. Lying can be a difficult habit to shake when it's been repeatedly engrained into our psyche. Most of us know we can't evade the ramifications of lying forever – eventually we're going to get caught out. Yet, facing up to the truth often means a loss of some sort, and so fantasy can seem the more attractive option.

If evading the truth is a key area for us, we tend to surround ourselves with other people who are also dishonest with themselves – to avoid being challenged or confronted. Even if those around us do attempt to confront us with the truth as they see it, we'll generally refuse to face it until we're ready, anyway. It's important to acknowledge that peeling back the layers of denial is a process, and rarely happens all at once. Author Melody Beattie describes denial as a 'protective device, a shock absorber for the soul', but in spite of any intervention from others, we won't remove this protective layer until we feel secure and resilient enough to do so – and that's OK. We may feel we're getting too many benefits from the situation as it is, that we're not yet ready to walk away, or stubbornness and pride may be blocking us from seeing the whole truth. Being ready to let go of denial happens in *our* time only.

If the subject of our denial is not our own problem but belongs to someone else that we care about, we may find ourselves controlling and manipulating their behaviour, lying and covering up for them, and generally making them the focus, leaving very little time for our own wellbeing. The same rule that applies to ourselves applies to others – instead of shaming or trying to control them, the best thing we can do is to allow them the time they need to face up to their own truth.

At this point, some of you reading this may know that you're far from being willing or able to look honestly at your situation. If that's you, we suggest that you close this book here. Put it back on the shelf and come back to it when you're ready, as the rest will be of little service to you until that time.

If you feel the words so far in this book have spoken to you, we encourage you to keep going. Regardless of the mess you might feel you're in or the truths you've refused to face up to this point, you must treat yourself with compassion now. You did the best you could with the information available to you at the time.

Finally, for those of you who are wondering quite how denial has operated in your life, know that you don't have to be at the extremes of rock bottom to want to improve yourself. Denial plays out just as readily in our day-to-day existence: in the way we choose to keep dating those who are emotionally unavailable, or in the way we spend money that we don't actually have in our bank account.

Whatever scale our denial operates on, there's one thing which we can all be sure of: reality *always* wins out in the end. By staying stuck and keeping our eyes closed to the truth of a situation, we prevent ourselves from making course corrections and growing along the way. When we're brave enough to step out of denial, we're brought our most important lessons, the ones that have been waiting for us all along – the gifts that, until now, we've not been ready to receive.

The questions below require you to be very honest with yourself. They will enable you to see exactly where you are today, based on the facts alone.

EXERCISES

1) As a child, what do you remember lying about and *why* do you think you told each lie?

2) Drawing out the table below in your journal, write down any lies – both major and trivial – you recall telling recently.

NATURE OF THE LIE	WHO I LIED TO	REASON BEHIND THE LIE	CONSEQUENCE OF TELLING THE TRUTH
1. *Lying about my spending habits: I've not been truthful about how much I've been spending on clothes and nights out.*	*My mum.*	*Because I want her to help me out financially.*	*She won't help me if she knows the real reason I'm getting into debt.*
2.			

Can you spot any patterns? Look closely at the reasons for being deceitful and the consequences you fear.

3) Write down three separate experiences from your life that challenged you. In each situation, think about your response. Did you face the situation head-on or do everything you could to avoid dealing with the truth?

CHAPTER 5

RESENTMENT

Persia

'The envious die not once, but as oft as the envied win applause.'

Baltasar Gracián

'm reading my new script on the top deck of the 65 bus on my way home from Tiger's parents' house. Tiger and I have now been together for around three months, and I've just been cast as Vera Kommisarevskaya – the first actress to ever play Nina in Anton Chekhov's *The Seagull.* It's for a new writing piece based around Chekhov's most famous play, and will be premiering at the Menier Chocolate Factory in London Bridge in a few months' time.

Vera is thought to have had a brief romance with Chekhov when she was playing Nina in 1896 in St Petersburg. She was a tragic figure who became unhinged when, at only eighteen, she found her husband in bed with her sister. Vera also lost her little brother Grisha in a drowning accident when he was a baby, and used her pain from this experience to begin the Stanislavsky method of acting. This requires an actor to go within themselves and draw on their own emotional suffering to make the performance more believable.

Like Vera, I too lost a little brother. When I was about seven, my mum had a baby that was three months premature. He died several days after birth. I can still vividly remember the moment Mum and Dad came through our front door, no baby in sight, and had to tell their two young daughters that their brother was in heaven. They had a second boy a few years later, also three months premature. For those three months, my parents would go to visit him every single day in intensive care. He survived, the miracle of the family, and was the driving force behind their success in getting sober.

To bring the role of Vera to life and give her some colour, the director of our production has chosen to merge this historical figure with the character of Masha from *The Seagull*. Masha is a depressed alcoholic and snuff addict who only wears black, and is tormented by her unrequited feelings for the soulful and misunderstood writer Konstantin, and irritated that instead she's being pursued by the boring local schoolteacher.

When I was living with Joey in north London last year, I had my very own Masha experience. An artist I'd been dating had mysteriously stopped responding to my texts. After finally accepting that he'd had all he wanted from me, I took myself off to the nearest Debenhams and bought an entire set of black linen, resolving to take to my bed to grieve this rejection. Joey walked into my room one lunchtime to find me sat in bed, watching back to back *Sex & the City* episodes and drinking Merlot straight from the bottle. When she asked why I'd bought black linen, I responded with Masha's opening line from *The Seagull*:

'Because I'm in mourning for my life.'

We both fell about laughing. I didn't think about the Artist again after that.

Although things appear to be going relatively well for me right now, this is not where I thought I'd be at twenty-five. I may have a boyfriend and an acting job – but Tiger's a drug addict on very shaky ground, and is growing more distant from me with every day that passes. My acting job may move me artistically, but it's unlikely to progress my career any further, because I doubt that any of the big casting directors will bother coming to see a fringe production.

It's slowly starting to dawn on me that it's unlikely I'm going to make it as an actress in the UK. I'm just not getting seen for any of the big stage or screen work, and I don't see that changing any time soon. I feel that my only hope of moving forward in my career is probably to try my luck in the States, where I've had a small amount of interest from music producers and other industry people.

America has become this distant magnetic force, pulling me towards it with promises of a life beyond my wildest dreams. I have enough self-awareness by now to know that this is just me doing another *geographical* – running away to the other side of the world in the vain hope that, there, things will be different: I'll be happy and successful and make entirely different choices in life and love.

As I'm sucked down into the depths of career anxiety, I decide to turn up the volume of self-flagellation by googling one of my oldest childhood friends – Jessica. 'Compare and despair' they call this in the Twelve Steps.

I've known Jess since I was thirteen. Growing up, she was always an avid supporter of my acting pursuits (and I of hers), even turning up to watch my humiliating turn as the role of The Sausage in a school production of the Brothers Grimm fairy tale *The Mouse, The Bird and The Sausage.* (To be fair, despite looking like a human-sized poo, I was told by my form teacher that I brought a real sense of vulnerability and grace to the role.)

A year younger than me, Jess also came to study English Literature at the same university when I was in my third year. Although I've acted with her several times, I've always felt inferior next to her. She's everything that I am – only better. More beautiful, more intelligent, more talented and more funny, she even won the heart of my ex-boyfriend only a few weeks after we'd broken up during sixth form (in Jess's defence, I *had* slept with his best friend while we were still going out – we clearly weren't all that into each other).

I was so livid that Jess had managed to get a first in her degree – while I had missed this achievement by one measly mark – that I'd told everyone that I, too, had been awarded a first. This lie backfired disastrously, however, when the tutor agency I worked for contacted the university for a reference, only to discover that their new star tutor was not such a star after all.

To add insult to injury, Jess was taken on by one of the top acting agents in the world while still at uni – before I'd even left drama school. With several leading roles in the West End and on screen, she's now cropping up on every red carpet and in every magazine, and her new boyfriend is beautiful and famous, and it's killing me.

We've barely spoken since I went out and joined her for pilot season in LA in February – a few months before Tiger and I started dating. Fresh off the back of my detox retreat in Thailand and first Al-Anon meeting, I turned up to the apartment she was staying in armed with several of my mother's self-help books. In my head, I was ready to make my acting dreams manifest. In reality, Jess's boyfriend showed up out of the blue, meaning that I had to find myself somewhere else to stay for the next three weeks.

Ever the resourceful traveller, that very same night I hooked up with a friend of a friend – an actor who'd just moved to LA himself. Both feeling lost and out of our depth in this strange, strange place, we clung to each other for safety amid the chaos of Hollywood, despite having very little else in common.

The next two weeks saw us jumping from grotty hostel to glamorous Oscar party to a different grotty hostel, as I tried to trick myself into believing my lifestyle bore at least *some* resemblance to Jess's.

It wasn't all bad, though. In those three weeks, I did manage to bag myself an acting agent (albeit, a bit of a naff one). When I returned to London, I swiftly signed myself up to a US visa handling company, and set about collating the necessary paperwork with the intent of moving out there by the end of the year.

But then I fell in love with Tiger, and so the visa process has inevitably taken a back seat, as has my friendship with Jess; being around her makes me feel too inadequate.

An acting teacher from drama school once told our class to remember that other people's successes are not our failures. But that's hard to do when you live in a culture that insists that what you do and who you know is more important than who you are.

I've completely lost my identity as the 'successful' one, and it's eating me up inside. All that's left for me to be is the 'ridiculous', 'fun' one. I tell myself that maybe my LA lover was right – that I'm successful simply by association with Jess and her friends. But really, we all know I'm just a social-climbing hanger-on, and nothing makes me feel smaller or more ashamed than this.

In a few years, I'll learn that Jess feels as bad about herself as I do – just from a different side of the fence: the more successful she becomes, the more anxious and insecure she feels.

I love her, but I can't be near her right now. *Not until my life is more impressive*, I tell myself.

LA it must be.

But, LA means no Tiger.

Joey

'Thou hast not half the power to do me harm

As I have to be hurt.'
Othello, William Shakespeare

P-dawg,

I think we are both aware that our friendship is not what it was – that makes me feel sad, particularly as I know that some of that is a consequence of my actions over the past few months. You have been one of the closest friends I've ever had so it does matter a lot to me. But I don't really want to analyse that if I'm honest, I don't think friendships can be forced. We both have to be in the right place mentally and emotionally, and at the moment, I don't feel either of us are. Which is not a happy thought, but a true one I think.

What I do really want to say – and I hope you will know this is coming from a place of love and not negativity – is that I am worried about you. I saw, more than anyone, how beautifully at peace you were after Thailand. I really saw my best friend starting a long but important healing process. Yes, there were some difficult feelings come up but, as you said, after keeping out the demons with drugs/booze/men for a while, things were finally being dealt with head on. I found this so inspiring and it was amazing to see you so positive and, pure, I think is the right word.

I can't really comment on the past few months, because our time together has been minimal. But from hanging out this weekend, I do feel that you have gone back maybe more than you should have to the old ways.

Now, I am not criticising or judging you, although I am sure you will feel that way reading this. I am your friend and I love you and I want to be honest about what I see. Having not seen you much over the last few months, the change is all the more noticeable to me.

I know you said you're at your happiest right now – if that is really how you feel deep down, then disregard this message as a friend over-reacting. Only you know if I have the wrong end of the stick or not.

I just want you to know that I see someone who is slightly less on track than she was.

Right. I think I've rambled enough. Night.

I really hope you take this message the right way x

My default is to be intimidating and accusative when I'm feeling pushed out, and I'm surprised by how gently this email reads. Neither Persia nor I have been in a particularly great headspace of late. We spent a year living together and spiralling destructively downwards, bonding over the fact we were both feeling lost and miserable. It's taken a while for me to come out of my black hole after the break-up with Rory, but when Persia returned from a trip to Thailand with her dad earlier this year, I was inspired by the change I saw in her. Her resolve to live more positively was contagious, and sharing a flat together, the effects soon began to rub off on me as well.

However, when I saw her on Saturday night (while her new boyfriend, Tiger, was away on a meditation retreat in France), she seemed really anxious and spent pretty much the entire evening obsessing about him and trying to get hold of MDMA. Drugs are something that Persia has always done more than me, but she'd reined it in massively since her return from Thailand. The two of us were inseparably close before Tiger came on the scene, but since they got together I've barely seen her at all. In fact, I haven't even met the infamous Tiger yet. I can feel she's slipping away and it hurts, because this isn't the first time it's happened in our friendship.

I haven't always dealt with my friendship dilemmas as gracefully as this evening's email might suggest. A few months ago, Persia told me about an idea she'd heard about in one of the Al-Anon meetings she attends: when someone hurts you, in order to prevent resentment and anger from taking you over, learn to 'detach with love' from that person.

I find this a hard idea to get my head around, because when I feel hurt, my instinct is to detach with a machete. My resentment towards a person can feel so all-encompassing that I can *literally* cut them out of my life. No discussion, no negotiation – decision made. I've always seen this as a sign of strength, of 'not taking shit'. I can be very cut and dried when it comes to other people's mistakes. I don't find it at all easy to let go of resentments. Like an elephant, I remember *everything*.

During high school, one of my close school friends, Elle, also displayed signs of having an unhealthy relationship with alcohol – she was the friend who, on a college trip, I'd escaped and pulled an all-nighter with in a transvestite club in Berlin – nearly resulting in us being unable to sit our AS level exams, due to suspension. The plan had been to go for a 'quick drink' in a bar across the road, but somehow our 10.30 p.m. departure time turned into a messy 7 a.m. return. Meanwhile, our friend Kitty (who we were sharing a hotel room with) had been awake all night, unsure of whether to raise the alarm and alert the staff or sit it out, hoping we'd make it back safely and in time for the group breakfast. Upon rolling back into the room at 7 a.m., Elle and I were relieved to discover that Kitty had opted for the latter. The following day, however, traumatised and having had no sleep, she disclosed the situation to another student, and from there word of the incident unfortunately spread back to the teachers.

Instead of being accountable for my actions and the ensuing punishment, I went ice cold on Kitty for months. The fact that the consequences I was facing had been as a direct result of my own actions went straight over my head. In my mind, it was her fault that I was in trouble, and my job to make sure she knew it.

As the years rolled on and we all went our separate ways to study degree courses at different ends of the country, I could see that Elle was growing even more reckless with her drinking than I was. During the second year of my training at drama school, I was really struggling to cope. I was trying to decide whether to stick it out or admit defeat, leave and try and get a place at RADA – which I felt might be a better fit for me.

Around this time, my group of school friends and I travelled back home up north one weekend, to celebrate Elle's birthday.

Feeling mentally delicate, I promised myself I'd stick to a limit of two drinks only on our night out. For me, the third or fourth has always been the point when my 'f*ck it' button gets pushed – and so two felt like a safer bet. Elle wasn't impressed by this decision and offhand, drunken comments were cast my way for most of the evening about 'how much more fun' I was when I drank. In my overly sensitive, sober state, her words stung and although I put a brave face on (because it was her birthday), inwardly I wanted to punch her.

After a confrontation back at her house in the early hours, I drove myself home in the middle of the night and, despite several phone calls, texts and even an intervention from her mum, Elle and I didn't speak again for *five years*.

My tendency to detach with a machete is a sure way of creating as much distance between myself and the offending party as possible, allowing myself to feel back in control.

When challenges arise in either my friendships or relationships, I find myself to be one of two extremes: either frantically clinging on or aggressively isolating from those who I feel have hurt me. Neither response comes from a place of peace, balance and clarity, but instead desperation, impulsiveness and force.

I read over my email to Persia one final time. I don't want to cut her out of my life, but her inconsistency as a friend is making me lose patience. The feeling of being abandoned has never been comfortable for me, but if it's going to happen, I'd much rather initiate it.

It's 2.32 a.m. as I press 'send' on the email. I close my laptop lid and the room fades to black.

You

'You can't hold a man down without staying down with him.'
Booker T. Washington

On a good day, we may believe that we can't think of any resentments to speak of. Understanding how resentment takes root in our lives is not something many of us will have dedicated much thought to. However, ask us on a bad day who or what we feel resentful towards, and most of us will be able to reel off a considerable list.

'Resentment', or *re-sentiment*, originates from the French word *'ressentiment'*. If we break it down, it's composed of two ideas: *'re'* refers to the idea of something repeating itself and *'sentiment'*, to our feelings. In essence, that's what resentment is: revisiting old feelings or wrongs from the past. In many ways, resentment is the main culprit in keeping us stuck in negativity, due to the toxicity it inflicts on our inner life. Some say 'resentment is like drinking poison and expecting the other person to die'. We cannot punish another person without punishing ourselves, since holding on to negativity is toxic for *our* soul.

What is the purpose and benefit of working through our feelings of anger and resentment? Well, when we don't the negativity festers, blocking us from living with honesty, tolerance and an open heart.

If we notice a splinter piercing the skin of our palm, our impulse would be to extract it quickly, to avoid discomfort and infection. Replacing the splinter with resentment, why, when it causes sickness to our soul, do we not seek to eliminate our negative feelings just as fast? Removing a splinter of wood from our skin, of course, is an easier feat, but we could choose to cleanse our minds from negativity with the same tenacity.

Negative feelings are part of the human experience and it's important to acknowledge that it's *OK* to feel them. It's natural to feel angry and resentful at times; sometimes the circumstances in our lives absolutely call for it. The question is not so much *to feel* or *not to feel*, but *how* we choose to express, and heal, those feelings.

Perhaps we react explosively to people and circumstances, providing ourselves with momentary relief, but often causing an already fraught situation to worsen. Or, afraid of being controlled by our emotions, we may withdraw into our shell and refuse to deal with conflict entirely. In doing so, we find ourselves at the mercy of our feelings anyway, because in refusing to process them, our anger quietly solidifies into unresolved, deeper-rooted resentment instead. Steely silence and shutting down can be just as cruel as harsh words, tantrums and door slamming, as they both derive from the same intent: a desire to punish and control.

In Twelve Step philosophy, resentments are referred to as the 'number one offender' for spiritual unbalance, and they're generally assigned to three core categories: people, places and institutions.

More often than not, it's people that we hold the majority of our resentments towards, whether for their success and what they have, or what they may have done or failed to do for us. In our closest relationships, in particular, it's often the smaller things that are most difficult to forgive: a sarcastic comment from our boyfriend in front of others or a friend turning up half an hour late to dinner. This often triggers an argument in which a whole host of past grievances are dredged up and used as weapons. The sarcastic comment is another example of how our boyfriend always disrespects us in front of loved ones. The friend turning up late is yet another indication of her complete lack of respect for our time.

We may also hold bitterness towards places: a shop that wouldn't refund our purchase or the country we got mugged in. Or institutions: the NHS's failure to save a loved one or the lack of support we received when we were at school.

Consider the process of weeding a garden. To make sure you weed properly, you need to grab each one by the root, extracting it from the earth, ensuring not one remains – since there's little point in weeding at all if you leave any behind, as they'll grow back before you know it. The process of rooting out resentment is very like this: you must be thorough in looking at the past grievances you're holding on to and pull them up by the root, effectively clearing the wreckage of your past once and for all. Once you have dealt with the resentments from your past, be they large or small, the work then lies in the ongoing maintenance of your garden. As soon as a new little shoot of resentment appears, you can identify, deal with and prevent it from taking root in your soul.

When you dig deeper, and look at the root of your resentments, you may find that self-pity and pride play a major part. In feeling resentful, we tend to adopt the victim mode of '*Poor me*' and '*How could they do this to me?*' or, the indignant stance of '*I would never do something like that*'. In being judgemental, we take a position of superiority, while belittling the identity of the offending person, place or institution, often – it has to be said – without having the full facts in hand.

Most of us have been guilty of misinterpreting a perceived wrong at some point, and, in obsessively playing it over in our heads, allow the offence to take on a life of its own. Even when another person is at fault, by giving the issue undue focus in our minds we can easily lose perspective on the situation. Having an imaginary argument in our head may allow us to control what each person says and who 'wins', but it also results in quickly losing our foothold in reality.

There are also occasions where something is completely unacceptable, and in those instances we needn't tolerate it – we're free to take decisive action. This may come in the form of calmly addressing a situation, setting a boundary to protect ourselves in the future or, in more extreme cases, removing ourselves from a dynamic completely. Whatever may be necessary, we can take the appropriate action, and then work on releasing ourselves from any lingering negative feelings.

It's often claimed that 'expectation is a premeditated resentment'. Therefore, in exploring how negativity plays out in our lives, we can look to our expectation as a possible source. Working to release expectations, especially around the things in our lives that perpetually disappoint us, can help protect us from feeling unnecessarily hurt.

If we buy a generous birthday gift for a friend, we can choose to give it freely and without expectation of anything in return. In doing so, we leave no room for disappointment when our friend doesn't display huge amounts of gratitude (which may not be in their nature), or reciprocate with a gift equally as expensive when our own birthday comes around. Similarly, if we know from past experience that *every* appointment we book at the doctor's surgery runs thirty minutes later than scheduled, we can allow space in the diary to accommodate the probable delay and arm ourselves with the patience required.

In becoming willing to deal with our resentments, we may even find ourselves prepared to step into the shoes of the perpetrator. Are we able to acknowledge that they too may have weak spots and insecurities? Can we identify why they may have felt driven or triggered to do what they did? Were we in their position, can we be sure that we would not have done the same? In fact, can we *honestly* say we've never done similar?

Often, it's those of us who have exceptionally high standards of ourselves that seek the same standard in the people around us. When we don't find it, the hammer of condemnation can come down with almighty force. It's not our business, however, to judge other people's choices. If peace of mind is what we're seeking, we must simply take responsibility for our own behaviour and remain focused on releasing our attachment to anyone else's.

A desire to retaliate and cause pain to an offending party in the way that they've caused pain to us is understandable, yet it's not our job. It helps to be mindful that, very often: 'hurt people hurt people'. Balanced, loving individuals rarely intend to inflict pain on the lives of others.

Finding it in our heart to wish those people well is not easy, but with the guidance of the second section of this book, it's possible. Having acknowledged our resentments in the exercises below, Part Two: The Solution, offers the opportunity to have them lifted from us.

EXERCISES

1) Often, when resentments are written down they lose their power over us. In your journal, draw out the table below and list as many resentments as you can think of. The fourth column remains blank until a later chapter.

I'M RESENTFUL AT	THE CAUSE	HOW DOES IT MAKE ME FEEL?	
1. *My friends.*	*They've booked to go on a girly weekend away and I haven't been invited.*	*Rejected. Disrespected. Afraid that I'm getting pushed out of the group.*	
2.			

2) Resentments are often linked to your fears and unresolved wounds. Can you see any patterns that show up time and time again?

3) Do you have a tendency towards people-pleasing (e.g. saying or doing something that you don't actually want to)? Why do you do it and how does it make you feel?

An example: I often agree to hang out with my housemate when I don't have the time to. I do it because she likes the company and I don't want to upset her by saying 'no'. As a result, I'm falling behind on the course I'm studying for and now feel angry at her for this.

4) Write down an example of a time someone you know experienced success. How did it make you feel? How did you react?

PART TWO

THE
SOLUTION

There is a famous children's book called *The Very Hungry Caterpillar*. It follows a caterpillar who experiences continuous hunger. He eats and eats, but never feels satisfied. After five days of gorging, he begins to feel sick. When his illness passes, he spins himself a cocoon and, two weeks later, emerges as a beautiful butterfly.

The insect's transformation is an analogy that's often used in reference to spiritual transformation – a journey from the dark to the light. However by the time you're ready to spin your own cocoon and 'hope for the best', its not by chance, but by necessity.

Having undergone our own 'spiritual metamorphosis' of sorts, we can really relate to the caterpillars experience. At our lowest point, having exhausted ourselves gorging on anything and everything outside of us to try and fill the void within, it slowly began to dawn on us that our old way of doing things simply wasn't working anymore. Albert Einstein is thought to have said, 'The definition of insanity is doing the same thing over and over again and expecting different results'. Realising that we'd been banging our heads against a brick wall of our own making, we could no longer deny that we were rapidly hurtling ourselves towards a very dark place.

But, what do you do when you know you can't go back, but you have no idea how to move forward – or what 'forward' even looks like? How can you know that you'll emerge from your cocoon at all? Because, if we're honest, when you're in there, it can feel lonely, hopeless and – worse still – permanent.

However, when you've experienced enough pain and disappointment, you'll likely be ready – and willing – to try something different.

Often, when you arrive at this point of surrender, you begin to realise that your real problem is not what's been going on *outside* of you – the job you despise, the relationship that broke down, your addictive vices – but what's been going on *inside* of you. And inside all of us, there's really only ever one toxic thought (though it may manifest itself in various different guises) playing over and over like a broken record, causing us to act out in all manner of unhealthy ways:

I am not enough.

We don't believe we really deserve the happiness we so desperately crave, so we keep ourselves stuck, and we keep ourselves small. We waste time and energy trying to change everything in our outer realities – our bodies, our careers, our lovers – to try and make ourselves *feel* enough. But even when we manage to succeed in our external endeavours, we still feel like a failure on the inside, because either we don't feel satisfied with what we have, or we don't really feel worthy of it. Then in steps self-sabotage, to ensure that our outer life matches how awful we're feeling on the inside. That way, at least our lives will make some sense to us.

So, what's the solution? Well, it's actually quite simple – simple, but not easy. As we stated in the introduction, what we've learned ourselves is that if you focus on the insides, the outsides will take care of themselves. Happiness is an inside job, and as this second part of the book explores, it's one that's centred around developing a spiritual connection of your own understanding. Through the application of universal spiritual principles and tools that help heal the internal wounds from your past, you're then more able to step away from the self-destructive patterns that have been sabotaging your present. When you shift your inner perspective like this, you'll start to see your outer reality heal, too – and we'll be focusing on that external aspect in the final part of the book.

For some, this section will be the most challenging. For others, it will be a huge relief. Regardless of which camp you fall into, we want to be clear here that the spiritual journey you're about to embark on is not one that is religious in nature. There are no rules or dogmas. Instead, this experience is an intensely personal, creative and freeing process in which you'll simply be guided to connect to a sense of love, peace and joy that already exists within you – you perhaps just don't know how to access it yet.

This may all sound really confusing, scary and 'out there' – particularly to those of you who are new to or uncomfortable with the word 'spiritual' – but it will become clearer and less esoteric in the coming chapters. At this point, all you need to have is an open mind and a willing spirit, as you step inside your own cocoon.

CHAPTER 6

POWERLESS

Persia

'There are times when we must sink to the bottom of our misery to understand truth, just as we must descend to the bottom of a well to see the stars in broad daylight.'

The Power of the Powerless, Václav Havel

'm standing over the sink in the dimly lit kitchen of Tiger's parents' house, scraping dog shit off one of my new suede boots. It's 6.30 in the morning, and the house is silent. While I was on my way to the bathroom twenty minutes ago, the dog squeezed past me into Tiger's room and shat all around his bed while he was still fast asleep. I only realised after stepping in some – thankfully, *after* I'd put on my shoes.

Under normal circumstances, I'd have turned the lights on, woken Tiger up and sorted out the dog and mess. But the last thing I want to do this morning is have to interact with Tiger – especially over dog shit.

Last night, I discovered that he cheated on me a month ago while he was on a meditation retreat in the south of France. He didn't tell me this – I went through the diary on his computer at his parents' house while he was out.

Although I've been regularly checking his phone, Facebook and email ever since we first got together, I really ramped it up after he got back from France and I'd seen this girl sending him private messages and asking for his address. I told myself that the messages were just platonic, but deep down I knew the truth, even then; it takes one to know one.

I've always gone through my boyfriends' stuff; it gives me a massive hit of adrenalin. Because I've cheated on pretty much everyone I've ever been with, I developed a need to cancel out my own guilt by attempting to uncover some hidden secret that they might be keeping from me. *If I can lie so easily, maybe they can, too?* Of course, if you go looking for evidence of someone's betrayal, you'll usually find some – even if it doesn't turn up in the form you expected. The strange thing is that, often, you actually *want* to find some-thing bad – as if the ends will somehow justify your boundary-crossing means.

However, what I read in his diary last night was far worse than I'd anticipated. It was an in-depth account of the amazing sex he'd had with the girl from the meditation retreat, and how he thinks he's fallen in love with her.

I was dumbfounded. Every cell of my body felt like it was in shock. I had no idea what on earth I should do, especially considering that in a matter of days, Tiger would be leaving to walk the Camino de Santiago pilgrimage in Spain for two months.

When Tiger got back from work last night, I told him everything – my stalking, finding his diary entry – all of it. The next few hours passed by in a blur of tears, screaming at each other, extended periods of silence and finally, angry emotional sex, before I crawled on to the sofa in his room and fell asleep, exhausted.

As soon as 6 a.m. came around, I quickly got up and dressed, desperate to get out of the house before he woke up. That's when I stood in the dog shit.

When the worst of it is off my boot, I put it back on and make my way to the front door. Tiger is standing on the stairs.

'Pers, did you just *shit* all over my room?' he asks, trying to get me to smile.

'Wish I had done,' I mumble, as I pick up my bag and walk past him out into the chilly September air. My one saving grace is that this morning there happens to be a breakfast Al-Anon meeting in Knightsbridge, which I've been to a few times before. The meeting's in a beautiful old church, which reminds me of the one that mine and Salena's primary school carol service used to be held at.

A moment after I've sat down in the meeting, a stylish older blonde woman with bright blue eyes asks if the seat next to me is taken. I shake my head and she sits. Her name is Bella. She tells me that she's been coming to these meetings for over twenty years now. Her ex-husband (and the father of her three sons) was an alcoholic, and the drama and violence that resulted from his addiction had left her almost suicidal. Al-Anon had quite literally saved her life.

After the meeting, I talk through mine and Tiger's situation with Bella. I realise that, for the first time in my life, the shoe is on the other foot. Tiger has only done to me what I've done to countless others before him, and I now finally understand that we both have a serious addiction to cheating and falling in love.

What hurts more than anything else is knowing that I've caused this kind of pain to so many of my previous boyfriends and was completely oblivious to it. It's like I'm suddenly experiencing the backlog of all that guilt and remorse now, and I never, ever want to cause someone to feel like this again.

Bella reminds me that I don't need to make a decision about Tiger and I until I'm ready. All I need to focus on for the remainder of the day is taking care of myself; the right course of action will become clear eventually.

Though my heart still feels like it's been shattered into a million pieces, I turn my phone off so that I don't have to think about whether or not Tiger's going to bother getting in touch. I take myself for a long walk in Richmond Park, where I sit and cry for a while. When I get home, I have a bubble bath and watch a romantic comedy in a vain attempt to cheer myself up a bit. I still feel awful, but at least I'm not out drinking and trying to find a new man to take my mind off my pain.

I go to bed early and am awoken in the middle of the night by a dream in which I'm talking to Tiger. I switch on the bedside lamp and grab a notebook and pen. Words that don't feel like my own pour out of me on to the page:

T,

I don't know how it's possible that this time yesterday I was screaming at you and felt as though my heart was physically breaking, and now I somehow feel the calmest and clearest I have done in a very long time.

I didn't think I'd be able to say that I've honestly come to accept what's happened, but I have. I'm even grateful for it, because it's forced me to look at some very painful truths about myself. Finally got a taste of my own medicine, didn't I?

Maybe the next two months apart is a gift for each of us. I dreaded it at first, because in many ways I've become addicted to the way you make me feel – good and bad. But clearly, we both need this time to be on our own. I've never really been on my own before; there's always been someone waiting in the wings.

This time, I'm going to choose something different. I'm not going to pick up drugs or find a new man to replace you. I'm going to start working the Twelve Steps in Al-Anon instead.

There's a huge part of me that wants to try again when you're back from the Camino, as I feel that deep down, our story is not meant to end just yet. But I trust that, after our time apart, we'll both know what to do.

I'm so grateful for the summer we've had together, and for the things I've learned about myself and relationships from being with you. Thank you.

Have a beautiful trip.

P xxx

The next day, I drop the letter through his parents' letterbox – several hours after receiving the following email from him:

Dear Persia,

You mean the world to me and I don't want to lose you. What I did in France was unforgivable and leaves me feeling like a fickle scumbag. I don't want to be that anymore. I don't know if it's that easy to just change a lifetime's bad behaviour, but I never want to put anyone through this again.

I feel incredibly muddled by all this and spent the whole of yesterday feeling as though my head was going to explode. I battled so hard to get this much sobriety under my belt and I feel it slipping away.

I don't think I'm ready for a relationship, I don't think I ever was. These kind of emotions are too strong and I know now why they don't recommend them for the early stages of getting sober. It's so painful – and it's even worse when you know it was all your doing.

I need to change something deep within me, otherwise I'm going to go through life doing the same thing in every relationship. And in that sense, the Camino trip couldn't have come at a better time – the perfect opportunity for some solitary soul-searching.

I want you to know I'll be thinking of you always while I'm away, you'll be at the heart of my thoughts and the thoughts of my heart. You have so much life in you Persia and so much motivation to better yourself and understand the world. You are beautiful from the inside out, and it's been an honour to have been let in and have a chance to see the real you.

Forever holding a place for you in my heart,

T xxx

The next day, Tiger departs for the Camino, and I begin what turns out to be in many ways one of the most challenging, but important periods of my life.

As well as starting weekly therapy, I also attend around four Al-Anon meetings a week, and ask Bella to be my sponsor. Much like in AA, a sponsor in Al-Anon is someone who's been attending meetings for a while and working through the Twelve Steps themselves. They serve as a support and mentor figure to help you along your own spiritual path.

I find myself ringing Bella most days, mainly because it helps stop me from going back into self-sabotage mode.

I don't think I've ever felt more powerless in my life. It's taking every ounce of strength I have not to throw this whole spiritual stuff out of the window and go and find myself a new lover to ease my anxiety. But I keep going, regardless.

Joey is also being a huge support to me at the moment. Having barely seen her since Tiger and I got together, I'm grateful that she's willing to be here for me. In many respects, our friendship has never been stronger; we go out regularly for long dinners, and she takes me to an amazing gig by an up-and-coming musician called King Charles, which lifts my spirits considerably. I promise myself that whatever ends up happening with Tiger and I when he's back, I won't sideline Joey again like I did this summer.

A couple of weeks before Tiger's due home – and just when things are starting to feel a little bit easier, I get my first call from him since he's been away. He tells me he's relapsed and is having a panic attack. I try to calm him down, but my words have little effect. I hang up the phone and the penny finally drops: *I'm never going to be able to change him.*

Joey

'I am so tired – so tired of being whirled on through all these phases of my life, in which nothing abides by me, no creature, no place; it is like the circle in which the victims of earthly passion eddy continually.'
North and South, Elizabeth Gaskell

'I think you should go home,' Persia advises stonily.

'Yes,' I reply.

Observing the steely tone in her voice and the way that both she and Tiger are staring unfavourably at me, now feels like a good time to leave. I bundle myself into a nearby taxi and swiftly depart the scene.

The evening didn't start well. The two of us had planned to meet for a girly catch-up before heading over to a warehouse party in east London, where we were meeting Tiger and his cohort. I'd felt Persia was rushing our time together in order to get there and predictably, when we did, Tiger was running hours late. I spent most of the evening drinking down my irritation at Persia for spending so much time on her phone texting Tiger, instead of being present for me – the one who *had* showed up.

So far in their on/off relationship, Tiger's behaviour has been far from ideal. Although other friends have warned Persia away from him, a month after he returned from the Camino, she made the decision to take him back. I get it: she isn't done until she's done. However, after growing close again while Tiger was away for two months, now that they're back together I can feel Persia disappearing once more. I'm not entirely blameless in this situation, of course; every time she returns, I receive her with open arms. Usually, if you spot it, you got it. I know I've been guilty of neglecting my own friendships before on account of a romance. Unfortunately, the inconsistency of our dynamic plays straight into my fear of abandonment, and I'm now acutely sensitive to any sign that it might be happening again.

Slumped in the back of the taxi, I try to make sense of the events that have unfolded over the last few hours. Not knowing anyone else at the party tonight, I found myself alone a lot while Persia stalked around after Tiger, who was always on the move. At some point they had a huge row, which prompted her to book a taxi for the two of us to head back to mine. By the time the car arrived, though, they'd disappeared off to make up and she was nowhere to be seen. Fed up, I found a random duvet cover and took refuge under it on the floor, with the warehouse party still very much going on around my head. By this point, it must've been nearly 5 a.m., and we'd been drinking since early the previous evening.

Under the duvet, in a state of semi-consciousness, I remember having a vivid dream that I was making out with Tiger there on the floor, when suddenly, Persia lifted the covers and tried to pull me up. It was only then that I looked down to see that somebody had been lying there next to me, and I didn't recognise him *at all*.

Confused, I told Persia what I thought had been happening: I thought it was Tiger I'd been kissing. Her face promptly dropped. Clearly it was *not* Tiger – and it was no vivid dream I was having.

Furious, she walked off, and still disorientated I turned to Tiger:

'Tiger, I love you,' is what came out.

He laughed uneasily, patted me on the back and headed outside after Persia. Following them out on to the street, it was at this point that I took my cue and bundled myself into a taxi.

What. A. Bizarre. Turn. Of. Events. It feels as if I'm in some sort of in-between state; I'm not asleep but it doesn't feel like reality either. I lurch forward to check with the cab driver, 'Is this real?'

He assures me that it is. Feeling a sudden wave of panic, I reach into my bag for my phone to ring Persia and try to explain, but it's not in there.

By nature, I'm a control freak. I'm used to having all my 'T's crossed and 'I's dotted. Yet, despite my previous success at keeping a lid on things, it all seems to be coming out sideways recently.

I've upped my catering shifts since Rory broke up with me, mainly to stop my mind obsessing, but also to try and sort out my finances. Working at parties and events often means late nights and a glass of wine or two on the job, and I've no idea why but there've been a handful of married men making passes at me lately. I honestly don't think I'm inviting the attention. I mean, I'm not even attracted to most of them. Maybe they see some kind of brokenness in me, a weak spot? I feel like a little girl when advances are made, and don't deal with it well at all.

A tarot card reader in Camden (who I've visited sporadically over the past couple of years when I've felt unsure about the future) said recently that, when she looked into her crystal ball, she saw an image of a fairy with a broken wand. Something about that image resonated: that's exactly how I feel. I just don't know how to get my wand working again.

I'm not sure if it's the result of my diet, drinking, gradual descent into depression, or all three, but I've also been struck, at the age of twenty-three, with acute acne on my face. Huge, under-the-skin, painful bumps across my cheeks. It's as if my inner turmoil is literally coming to the surface, and at a time when my acting career already feels completely out of my hands, it's not helping matters.

I seem to have entered one of the only professions where initiative isn't at all proportionate to reward. No matter how much you might have prepared, if your face doesn't fit or someone reads the part better, you're not going to land the job. And you rarely get any feedback, either. I'm repeatedly at the mercy of this – I feel I'm putting so much out there and *nothing* is coming back.

Since I graduated from drama school, the only job I've been paid a reasonable wage for was a commercial – many months ago now. It was for Alpen cereal and was shot in the Ukraine. I had assumed (with my impressive tolerance levels) that I could keep up with the locals at the wrap party, where there was an abundance of vodka gold circulating all evening. I misjudged that. The trip culminated in me retching on all fours outside the airport the following day, vomiting inches away from the director's shoes as he tried to shake my hand to say goodbye. Not quite the picture of balance and radiance that I was going for as an Alpen advocate.

Thankfully, this episode hasn't got back to my agent, who needs no further ammunition to dislike me. They make no secret of the fact they find my eagerness irritating. Any email I send flagging up an audition I'd like to be considered for is met with either a cold response, or no reply at all.

Nevertheless, they're a reputable agent and I'm lucky to be on their books, so I'm trying to keep my head down. I recently got down to the final two actresses for roles in separate theatre productions, but found out this week that I landed neither. This wouldn't be so much of a blow if, earlier this year, I hadn't secured the female lead in a feature film set in Varanasi, India, only to be dropped from the cast weeks later. A new director came on board and he said, I quote, 'I don't like her face.' I was, and still am, mortified by this. Apart from Mum, I've told no one the real reason why I was turfed off the project – not even Persia. It'll be a few months from now that a letter from my agent arrives through the letterbox informing me that my representation has been officially terminated.

This situation is only made more unbearable by Olivia's recent rocket to stardom. At this point, neither myself nor the two boys we moved in with after graduation fully understand what a huge deal her break will turn out to be. She'll go on to become Hollywood royalty, and one of the most talked about actresses in the world.

In the years that follow, I'll refer back to this period as my 'divine storm'. In essence, a divine storm is a period of life where you feel like literally *everything* and *everyone* (including the Big Man himself) is against you.

The taxi must have delivered me home from the warehouse party safely, since I've woken up today in my own bed. I manage to borrow a phone to contact Persia, but she ignores my calls – which only makes me more determined to reach her. I persist and she finally picks up, on my thirtieth or so attempt. The conversation is short and cold. She tells me that I 'need help' and 'should look at my drinking', before handing the phone over to Tiger.

'I want to speak to my best friend,' I say.

'I don't think she is anymore,' he replies, in a voice that doesn't sound too far off smug.

I am *IRATE*. After consistently being there for her, having the two of them turn on me like this really does feel like the final nail in the coffin. Everything I touch seems to end up spinning totally out of my control.

You

'The realisation that he was utterly powerless was like the blow of a sledgehammer. Yet it was curiously calming as well.'
The Unbearable Lightness of Being, Milan Kundera

Life is like a river; it gently meanders and flows for miles and miles, eventually finding its way to the sea. As we're each carried down this river of life, we often find ourselves becoming afraid.

What if the river takes a wrong turn? We fail to see that there is no such thing as a wrong turn for a river – it's all just part of the journey. In our fear, we panic and grab onto the riverbank. We kick our legs furiously, trying to turn around and swim against the tide in a vain attempt to take back control. But all this does is exhaust us and prevent us from enjoying the ride.

As we've already explored in the first section of this book, the majority of our struggles come as a direct result of trying to make things happen in the way that we think they should. We tell ourselves that, if *I* do not hold it together, if *I* do not take control, everything will crumble. And maybe that's exactly what needs to happen, for in trying to control things so rigidly, we may be preventing what needs to naturally occur from taking place – or at least prolonging the inevitable.

This tends to play out most commonly in our relationships, for example: many of us believe that it's our responsibility to fix other people's problems. We try to cajole and coerce our family, friends and lovers into our way of thinking or doing things, only to find them withdrawing from and resenting us – which makes us, in turn, feel hurt and angry.

We often tell ourselves that our attempts to control others or certain outcomes comes from a loving, well-meaning place. This may be so to a certain degree, but more likely it's because *we'll* feel better if things pan out the way we think they ought to.

One of the most painful yet life-changing lessons we've learned over recent years is that we are all powerless over pretty much everyone and everything, except ourselves. In our experience, this revelation usually hits when you're at your very lowest – when you feel so desperate and hopeless that surrender becomes your only option.

It often takes us a while to get there, because our culture is constantly trying to persuade us that a strong sense of self-will is the solution to our happiness and success – and to some extent, it is. However, there comes a point in life when you realise that there is an awful lot you can't control, no matter how hard you might try.

While it may be your last resort, coming to accept your powerlessness turns out to be a huge relief and blessing, because it means that you can finally stop trying to swim against the tide. A heavy burden is lifted from your shoulders, and you become free to focus all your attention on the one thing you can actually change – yourself.

All that energy and effort it takes to try and control every element of your life – your job, your weight, your relationship, your friendships, your social media profile – you can just *stop*. Stop fighting your appetite. Stop trying to manipulate the person you're dating into falling in love with you. Stop worrying about how you're ever going to afford a mortgage. Just for *this* moment – *stop*.

Worrying, obsessing, controlling and manipulating are all pointless activities. They deceive you into thinking you're being productive and making progress, but what you're really doing is pushing all the things you really want away, because you're coming from a place of fear. This anxious energy it makes very difficult to arrive at rational decisions, and so you often end up making an already trying situation even worse.

When you stop meddling in other people's affairs, you free up a load of energy to focus on what you want for your own life, and personal clarity is an incredibly creative and productive force.

What most of us want to experience as human beings is a sense of peace within ourselves. We've all had those moments – however fleeting – when the world just seems to stand still. We can catch our breath, and no matter what's going on outside of us, we feel totally calm, centred and grateful. This is because we are present in the moment; we're not trying to make it anything other than what it is. The goal is to try and experience this feeling more and more, so that our lives begin to find a sense of flow.

One way of practising powerlessness is by striving to live our lives *one day at a time*. We are powerless over the future, except to the extent that the choices we make *today* will affect it. Life becomes much more manageable when, instead of letting ourselves become totally consumed and overwhelmed by the magnitude of a situation (whether that's getting over a painful loss, completing a huge project at work or moving house), we focus on what small action we can take today to move us in the direction we want to be heading in. And, we also need to get very clear about what our limitations are within this day (or even just this moment) – what we *can't* control right now.

Although your first experience of powerlessness tends to come through one major (and painful) situation, eventually you start to accept powerlessness as part of the more intimate details of your everyday life. *I am powerless over whether or not there is a parking space right when and where I want it. I am powerless over the price of public transport. I am powerless over my friend's negative mood.*

At the end of all Twelve Step meetings, the group says the following words together – originally written by American theologian Reinhold Niebuhr. Whenever we've found ourselves feeling anxious about the future, repeating these words always helps to calm us down and shift our perspective:

> *Grant me the serenity to accept the things I cannot change,*
> *The courage to change the things I can,*

And the wisdom to know the difference.
No matter how big or trivial a problem we may face, we must accept what we are powerless over, relinquish control and strive to change only the things we're able to in this moment.

EXERCISES

1) How do you feel about the idea that you're powerless over the other people in your life? Does it make you feel scared? Anxious? Relieved?

2) Write a list of all the things you're stressed or worried about. Identify which ones you have no real control over, and scribble these items out as a reminder to yourself that you are powerless over these things, and can therefore choose to let them go.

3) Then, look at the remaining items on your list and note down a small action step you can take for each to move you forward in that area. Make sure you give yourself a time frame and schedule it into your diary to help you stick to it – e.g. Feeling anxious about my weight – cut out cake and biscuits starting tomorrow for the next two weeks.

CHAPTER 7

HIGHER POWER

Joey

'To one who has faith, no explanation is necessary.
To one without faith, no explanation is possible.'

St Thomas Aquinas

've been lying in bed for what seems like an eternity. The more I think about it, the more I'm convinced that someone put something in one of my many drinks at the warehouse party two days ago. I can still feel my heart pumping in my chest.

Persia and I haven't spoken since our short conversation yesterday, which is definitely not helping my anxiety. I'm supposed to be going on a date later this afternoon with a guy named Josh – it's a blind date, set up by a mutual actress friend. I slip my arm out from the covers and pull my phone back inside with me.

'Hi, I'm so sorry, but I'm not feeling well. I think we're going to have to reschedule today.' I type.

A millisecond before pressing send, a message pops up on my phone. It's from Josh.

'Hi Jo, are we still on for 4.30 p.m., outside South Kensington tube?'

I sit up in bed and scramble over to the mirror: I look like a revived corpse. Despite the horror staring back at me, something makes me turn back to my phone.

'Yes x', I reply, deleting the message that was so nearly sent in its place, just a minute earlier.

A quick shower, a smattering of make-up and two pieces of toast later, and I'm travelling down the Piccadilly line. I spot a guy waiting at the top of the stairs of the underground, with a small artificial red rose behind his ear. I'm not sure why, as I've never seen Josh before in my life, but I know it's him. He seems to share this knowing, as he clocks me instantly, breaks into a smile and wanders over. This is a lucky dip gone right. Josh is tall, athletically slim with dark hair, and golden skin. He is thirty-two but looks younger than his years. There's a glow and brightness about him.

Making the most of Christmas time in London, we go ice-skating on a nearby rink, before heading to the pub for some food. A sign just behind Josh's head is glaring at me – it's advertising mulled wine, my absolute favourite tipple during this season. Although I'd usually jump straight on the wine wagon on a first date to take the edge off my nerves, I'm not actually sure I can stomach it.

The waitress comes over and stands beside us with her notepad poised. I glance back to the sign, hesitating.

'Er . . . an orange juice?' I ask, as if looking for confirmation.

Josh cocks his head sideways in surprise and orders himself a Diet Coke.

I've often heard the old adage, 'When the student is ready, the teacher will appear'. What should be added to that, is that you might not come to realise that *you* are the student, or *who* your teacher is, for quite some time.

A connection to God, or a power greater than myself, is not something I explored in the early stages of my life. Growing up, the only time our family ever visited church was for the Christingle service, where Dad used to joke we'd go to get our free orange. Questionable humour aside, my parents are full of integrity and kindness, but faith in an entity that couldn't be seen was never embraced in our household.

One Christmas, at the age of about eight, I remember when my grandma learned that I was yet to be christened. Although I'm not sure she was actively practising a faith herself, she took offence to my parents' lack of diligence.

'But she'll go to HELL!' she exclaimed, over Christmas dinner.

I left the table and ran upstairs, howling in distress. I'm not actually sure why, as I didn't believe in God, heaven or hell, but it seemed like an appropriate response at the time.

Years later, during high school, there was a boy in my class who made no secret about the fact that he was on fire for Jesus. I was one of the wilder teenagers in among a very middle-class and sensible year and, possibly because of this, he made me the sole focus of his conversion efforts. Regularly serenading me with song, his enthusiasm both amused and bewildered me. I was intrigued by the unshakable faith he possessed, but upon enquiry it made no logical sense to me.

It wasn't until I was sixteen that I had my first undeniable 'otherworldly experience'. I was visiting my cousin Natty in Texas and we did a Ouija board – which was incredibly bizarre and not something I'd recommend or repeat. There is no doubt in my mind that we connected with spirits that day, and I felt quite out of sorts for a long while after. However, one question that we asked those we spoke with was:

'Does God exist?'

The answer that came back: 'Yes.'

I wrote about this experience in my diary at the time but forgot all about it, until rereading the entry many years later.

By the time I was in my third year at drama school, something odd started happening to me. I began waking up in the middle of the night to see a giant spider hanging off the lamp beside my head. I would squeeze my eyes shut, convinced that I was having a nightmare, but when I reopened them, the spider was still there, inches from my pillow. My heart would pound so hard that my whole head pulsated. I'd try to move, but I couldn't – it was as if I was paralysed. At some point, the paralysis would release its hold, and as soon as I could switch the light on I'd find there was nothing there.

The third time this occurred, it was accompanied by a crashing sound and a thud – as I landed on the floor on the other side of my room. Startled, I ran my fingers across the wall in search of the light switch. The spider had once again vanished, but all the perfume and cosmetic bottles on my desk were scattered and smashed on the floor. I felt my hip throbbing and lifted up my t-shirt to see my skin was swollen and red.

Concerned that I was losing my mind, I booked myself an appointment with the doctor. There was no medical explanation, but it was suggested I was going through a period of change (this was true – I was coming out of my longest and most stable relationship to date, which had been my lifeline during those tumultuous years at drama school) and I was advised that the episodes should pass in time. With no further light shed on the issue, I turned to the twenty-first-century alternative GP: Google. Within seconds, I'd found reams of information listing symptoms exactly like my own – the feeling of being immobilised, yet awake and fully conscious of what was happening. This experience was commonly referred to as 'sleep paralysis', with the most reported sighting being spiders or black mounds.

As I continued to read more about it, I learned that 30 per cent of young adults are affected by sleep paralysis. While the medical profession had little in the way of explanation, it had recently been listed in a manual by the American Psychiatric Association as an issue of 'spiritual emergency'. Sleep paralysis was described as a symptom of an 'impending spiritual awakening', resulting from a crisis about the meaning of life and existence, and commonly occurring during times of transiting into adulthood, parenthood or mid-life. I read on, and an extract from another book *Sleep Paralysis: A Guide to Hypnagogic Visions and Visitors of the Night* stood out:

> Seen in this light, Sleep Paralysis can serve as a metaphor for the fact that our old defenses are no longer functioning as well as before. When this stress manifests as Sleep Paralysis, the body is paralyzed, the mind is in fight or flight, and there's nowhere to run. So, instead, we must take a stand. For some, this looks like courage. For others, it is faith.

Shame around my past behaviour had kept me from ever entertaining the idea of faith as the years went on. As a teenager, I had hung out in the graveyard of the church near my house, smoking weed, drinking and hooking up with local boys. Having acted disrespectfully on sacred ground made me think that, if there were a God, He'd know and wouldn't want anything to do with me. On occasion, I had joked that should He actually exist and want to reach me, He'd use my Achilles heel – a man – to draw me in.

The waitress places my orange juice in front of me and Josh glances down at it.

'You're not drinking?' he asks.

'Not today I – I've been having a bit of a bad time recently with going too far.'

And with that, I verbal diarrhoea the *entire* warehouse party story at him. He sits quietly taking it all in, his brown eyes calm and present, as I ramble on.

'Nothing so bad that it can't be fixed,' he says. 'I suppose I should tell you now, I haven't had a drink in four years. I'm in AA.'

Persia

'When you really want love, you will find it waiting for you.'
De Profundis, Oscar Wilde

I'm sat on the floor of a large church with Tiger on a Sunday evening. It's my first proper church service in years. Cushions are scattered across the carpet and candles fill the little alcoves in the walls, as the smell of hot mulled wine, sandalwood and old, musty books wafts through the air. Hundreds of other people my age pour in through the big red double doors at the back, as about eight young, good-looking musicians mill about on the stage, tuning their various instruments.

After five minutes or so, the lights are dimmed and a spotlight is brought up on King Charles – the dreadlocked hipster singer that Joey introduced me to while Tiger was away on the Camino in Spain, just after I'd learned he'd cheated on me.

The congregation grows quiet, as King Charles begins a haunting rendition of 'O Little Town of Bethlehem'.

It feels a little strange – if not inappropriate – to be sat in the House of God, considering I'm still hungover after the theatrics at the warehouse in the early hours of yesterday morning.

I'm beyond confused about the whole situation, to be honest. On the one hand, maybe Joey's odd behaviour was just a strange manifestation of her anger that Tiger and I are back together. That would make sense, seeing as she'd been the one to pick up the pieces after his betrayal.

At the same time, though, I'm finding it really, really unsettling that she told Tiger she loved him – especially after she'd had a dream that they were hooking up. When the two of them first met several months ago, Joey had made a point of telling me how attractive she found Tiger. What if she's had feelings for him all this time, and they accidentally came out when she was drunk?

Whatever the truth may be, she made it much worse by calling me non-stop yesterday – after I'd specifically asked her for a few days' space to process the weirdness of the situation. This is where Joey and I are most different: when she's in fear, she clutches; when I'm in fear, I run.

I even ran from Tiger when he tried to win me back after his relapse on the Camino. He was – understandably – not in a good place when he returned home, and so initially told me he wanted to break up. However, after seeing how much stronger I was feeling after two months of therapy and Al-Anon meetings, he quickly changed his mind and begged for us to give it another go.

I managed to stave off his advances for a good few weeks, during which time he wrote me poems, sent homemade gifts – he even turned up to my house at midnight one evening, and stood below my bedroom window with a ghetto blaster on his shoulders playing Bon Iver's 'Skinny Love' as he screamed 'I LOVE YOU PERSIA LAWSON!' at the top of his lungs. Eventually – after he'd promised to go back to AA and do all he could to make us work – I finally caved.

Tiger's efforts in our relationship since then have been somewhat sporadic, but like anyone who's hopelessly infatuated, I tend to downplay the bad and make more of the good than perhaps I ought to.

Tonight is a prime example of this: I'm delighted that Tiger remembered how much I love King Charles and brought me to see him play here – particularly as churches really aren't Tiger's thing.

I, on the other hand, love them – always have. I think they're one of the most calming places in the world. The problem is, church means institutionalised religion, and I've got a fair bit of baggage around that – religion, but not *God*.

Unlike many people who find themselves in a Twelve Step meeting, I've never really had an issue with the concept of God. To me, it's always felt normal. This is partly because of my upbringing: my mother was raised a Catholic in Belfast, so my sister and I were christened together when we were toddlers and both went to a very traditional primary school. The daily morning prayers and hymns there had taught me that if I was sad or scared, I could pray to God, and He would make me feel better. So, whenever my dad disappeared for days after a fight with Mum, my sister and I would stand at our bedroom window and do just that – and Dad would always come back.

It was a simple relationship, but it worked: I asked for something, then waited patiently for an answer, never questioning that there was someone out there taking care of me and my family – however bad things got. I even had my favourite poem 'Footprints' by Mary Stevenson taped to the inside of my hymn-book to remind me that through the most painful times, God was carrying me.

Things *did* get bad for us, but there were many miracles, too – the main one being the survival of my second little brother, despite being exactly the same number of months premature as the baby we'd lost several years earlier.

In short, I now have the family that I could only have dreamed of on those dark, lonely nights as a child. If you'd lived in my house for just a day back then, and then fast-forwarded fifteen years or so to visit our family home today, I'm sure you'd call this miraculous too.

Aside from my family's fortuitous experiences, I also felt something was at work in my life to protect me from the numerous life-threatening (or at least life-sabotaging) situations I kept propelling myself into headfirst over the years. When I was living in Moscow, I took a drug called 'Siberia' with my boyfriend, his Russian friend and two other English guys on my acting course. We were told that the drug was a mixture of LSD, speed and ecstasy. An hour after taking it, we found ourselves driving down a main road near Pickled Lenin's mausoleum in Red Square at nearly a hundred miles an hour. The guy driving was hallucinating and veering all over the road, as I hung out the sunroof singing Robbie Williams's 'Angels' at the top of my lungs. Somehow we didn't die, and somehow we weren't even arrested (even though a night in a Russian prison cell may have been just what I needed).

I came to believe that I was either a real dab hand at escaping the consequences of my hedonistic and self-destructive lifestyle, or – very much like my parents – something out there was protecting me, mostly from myself.

Ironically, being in a church again, while it has made me feel very connected to the God of my own understanding, it has also made me question if I still identify myself as a Christian like I did when I was younger. This is probably because, over the last few months, I've been reading books and exploring practices of other religions – mainly Buddhism and New Age spirituality – and I've really loved it. To me, learning wisdom from other cultures and philosophies supplements and deepens my connection with my Higher Power, rather than muddying or weakening it.

While Tiger was on the Camino, I read a book called *Love Wins* by Rob Bell – a pastor who's often been described as a heretic for his controversial approach to Christianity. The views in this book are sometimes referred to as being 'Christian Universalist' in nature. Christian Universalism includes the belief in the idea of universal reconciliation – in other words, 'God will restore the whole of mankind to holiness and happiness'. I think that sounds nice, and very liberating. Seeing as the idea of having to abide by a strict set of religious rules and ideologies – many of which I can't bring myself to agree with – immediately fills me with dread, 'nice' and 'liberating' is good enough for me.

So, if I absolutely *had* to put a label on my faith today, a Christian Universalist may well be it. While some of the more devout followers of any religion may find my selective approach to spirituality offensively casual, for today I've given myself permission to follow the Twelve Steps's suggestion to 'take what you like and leave the rest'. I can't pretend to agree with (let alone put into practice) everything I read in scripture, just because I'm told to; I have to *feel* that what I'm reading is 'right' somehow, and I work that out by asking myself one very simple question: *Does this feel loving?*

Lots of bits in the Bible and other religious texts do, and lots don't. For now, I'm just trying to work on practising those bits that *do* – for example, turn the other cheek, love your neighbour as you love yourself, don't commit adultery.

When all's said and done, I simply think that God/Christ/ the Spirit – or whatever else you want to call 'It', resides in any moment or expression in which love is present.

This idea is summed up perfectly in one line in the Nativity sermon Tiger and I are watching, which is being given by an artist called Charlie Mackesy:

'God is love,' he says. 'The rest is detail.'

You

'I believe in God, but not as one thing, not as an old man in the sky. I believe that what people call God is something in all of us.'
John Lennon

When it comes to the idea of God, so many of us throw the baby out with the bathwater. A whole host of personal and historical evidence leads many of us to conclude that God equals religion, and religion equals wars, death, conflict and awkward conversations at dinner parties, so it's understandable that we'd feel uncomfortable at the very mention of the 'G' word. All we ask is that you keep an open mind, then take what you like from the following pages and leave what you don't.

As we see it, there are two main positions on resisting opening up to a spiritual faith. The first is a simple and straightforward atheistic stance – a lack of belief in a God of any kind. The second is not that we are closed to the possibility that there *could* be a God, but that we struggle with the negative connotations associated with this idea because of our own personal experiences. We may have had a strict religious upbringing, for example, and therefore equate God with rules and regulations that we have no interest in trying to abide by now that we're adults. God to us may appear to be a punishing, cruel, angry force – no wonder we'd want to reject the idea entirely.

Considering that one of us grew up in a family that were atheist, and the other in a dysfunctional household where addiction caused much pain and suffering, we've battled with this concept of 'God' significantly ourselves. We had so many questions that baffled us: *Why would a loving God allow natural disasters and suffering? With so many religions, how can you know which – if any – is the 'true' one? How can I possibly believe in something I can't see?*

There are thousands more questions – and answers – surrounding the issue of whether or not there is a God. And if there *is* one, what 'It' might look like – for example: the controversial issue of God's gender. Throughout these pages, we tend to refer to God or a 'Higher Power' more traditionally as a 'He', simply to make referencing more straightforward, but please feel free to substitute that pronoun for a 'She' or 'It' – whatever works for you.

It would be impossible for us to try and tackle all of these questions and issues in this short chapter – in fact, even if this entire book were dedicated to the subject, we'd still fall short. Our goal is simply to help you love yourself more. That's it. If you've related to any of our own stories so far, then you'll probably identify with feeling a profound lack of self-worth at some point in your life. In our experience, this lack of self-worth was the one single cause of every external problem that we went through. It affected our relationships, our bodies, our careers, our mindset and our outlook on life.

The solution to this problem for the both of us was in developing a spiritual connection *of our own understanding.* This worked so well for us, because it allowed us the space and freedom to decide what that spiritual connection looked like for us as individuals. What we were seeking was *help*: we wanted to stop feeling afraid, depressed and anxious all the time, and instead to experience more joy, peace and happiness. Coming to believe in what we refer to as a 'power greater than ourselves' – one that loves us and wants the best for us – has helped us to achieve this.

For those of you who are atheists – or who don't have an interest in starting a relationship with any kind of Higher Power – it's helpful to remember that there are many people who successfully walk a spiritual path by thinking of their 'Higher Power' simply as the energy of a collective of like-minded people, as nature, or as love itself.

For those of you that are open to the idea of God in a more traditional sense – as an omnipotent being, Creator of the universe – but who struggle with the religious or negative implications of such a God, we encourage you to consider redefining and simplifying your idea of what a Higher Power could be.

Similarly, if you've come to these pages already having a very clear and solid relationship with a God (in whatever shape or form that may take for you), we hope that the ideas in this chapter will complement and maybe even challenge your personal beliefs in a positive and beneficial way.

Our understanding and relationship to this power is intensely personal; there is no right or wrong. Not one single person on the planet can actually prove or disprove 100 per cent the existence of God, therefore, we are – if we choose to be – totally free to explore what works for us. What has been most effective in helping us solve our own problems, is actively *choosing* to believe in a loving and supportive Higher Power.

One of the fundamental elements in developing a relationship and connection to this Power is in the way in which we love and value ourselves. When we treat ourselves badly – whether that's through self-destructive behaviour or negative self-talk – it's very hard to imagine that we could be loved at all.

However, the more you practise self-care, the more you'll find yourself opening up to the possibility that you are *deserving* of love. Meditation, journaling, walking in nature and listening to uplifting music, are extremely effective and simple ways of practising self-care and beginning to experience a sense of this spiritual connection. Meditation in particular has been scientifically proven to help reduce stress and anxiety, and help you to experience an improved sense of health and happiness. By slowing down, quietening your mind and turning your focus inwards, you are then able to become centred and present enough to hear your own personal truth and intuition, which holds many of the answers that you're seeking.

At the beginning of developing a spiritual connection, it can often feel as though you're pretending. That, in itself, is part of the process. Over time, however, the more you commit to the practices that help you to connect to your Higher Power, you'll likely see little miracles begin to occur in your life, which we'll explore in the next chapter. These positive results serve to slowly and gently encourage your belief to grow.

It's a process that can take time, so be patient. The effort that you need to invest, if you want to experience this sense of peace, joy and flow, requires you to get quiet and go within, which is where your Higher Power really resides – *inside of you.* The following exercises will guide you to do this.

EXERCISES

Higher Power Blocks

What (if any) is your experience of God or a Higher Power? Think about your childhood, any positive or negative thoughts and feelings that come up for you around faith.

MORNING 'QUIET TIME' PRACTICE

We suggest that you try the following meditation (as well as the other two exercises below) every day for the next month. We can almost guarantee that you'll see at least some positive results – make sure you keep a running document of them in your journal.

Connection Meditation

1) Go to www.theinnerfix.com/meditation

2) Sit upright with your legs crossed and palms on your lap facing upwards, and breathe slowly in and out – as you breathe in, your stomach expands; as you breathe out, your stomach contracts. The recorded meditation will guide you to focus your attention inwards.

3) When you've finished the meditation, feel free to write down any thoughts or feelings that came up for you in your journal.

Valuing Yourself

Open your journal and write down three things that you love about yourself. These can be anything – from the big to the small. For example, your eyelashes, your loyalty to your friends, your handwriting – *anything*. But they must be three *different* things every day for a month. You may feel like you're running out of things in the first week, but keep digging.

One Loving Thing

As mentioned in the introduction to this book, we really want you to commit to doing one loving thing for yourself every day – however big or small.

Examples may include:

- Arranging a phone call or date with a friend who always leaves you feeling positive, inspired and joyful.

- Booking a doctor's appointment to check out that ailment you've been pushing to the back of your mind.

- Going for a long walk in the park at sunset.

- Allowing yourself an evening of watching your favourite box set back to back.

CHAPTER 8

HAND IT OVER

Persia

'Let go, or be dragged.'

Anonymous

'm sat on the Overground train going east from west London to pick up my stuff from Tiger's warehouse, where I've been living for the past few months. It's 1ˢᵗ May – exactly one year since we first got together.

Last night, he broke up with me over the phone, saying I wasn't healthy for him, and that he needed to be on his own.

I haven't eaten, I haven't slept, and I just ran out of an audition because I blanked during my monologue – which is something I never do.

The last five months have been a messy blur. After Christmas, our relationship slowly began taking precedence over the spiritual connection I'd established while Tiger was on the Camino. My Al-Anon meetings were no longer a priority and, as a result, all the inner strength I'd built up during that period slowly started to dwindle. Once again, Tiger had become my world, and I lost all my autonomy as my life began to orbit around his far more dazzling one.

I was back to feeling like a hopeless love junkie, and it didn't take long for the effects of my self-neglect to show: I was anxious, needy and constantly on the lookout for evidence that he was about to leave me. With every day that passed, I could feel him slipping further away. Which is probably why, despite my previous protestations about Tiger moving to the warehouse, I soon found myself living there right alongside him – in a freezing, five-foot-high, windowless basement that you could only enter by jumping through a trapdoor in the main living space. *Not ideal.*

There was so much being left unsaid between us, but I didn't dare give lip service to my concerns for fear of what I might find out. Not one bit of me was ready to have confirmed what I already knew deep in my bones: Tiger was using drugs again and likely cheating on me, too. But I couldn't – I *wouldn't* see it.

So, instead, I drew false confidence by getting back on the cocaine, which rather than making me feel better only served to heighten my anxiety. Where comedowns had once been a twenty-four-hour malady at worst, I was now struggling through three whole days of the most debilitating paranoia that I'd ever known. It was as if my body was screaming to me: *Get out, get out, GET OUT!* But, even in my sorry state, the concept of leaving him was inconceivable. I *had* to make this work.

A few weeks after the whole warehouse party drama with Joey at Christmas, I received another lengthy email from her – very different from the gentle, concerned one she'd sent in the summer when she was worried I was returning to my old ways. In this latest email, she gave a blow-by-blow account of the events of that evening in the warehouse from her perspective. It hadn't been an easy read, not only because I could feel her anger at me pouring through every sentence, but also because much of what she said was painfully on the money:

> I'm thinking, hang on Tiger, who has been there every time to pick up the pieces when you f*ck Persia over? Me. And who gets ignored and pushed aside once it's all OK again? Me. This is the guy who shagged someone else while he was going out with you, went away for six weeks with no contact until he was on the point of relapse, and then doesn't bother to get in touch in the following days to let you know he isn't dead. Then he comes back, BREAKS UP with you, and then changes his mind.

Reading those words made me feel like more of a fool than I think I've ever felt, so unsurprisingly I was not all that eager to throw myself back into my friendship with Joey. Having her back in my life would've been a constant reminder of Tiger's repeated fuck-ups. I think that's why I've kept her at arms' length for the last five months; it made it easier to kid myself that he and I were happy.

And yet, you can only hide from the truth for so long. A few weeks ago, what was left of our crumbling relationship finally fell apart while we were on a trip with some friends in Paris.

The holiday was a disaster from start to finish: Tiger had cycled over from London without any training whatsoever, so was a broken man by the time I met him at the Champs Élysées.

On the second evening, paranoid that Tiger fancied one of the girls he'd been cycling with, I decided to get so embarrassingly drunk that I ended up kissing a Frenchman right in front of him. He responded by buying some weed and smoking it en route back to our hostel, and I stumbled behind him slurring insults, completely oblivious to the fact he was getting high right in front of me.

The next day, I was so severely hungover that as soon as we arrived at the house we were to be staying in for the next few nights I vomited into a saucepan, while Tiger sang 'All You Need Is Love' by the Beatles at full volume, so that our hosts – who were stood right outside our door – wouldn't hear my retching.

On the Eurostar home, we both knew it was over. We sat in separate carriages and I cried for the entire journey, appalled and humiliated by my behaviour.

When I returned to my parents' house later that evening, I decided to give the relationship one last shot via a letter, which owned my part in our disintegration, but also served a straight-up ultimatum: go back to AA, or we're done for good.

In our phone call last night, Tiger gave his response, and it was, as I'd feared, the latter.

And so, here I sit on this train, preparing myself to see him for the last time.

A stickler for nostalgia, I'm listening to the playlist he made me last year, which is not doing much to relieve my sadness.

I can't do this. I really, really can't do this.

I squeeze my eyes tightly shut, and with all other resorts totally exhausted, I resolve to say a prayer (to myself, it's a packed train).

God, please help me. I'm scared. I'm so, so scared. I can't handle the intensity of these feelings. Please show me how to do this, because right now I can't imagine having enough strength to walk away. I've done everything I can to make this work. I finally get that it can't. I need a miracle. I'm handing this over to you now.

I open my eyes. My iPod's stopped playing. I press shuffle, and one of mine and Tiger's favourite songs comes on – 'If You Want To

Sing Out' by Cat Stevens, featured on the soundtrack to the film *Harold and Maude* that we watched the first night we got together.

As soon as the piano introduction begins, I feel a huge wave of euphoria sweep over me – a feeling I normally only associate with coming up on drugs. Out of nowhere, I'm suddenly bursting with excitement, and I know that what I absolutely must do is give Tiger and I the best send-off I can muster. 'Always end things well,' my mum once told me.

I get off the train and head straight to Tesco, where I pick up a bottle of Cherry Lambrini for me, and a can of Coke for him.

I let myself into the warehouse. No one seems to be in, so I climb down the ladder, through the trapdoor and into the basement we've been sleeping in together for the last three months. Tiger's back is facing the entrance. He's putting some of my clothes into a suitcase. The room is littered with candles and smells of burning incense and, ironically, Cat Stevens' album *Tea for the Tillerman* is playing in the background.

'Hey,' I say, smiling in the doorway.

He looks over his shoulder at me, eyes watering. He puts the clothes down, walks over and holds me for a very long time.

'I've bought us a farewell present,' I say holding up the drinks. 'If we're going out, we're going out in style.'

He looks at them and laughs.

'I thought this was going to be awful,' he says.

'It was,' I reply.

We end up having one of the best nights of our entire relationship. We order a pizza and watch *It's a Wonderful Life*. We laugh, cry, reminisce over our year together, and have the most loving sex.

Whatever he's been doing behind my back doesn't matter anymore. I know the coming weeks are going to be hell, and I just want our last hours to be beautiful, even if they're laced in a veil of denial.

I fall asleep in his arms. The next morning, we decide to go for a walk in central London, seeing as it's such a beautiful day. For a while, we stand and watch the London Symphony Orchestra playing in Trafalgar Square, and then Tiger takes my hand and we wander through the backstreets of Covent Garden.

As we round a corner near Embankment Bridge, we pass an old man sitting on the pavement writing poems – a kind of literary busker. I go to top up my Oyster card at the tube station, and out of the corner of my eye I see Tiger slip the busker some money and pocket an envelope. For once, I'm not suspicious about the transaction.

We take the train back to the warehouse. Tiger helps me carry my suitcases out of his Zen dungeon and into the boot of a taxi outside.

I climb into the back seat of the car and roll down the window.

Tiger takes my hand and looks at me with those intense green eyes of his.

'I love you Persia. I really do love you,' he says.

'I know you do.'

He slips an envelope into my hand, and walks back into the warehouse, as the taxi pulls off to take me back to my parents' house.

I open the envelope and use the light from my phone to make out the scrawled purple writing:

Farewell Blessing

Farewell, dear friend,
Your heart's desire
May Providence supply –
The flame of your life,

Its warmth and goodness
Has touched my life
And increased it.

Then let's not say:
There's an end –
That hopeless word –
And meaningless sadness:
For remembrance will keep you
In my affections
Always treasured.

Joseph M., May 2012

Joey

'I have been driven many times upon my knees by the
overwhelming conviction that I had nowhere else to go. My
own wisdom and that of all about me seemed insufficient
for that day.'
Abraham Lincoln

Something about Josh feels distant. He awkwardly bites down
on the side of his lip and keeps his eyes fixed on his hands,
which are clasped on the table in front of him. Conversation, so
far, has been strained. I've just arrived back from a three-week
trip in the US; the first week travelling down the Florida Keys
on the back of a Harley-Davidson with him, before he left to the
Bahamas for a friend's wedding.

Considering we've been together less than six months and

have just spent two weeks apart (our longest period of separation so far), the reunion is wholly underwhelming.

'Did you get with someone in the Bahamas?' The question trips off my tongue quite unexpectedly, for both of us.

'What? Yes, I mean, no,' he stumbles.

'Did you get with someone? Tell me the truth.'

Biting down harder on his lip, he nods, slowly.

'Are you going to see her again?' I probe.

'I don't know.'

I feel as if I'm weightless. I get up from the table, where we're seated in a café in Kings Cross, and prepare to leave.

'If it's any consolation – no, no, it doesn't matter, that doesn't help,' he mumbles, shaking his head.

I've no idea what he was going to say but I suddenly see red. I want to hit him. So I do. I hit him across the face – the thwack makes everyone in the café around us fall silent. It's as if everything is now in slow motion, and I float out, covering my stomach as if I've had the wind knocked out of me. Pacing up and down on the street outside in shock, I glimpse back to see Josh paying for the coffees that have been sitting patiently on the table between us, untouched.

I'm the first to admit that we may not score highly on the overall compatibility scale, but I've been learning a huge amount from this relationship. The week we recently spent together in Florida was a mixed bag – we had several petty fights, but also some really beautiful experiences.

Gradually, I've been dipping my toe into the spiritual pool more and more, and it's not quite as weird as I imagined. I've watched Josh's sober lifestyle with intrigue, as he wakes up day after day with no hangover – and in spending time with him, I've been more or less doing the same, and experiencing a much clearer head as a result. It feels like a new lease of life for me, as if I've discovered a lifestyle choice that I never knew was an option before: *To drink or not to drink, who knew that could even be a question?*

Meeting Josh has shown me what's possible. As the months have rolled on, I can see that, in cutting back on alcohol as I've now begun to, a void has been left in its place. It's becoming apparent that it might need filling with something else. I can jump from one comforting habit to another, or I can see what happens if I stay still and instead choose to fill it with something more spiritual in nature. After all, we're made up of mind, body and soul – I've just tended to neglect the soul part.

Despite the loaded word 'God' initially making my toes curl, I'm trying not to get too bogged down in the semantics, and am instead simply focusing on what the idea symbolises for me. It's taken a while to get over the fact that, just because 'a power greater than myself' has never graced me with a big reveal (bursting through the clouds with a booming-voice-type gesture), it doesn't mean it isn't there. For a while, I've been wondering if perhaps I've been forgotten – or worse, rejected – but actually, I don't think that's the case. I've just been pretty closed off to seeking any kind of spiritual connection up until now.

Something that's always bothered me about religion is how divisive it feels. Surely, if there is a *greater power* responsible for the creation of the universe, it's just *one* entity, one that we're all attaching different labels to? For me, the way I understand it is as a loving force (something bigger than I am). Or, as Josh describes it, a Higher Power (HP). The inclusiveness of that idea feels most expansive and true for me. Faith is such a personal journey, and I only know at this stage that I'm beginning to open myself up to it.

After an enlightening week with Josh and a few days visiting one of my oldest school friends in Atlanta, I then found myself in Texas for ten days. My only cousin, Natty – a born and bred Texan – also happens to be the proud owner of a bar in a small university town in the Deep South. It was neither of our faults (unfortunate timing I suppose) that she was looking forward to the arrival of her 'fun-loving British cousin', while I was on a somewhat precarious stint of not drinking. I instantly felt like I was a disappointment to her, as I spent long days and evenings in her bar sipping on Dr Pepper while growing more and more out of focus to everyone around me.

I also had an unsettling feeling about Josh, despite there being no tangible cause for concern. Intuitively, I sensed that something wasn't quite right, and I just couldn't shake it.

On day eight of ten, something inside me snapped. It was Cinco de Mayo (something celebrated heavily in Texas), and I was feeling increasingly separate and isolated by not drinking, while it was everyone else's main sport. Natty was throwing a pool party at her house and, without a second thought, I picked up a midday margarita. The next fifteen hours went by in a blur, until I came to the following day, wrapped miserably around her toilet, pleading for her to call an ambulance. I'd been vomiting on and off for so long that I was now just retching air.

Having returned to London – and reeling from my café confrontation with Josh – I lie in bed and, not knowing who to turn to, open my diary:

I feel low tonight. And quite alone. I am shocked how quickly someone can be in your life one minute, and the next, gone. Everything changes. And it feels so totally out of my control. x

I've barely spoken to Persia since the warehouse fight before Christmas, which was about five months ago now – the full length of time that Josh and I have been together. I suppose that's no coincidence. I've put all my energy into him and surrounding myself with the lifestyle I know I'd do well to embrace – which, rightly or wrongly, has meant time away from Persia. Meanwhile, I expect she's still clutched into the claws of captivity by Tiger. Whatever the case, neither of us has bothered to meet up.

I pull up the email exchange that took place between us much earlier in the year, following the warehouse party, and wince as I read the angry tone of much of my correspondence. Only feeling slightly relieved by the gentler closing words of my rant:

> You were my best friend and I really hate to think we've lost our bond. I have no idea what's going to happen and no plan. And no hope either way actually. I think our lives could carry on with or without each other. With – will be hard trying to move on and find the trust and normality again. Without – is probably easier for now, but I'm sure we both will have tinges of regret in time to come that we let such a friendship fall.

I know I need to take my hands off and trust this, if I'm to allow a Higher Power to guide the way. I'm not going to contact Josh or Persia. I plan to hand this over and surrender to whatever the outcome is to be. Perhaps this is a nudge from the universe, an opportunity to see how this faith thing works.

You

'Faith is the bird that feels the light and
sings when the dawn is still dark.'
Rabindranath Tagore

What a relief it is to accept that we are not masters of our universe.

But, at the same time, letting go of the idea that we *are* can be so frightening. It requires a huge leap of faith that things are going to work themselves out for the best.

As we've already explored, much of the power we think we possess is an illusion. In reality, we have little control over the past or the future. Most of our pain comes from our false belief that we do.

Our self-will usually leads us to stay stuck in a situation way beyond its shelf life. The more we cling – whether it's to a person, a job or an idea of what we want, the more we tend to push it away. We suffocate the very thing that we believe we most need.

The thing is, we don't always know what's best for us. We *think* we know, but we don't. When we're going through a troubling time in life, it's as though we're standing behind a big tapestry. Everything looks tangled and messy, and we can't see how any of it is possibly going to work itself out. However, further down the line, the gift of hindsight enables us to see the tapestry from the front. What had seemed so awful and confusing at the time was actually part of the process of creating the picture of our life – in which the painful and challenging experiences are also a fundamental element.

Just look back to an example from the past: that person you were once so in love with and couldn't imagine ever being apart from – what if you'd had that wish granted? With some distance from the relationship, you may see that, though you shared some incredible moments together, you'd never have been happy with them in the long run. Our soul-mates are not always meant to be our life mates, but the level of passion and intensity we experience with a person can cloud our judgement and trick us into believing that only they could ever make us happy.

In any given moment, we can never see the whole picture. The most wonderful, unexpected surprises could be waiting for us just around the corner, if only we were able to trust and have faith in the timing of our life. However, when things are rough, it's difficult to imagine that they could ever be better, or that the solution to our problems is more likely to come about by surrendering control rather than grasping for it.

When considering this idea, author Marianne Williamson talks about how it can be helpful to look towards nature – which holds many of the answers that most of us are searching for. Unlike humans, nature does not have free will, it simply follows its own internal programming to become the highest possible version of itself. Trees, plants, animals – even babies in the womb – all demonstrate this miraculous process. And yet, we think that once we arrive into this world, suddenly we're exempt from it? We are if we choose to be: we *can* choose to say no. We *can* decide to go off and do our own thing, rather than trust that life will gently carry us towards our greatest good, if we allow it to.

Although some may argue that letting go of control over elements of our lives or that of those we love may seem lazy or selfish, it's actually often the most helpful and beneficial thing we can do. For example, we may think our sibling is drinking too much, and in an effort to 'help', keep nagging them about the problem. However, this is more likely to irritate them and make them feel ashamed, meaning they might simply work harder to hide their drinking – or worse still, detach themselves from us completely. No one wins.

Perhaps it's time to try a different approach instead: that of *surrendering* our fears and problems, rather than trying to fix them all by ourselves. Even if you lack faith, you can *choose* to believe that you have a Higher Power that wants what's best for you. You can *choose* to hand over every single element of your life to that Higher Power – your fears, your dreams, your finances, your relationships. Instead of trying to nag that sibling into stopping drinking (or any other issue a loved one may be struggling with), pray that they receive their own guidance instead. Ask your Higher Power to help you 'detach with love' from them, so that you can stop getting so frustrated by their behaviour, and they can stop getting so frustrated by your judgement and control. If they feel your love and support, they're far more likely to take positive action or ask for help, than if you continue to chastise them. If nothing else, 'detaching with love' will help to ease your own anxiety, regardless of what's going on for the other person involved.

In order to experience the benefits of 'handing things over' and surrendering issues you're worried about in a practical and tangible way, we encourage you to commit to the Connection Meditation, Valuing Yourself and One Loving Thing exercises we set out at the end of the last chapter. Do these exercises *every single day* for one month. *One month*. That's no time at all, in the grand scheme of things. Even if, at this moment, you don't believe that there's anything out there listening, try it anyway – what have you got to lose? As the Indian proverb states: 'When we take one step towards God, He takes seven steps towards us.'

The more you cultivate this relationship with your Higher Power by praying and meditating, the stronger your intuition will become. *You pray to ask, you meditate to hear.* How many times have you said to a friend something along the lines of: 'I just knew in my gut that it wasn't right/he was the one/I had to give you this book'? That guttural response may just be our Higher Power guiding us to towards making the best, most loving decisions for ourselves, so it's wise to listen to those instincts.

We sometimes find that what our gut is telling us seems to be counterproductive. It tells us to walk away when it would be so much easier (and less painful) to stay. It tells us to go and introduce ourselves to someone at a party or work event, when we'd be far more comfortable shrinking back and staying small. It tells us to resign and follow our dream to travel the world for a whole year, when a big part of us would rather just stay in our job and complain about it, either because that takes less effort, or because our rational voice tells us we might not get another job and will run out of money.

Our gut is usually telling us something we don't want to hear because it's scary: let go, walk away, follow your heart. But ignore that voice at your peril, because it's not going anywhere – it will keep nudging you until you're eventually forced to listen to it. In our experience, your Higher Power wants what's best for you in the long term, and that might mean you may have to be uncomfortable in the short term.

Sometimes, we're very clear and certain about what our gut is telling us to do (or not do). Other times, we're faced with a situation in which we feel confused and baffled about the 'right' course of action to take and come to a place of decision paralysis. Every possible choice we can think of then contains another five decisions that branch off, and soon we become completely overwhelmed by the enormity of it all.

So, what are we supposed to do when the way isn't clear?

'If you don't know, do nothing.'

In our fast-paced, results-obsessed modern culture, *waiting* feels extremely uncomfortable and unproductive. Yet, it's only in the stillness that we generate through our daily meditation practice that the right answers begin to emerge. And they always *do* emerge, given the time and space they require. We just need to be quiet enough to listen.

In some respects, receiving spiritual guidance is similar to taking directions from a satellite navigator: whenever you 'take a wrong turn', the satnav simply renavigates to ensure you still get to your destination, albeit via a slightly different route. Similarly, it's reassuring to know that, whatever course of action you decide to take in any given situation, you can still get to where you want to go, so long as you keep coming back to your spiritual practice.

There are no mistakes; we'll learn the lessons we need to learn eventually – it just makes it faster and less painful if we commit to consistent meditation and surrendering practices.

Another issue that often comes up around this topic is how we can know the difference between our own self-will and attachment to a specific outcome of any given situation, and the more loving, healthy course of action to take. What we have come to experience in our own lives is that, when we feel calm and clear about a certain decision, then we know it's the right time to act. When we feel an impulsive or passionate impulse to take action, it's better not to.

If you're struggling to make a decision, return to the space of 'if you don't know, do nothing', and wait until you feel peace and clarity about it.

This doesn't mean that we all just need to passively sit back and let life happen to us. Rather, it means that we should give ourselves the space and time to make a decision that's informed by our intuition and the spiritual connection we've been cultivating through our meditative practices. These practices *are* our action – and will gently lead us towards the most loving choice for our specific circumstances in due course. For example, if we've been hurt by a close friend, instead of defensively reacting out of anger, we can take a step back and ask for guidance through our meditation, journal writing or any other spiritual practices. We'll likely then be able to see the situation in a clearer, more balanced way, and be able to respond – not *react* – more lovingly.

One of the clearest ways you can see evidence that you're being guided and that your spiritual connection is evolving is through an increase in your experience of coincidences and synchronicity. It's funny how, when you start paying attention to them (or writing them down), coincidences seem to pop up everywhere. A friend you haven't seen in years will suddenly call you out of the blue – just as you're checking their social media profile to see how they're doing. The tune that you've been singing all day will come on the radio. A positive quote on your social media feed will offer you the specific guidance you asked for that morning.

The above instances may seem somewhat trivial, irrelevant – or even a figment of your imagination. They may well be. But, then again, they might not. You get to decide. What if you chose to see synchronicity as a signal that you're becoming open to receiving guidance? After all, if you can access this guidance in the little things, you'll also be able to access it for the more important life choices and circumstances, too. At the end of the day, choosing the optimistic view is far more likely to help you feel happier and more hopeful, and even if that's *all* that happens, that in itself is a great result.

The exercises below will help you to do this.

EXERCISES

Connect the Dots

1) Look back over your life and make a list of all the strange coincidences and synchronicities that have occurred. Try and connect the dots. Are there any patterns that emerge? What significance might they have for you?

2) Write down three examples from your past where things didn't turn out the way you wanted them to at the time, but with hindsight you can see they actually turned out better. Be as specific as you can.

Surrender Box

1) Make yourself a 'Surrender Box'. On separate pieces of paper, write down anything that you're struggling with, or things you'd like to happen in your life, place them in your box, and make the decision to 'hand them over' to the care of your Higher Power.

2) After six months, open the box and read the different notes, writing down the outcomes in your journal.

Surrender Meditation

1) Go to www.theinnerfix.com/meditation

2) Sit upright with your legs crossed and palms on your lap facing upwards, and breathe slowly in and out – as you breathe in, your stomach expands; as you breathe out, your stomach contracts. The recorded meditation will guide you to focus your attention inwards.

3) When you've finished the meditation, feel free to write down any thoughts or feelings that came up for you in your journal.

Get In Nature

Make it your mission to get out into nature at least once a day. Go for a walk in a nearby park at lunchtime, sit by the river for ten minutes or practise yoga in the garden.

Being in nature reminds us to align ourselves with the natural flow and order of the universe. It reconnects us to our Higher Power, as we experience the peace, stillness and beauty of the world around us.

CHAPTER 9

FORGIVE

Joey

'Humanity is never so beautiful as when praying
for forgiveness, or else forgiving another.'

Jean Paul

'm stood waiting outside a terraced house, as Persia gets out
of a car a little way down the street and calls to me.

As our eyes meet, a huge smile spreads across her face. We
run towards each other and stand hugging for a long time. I
then take her hand and lead her into the house party, which is
now in full swing.

Someone offers us a warm glass of wine in a red plastic cup.
Persia accepts, but I shake my head.

'You not drinking tonight?' she asks.

'Not tonight.'

We make our way to one of the upstairs bedrooms to talk,
but it's already filled with people taking lines off CDs and
bedside tables. A friend of Persia's from uni offers her a line,
and this time it's her turn to refuse.

'Shall we get out of here?' I mouth. She nods.

This is the first time we've seen each other in months. I learned yesterday, when she rang me out of the blue, that Tiger has ended their relationship. I was on a break at work when she called, and when I saw her name flash up, I very nearly didn't answer.

'Hi . . .'

'Hey,' she said, before pouring out every detail of their break-up.

When she'd finished, there was a lengthy silence.

'What day was this? I mean, what date?' I asked.

'Uh, two weeks ago on Wednesday.'

'I don't believe it,' I let out a little laugh. 'That's the same day Josh broke up with me.'

'What!?' she shrieked.

It's so strange to think that Persia never even met him.

'I'm so sorry Jo – for everything,' she said solemnly.

'We've both been shit, let's be honest,' I reply.

We head back to mine and stay up talking into the early hours, going through everything that we've missed out on over the past six months.

The next morning, Persia takes me to my first Al-Anon meeting. Although I've been out with a lot of destructive men in the past, Josh was the first who actually identified himself as an addict, and so I finally feel as if I qualify to attend a meeting of this kind.

The theme is on forgiveness and detaching with love from those who have wronged you, which couldn't be more relevant to the both of us today. Considering what both of our exes have done, it's tempting to hold on to resentment and bitterness. But as we both learn in the meeting: in clinging we hurt, in releasing we heal.

It's a sunny afternoon, and after the meeting Persia invites me to a barbecue she's heading to. The people there are relatively new friends of hers – from church – and I can see that she's nervous about introducing me to them. As 'churchy types', I anticipate they'll be either extremely weird or extremely boring, but to my surprise they're neither. In fact, it turns out we have quite a bit in common. Though Persia doesn't know it yet, someone we meet at the barbecue, a guy called Sam, will later become her long-term boyfriend.

At home that evening, I open my diary to find an acting course scrawled across the pages of the coming week. I'd completely forgotten I'd booked it. It was actually Josh – an ex-actor himself – who suggested I do it. I signed up months ago, in the hope it might reignite my dwindling faith in becoming an actress.

I'm in no headspace to do anything outside of my comfort zone right now, but it's almost as if something has been at work recently. Persia and I have unexpectedly come back into each other's lives under the most bizarre circumstances, and there's a small part of me that feels pulled to trust in how things are unfolding. Besides, I've paid a fair bit of money for the course, and I won't get that back now.

Josh used to keep a hand-written note stuck above his bedroom mirror that was in his line of vision as he got ready every morning, which read: 'BE THERE'. If I can take one lesson from our relationship right now, I suppose it's the recommendation of this course and those words.

So, here I am.

The week ahead is essentially an intensive acting course merged with therapy, because, as our coach Tony from sunny LA, tells us:

'Our acting problems *are* our LIFE problems.'

Clearly a bit of a legend (who knows it), Tony paces the room intensely, one hand attached pensively to the side of his face. He's part way through guiding us to 'release the emotional burdens of our past'.

'OK people, I want you to list, out loud and all at the same time, *everything* that you know you need to forgive others for . . . GO.'

Within seconds, some of the group are rocking miserably on their hands and knees, muttering inaudible grievances to themselves. Others smack their palms against the studio floor, releasing guttural, primal cries from somewhere deep within. I, meanwhile, find myself rooted to the spot, feeling quite separate from the mass hysteria going on around me. It's ironic that, of all the people in this room, I'm not one of the ones bludgeoning my head against the floor, since it's not even been three weeks since Josh abruptly ended things between us.

We've had no contact since meeting (shortly after the face-punching episode) in the exact spot he stood waiting for me with a red rose tucked behind his ear six months earlier. Things had come full circle: this time, we were meeting so he could hand back my stuff.

Having composed one of my typically lengthy emails to Josh, Persia has managed to persuade me not to send it immediately and, instead, to mark a date in my diary a month from now. If I still feel the same about sending it then, I can do.

The email doesn't end up getting sent. In hindsight, this was a good thing. Unbeknown to me at this point in time, Josh will go on to marry the girl he cheated on me with – just five months from now. I'll unexpectedly stumble across their wedding photos, as a result of snooping around on Facebook.

Yet, here, in the midst of an acting exercise on forgiveness, I'm not sure I actually feel all that angry with Josh. Rather, I've turned the feelings inwards and taken it to heart. It's reaffirmed something I already knew: I was clearly not enough for him.

Although I've been feeling low, I haven't had a drop of alcohol since my bender in Texas and am pursuing no one new, despite there being several very tempting options waiting within fingers' reach in my phone contacts. I know that drinking and hoicking in a new love interest works temporarily – it always has – but I've arrived at a place where I'm at least trying to do things differently. I'm finding it hard; sitting with these feelings isn't comfortable. In Al-Anon, they say that with pain, you need to feel it to heal it. Well, I've definitely been feeling it, without the anaesthetisation of wine or a replacement lover, in a very raw way.

After Tony has finished taking us through the 'forgiving others' exercise, he asks us to turn our minds to everything we need to forgive *ourselves* for. The group once again throw themselves into the task, and this time I find myself reeling off anything that springs to mind. Before I know it, I'm swept up in recalling old memories and subsequent beliefs that I've been holding on to – almost all of them against myself. How being sexually assaulted at fourteen led to blurred lines around intimacy as the years went on, believing that my body could be used without my consent. How being cheated on led me to assume that I'm not worthy of commitment. I realise that hardly any of my resentments are against other people at all. I've somehow managed to turn even the stuff that others were responsible for, back on myself.

With the whole room electric with emotion, Tony instructs us to forgive ourselves, declaring:

'You don't have to hold on to these feelings about who you are or what you did – you get to choose again.'

And there, in the middle of a room full of almost strangers, I break down, but in this really beautiful way, as if something is being lifted.

Later that evening, I'm flying down Upper Street in north London, on my way to have dinner with Persia. I feel elated, as if I've been gifted a new set of wings.

'What the *hell* has happened to you today?' Persia asks, intrigued, as I flop down in my chair opposite her at our little table in the corner. I get her up to speed.

'I've never seen you this exhilarated in my life,' she says, practically speechless (a rare occurrence for her).

I take her hands and lean in, 'I feel like I'm learning so much at the moment – because I'm actually *open* to learning it. Josh and Tiger have already brought so many lessons, haven't they?'

'I know. I actually typed, "how to mend a broken heart" into YouTube the other day and the advice was atrocious. I felt more depressed at the end of the video than I did before I started watching it.'

'You're kidding! SO DID I . . .' I squeal. 'There's nothing useful at all!'

We both laugh. It's good to have my friend back.

'Maybe we can do our own video on it one day,' she says.

'They do say you teach best what you most need to learn . . .'

That evening, I lie in bed thinking of Josh. I miss him. My mind flits back to the first few nights, after we broke up. I'd hardly eaten and spent hours sweating, tossing and turning, running over thoughts, conversations and projections in my head. At times I almost felt delirious, it was as though the room and walls were moving in the darkness, like I was tripping. Such is the power that withdrawing from a loved one can have over me. It occurs to me that it's never really been about the other person. This obsessiveness is something in *me* – it must be – since it's the same for every break-up, and I'm the only common denominator.

Tonight, I do feel calmer, though. Sad, but calmer. I know I don't want this experience to close my heart. There's an overwhelming part of me that feels like saying, 'F*ck it' – I'm better off hardening and protecting myself from now on. I feel like I've been burned one too many times, so why shouldn't I?'

It's like I'm on the edge of a precipice, and there are two clear choices available to me. I can choose to see this situation through a lens of love, or I can close myself off, through fear. Love. Or fear. In my heart, while I sense it's the riskier option, I want to choose love. I want to live my life with hopefulness, not hostility.

Lying alone in my bed, I put my hands together, close my eyes and take a slow intake of breath. I'm not accustomed to saying prayers, but tonight I give it a try.

Hi, HP.
I'd like to pray for Josh. I hope he finds what he's looking for. I ask that I can forgive him. Please help me keep my heart open, even though I'm hurting.
That's all, really.

Nothing at all happens, and I soon drift into a deep sleep. During the night, I have one of the most vivid dreams of my life. Myself, Josh and his father (who died from alcoholism long before Josh and I met) lie on the ground with our heads facing in towards each other, almost in a star shape. In the dream, I'm observing the situation from a bird's-eye view. Josh's dad speaks, telling me his son never meant to hurt me. The three of us lie there, gazing upwards.

'I know,' I whisper.

I wake the next morning, feeling that a new level of peace has befallen me.

Persia

> 'Forgiveness is the fragrance that the violet
> sheds on the heel that has crushed it.'
> Mark Twain

It's early July, and I'm sat in a café with Joey after an Al-Anon meeting. London is overwrought with Olympic Games fever, and for the first time in a long time, we're both feeling happy and content.

Since we've been back in each other's lives, our days and evenings have been filled with yoga, running, meditation, healthy meals, Twelve Step meetings, and reading every self-help book we can get our hands on. I've even become a regular attendee at the church Tiger took me to last Christmas.

There have been good days, and there have been bad days. The sting of our mutual heartbreak has come in waves, but we've managed to successfully ride each one – largely thanks to our decision to stay away from our own personal Kryptonites – for Joey, that's alcohol, and for me, that's handsome strangers and cocaine (or, 'The Devil's Dandruff', as I now refer to it).

Something about that particular substance really triggers the 'Fuck It' button in me. The minute I choose to have some, my entire night becomes centred around when – and how – I'm going to have more.

I've done some pretty shady things while high on coke – or in my pursuit for the next line: I've flirted with drug dealers to get some for free. I've snuck off to grubby bathrooms with people I've just met to nab a bit of theirs. I've snorted lines off the most vile toilet seats imaginable and, worst of all, I've kissed men while my boyfriend was outside having a cigarette – just because I quite literally Did. Not. Give. A. Fuck.

In short, I become a real arsehole on cocaine, and in my opinion, so does everyone else. It may make you feel confident and invincible, but it also makes you insufferable to be around for anyone who's not also on the drug. Whereas with some other drugs, you could say, it's very much about how beautiful and amazing everyone else is, with coke it's all just 'me, me, me'. Add to that the prolonged anxiety it now gives me, I've chosen to steer well clear of this particular party favour for the foreseeable future.

As we're about to order something to eat, Joey puts her hand on my wrist. I can tell from the anxious expression on her face that she's got something to tell me – and that it's probably to do with Tiger. During the past few weeks, I've been hearing various rumours circulating about him, mainly about his drug-taking.

'Go on then, what is it?' I ask her nervously.

'You're not gonna like this,' she replies softly, 'but I'd rather you hear it from me than someone else: Tiger's Facebook status says he's in a relationship.'

Of course it bloody does.

I ask Joey to show me on her phone, seeing as I blocked Tiger on Facebook the day we parted ways.

My worst fears are confirmed: it's with the girl he cheated on me with last year at the meditation retreat in France.

I later learn that this girl moved into the warehouse only weeks after I moved out, and had also gone with him to the Secret Garden Party festival – the same place Tiger was sectioned just two summers earlier.

'It doesn't change your reality; he's not in your life anymore,' Joey says, wrapping a comforting arm around my shoulder.

I know she's right – and I knew this was coming – but it doesn't feel good.

That night, I go to a friend's thirtieth birthday party, and make some *bad* decisions, one of which finds me waking up at three in the afternoon in a drug dealer's flat in Elephant and Castle. I get dressed and quietly sneak out while the guy's in the bathroom.

On the bus, I call a friend from church, who tells me to meet her at the 4.30 p.m. service.

'But I can't! I'm in last night's clothes, I feel disgusting!'

'Exactly,' she replies, 'that's why you need to come.'

I spend the whole of the service weeping on her lap on the floor.

'When you're feeling far from God, guess who moved?' the speaker says. 'But, you can move back, too.'

Now that I've had my own 'relapse' of sorts – falling back into bed with a stranger to try and make myself feel better – how am I going to play it this time? Does it negate all the work I've done on myself so far? Shall I just forget all this self-love and healthy living shit, and dive back into what's easier and more familiar to me?

No. I can't go back to that. I can't – I *won't*. Two steps forward, one step back. That's how it seems to go, this journey towards personal enlightenment, or whatever else you want to call it. *Progress, not perfection.*

'Slipping up is part of the process,' my sponsor Bella always says. So I'd better embrace it, and I'd better get very good at forgiving myself (which is so much harder for me to do than forgiving other people). Twenty-six years of self-destructive behaviour is not going to just disappear in a few months.

Sometimes, my mistakes will be reasonably harmless to myself and others. Sometimes, they may cause pain. It's OK. *I'm doing my best, I'm doing my best, I'm doing my best.* Even when my best isn't perfect, *it's OK.* It may feel like I'm going round in circles, but I'm not. It's a spiral, and each time I go round, I'm slowly, gradually moving upwards (at least, I hope I am). *Just do the next right thing.* That's all you can ever do after you mess up.

When the service is over, I find myself signing up for the annual church holiday in a few weeks' time. I know I'm jumping from one extreme to the other, but I'll do anything to move back towards the happiness and peace I felt before finding out about Tiger's new relationship – even spend a whole week camping with a bunch of Christians.

On the way home, I get off the bus at Putney Bridge and take out the little pink gemstone that's been living in a pocket of my purse for nearly a year now. Tiger brought it back for me from the meditation retreat in France last summer – probably in an attempt to assuage his guilt over having cheated on me while there.

I lean over the side of the bridge and drop the pebble into the Thames.

When I get home, I write Tiger an email telling him I know about his new girlfriend. I explain that, although it obviously hurts, I'm not angry and I forgive him. But, I'd be grateful if he'd give me some space over the coming months so I don't have to see them together in the flesh (I'm not *that* strong). I also thank him for taking me back to church, and for being the catalyst that helped me reconnect to the spiritual relationship that helped me so much when I was little.

Two days later, he replies:

Dearest P. frisky,

Your astoundingly written mail brought tears to my eyes and as always, made me laugh out loud.

The last few weeks have been a bit of a rollercoaster for me, but I guess you'd be surprised if I said they hadn't; it seems to be the way my life's ride travels, like a yoyo. But, along with some crushing lows have been some glorious highs, so things could be worse . . . I have my health (give or take a few coughs and splutters in the mornings).

As you probably heard, things did get a bit wild for a time after we split. It was the standard story of giving a psychedelic journey a go again and having a few more licks of the disco lolly before putting it down. But, I found myself getting too close to the old me, and for that reason, I've taken a step back from the precipice, and am getting my feet back into the routine of life in the city and on the T.Total wagon (for the time being, anyway).

In regard to your wishes, I totally respect what you have asked of me, and will make every effort possible not to cross your path until you are ready for us to meet.

You are the person you have always wanted to become Persia. You're not the same individual that I walked with on that sunny afternoon in Richmond Park well over a year ago. You really have transformed into a beautiful butterfly, and I think I was the chrysalis: I was there to help with your transformation, but then came the time when you needed to break free from the chrysalis and embrace your new wings. However comforting it is to be in the security of the cocoon, why waste the gift of flight?

So go forth little P; flutter and test how far you can fly (just don't go too near to the sun, or you'll end up like me, with singed wings holding you down on street level among all the other mere mortals, drinking Frappuccinos and sipping on the system).

All the love I have to give,

Tiger xxx

You

'To be wronged is nothing unless you continue to remember it.'
Confucius

Forgiveness is a selfish act: it's not only a gift to the other person, it's a gift to ourselves. This is why the practice of forgiving is a non-negotiable element of every serious spiritual pathway. It's the key to ensuring the peace and happiness of both ourselves, and every person that we come into contact with. Although it may be a very challenging journey, without it we don't just stay miserable in our relationships and friendships, we stay miserable in every other area of our lives, so powerful and all-consuming is the nature of anger and resentment.

When we hold on to past grievances, the noose that we meta-phorically tie around our perpetrator's neck ends up choking us. We feel angry and bitter because of our own unwillingness to change our attitude about the past, and we project all of that negativity on to the other person, because we don't want to take responsibility for our own thoughts.

Many of us know deep down that the only solution to tran-scending this uncomfortable place lies in forgiveness, and yet so much of the time we'd rather stay stuck in our fury. Why do we do this when we know that it's completely futile and leaves us feeling bitter?

Sometimes, we can't see clearly enough to realise that it's actually far easier to let go, and other times, we get too much of a kick out of playing the victim to give it up so easily. In stay-ing angry, we get to feel powerful and in control by way of making the other person 'wrong' and ourselves 'right'. We get to feel smug and self-righteous – even tricking ourselves into believing that we're the 'bigger person'. That's the payoff. Yet, *we* remain stuck.

When our thinking is dominated by another's behaviour, it's a sure sign that we've lost focus on ourselves, and that we too have become spiritually sick. In order to bring ourselves back into balance, we must identify what part we personally played in the situation. Our initial response is likely to attribute *all* blame towards the person, place or institution in question, but if we're honest with ourselves, there's *always* something we can take responsibility for (no matter how small). We may have been aware of someone's untrustworthy reputation, but buried our head in the sand and ignored the warning signs until it was too late. Or, we may have been running late for work and in our haste neglected to buy a parking ticket, landing ourselves with a hefty fine – leav-ing us feeling really angry and resentful towards the traffic warden.

The point is, we're rarely, if ever, completely blameless. Looking at our part in any given situation is of huge benefit to us, because it means we need not go blindly through the same hurtful predicament again. If we're not feeling at peace about resentments from our past, the likelihood is that we have not yet acknowledged our part in it, and learned what we might have from the experience.

Although we sometimes tell ourselves that forgiving people who've injured us will make us look and feel weak and feeble, it's actually the other way around. The more we forgive, the stronger we look and feel. People who love and respect themselves practise forgiveness on a daily basis. They know that we're all just doing our best, however rubbish our best may sometimes appear to be. They are able to 'detach with love' from other people's mistakes or errors in judgement, and don't take everything so personally.

Whatever struggles we may have faced in our life, someone out there has experienced trials and tribulations so much worse than we could ever imagine. While it's true that all pain is subjective, it can sometimes help put our own issues into perspective by acknowledging those people who've clearly suffered more than we have, handling life with grace, dignity and an ever-expanding attitude of forgiveness.

Often, it's those who have much to forgive the world for who seem to extend forgiveness the most. Corrie ten Boom was a prisoner of war who, some years after the Second World War, came face to face with a guard from the concentration camp she was sent to, and where her sister had died. When the guard asked for her forgiveness, she grasped his hand and exclaimed, 'I forgive you brother, with all my heart!' She had realised that, 'Forgiveness is not an emotion, but an act of the will, and the will can function regardless of the temperature of the heart.' This is an extreme example, we know, but it powerfully illustrates how forgiveness is a radical act of self-love and healing, because in forgiving her perpetrator, Corrie set herself free.

Almost every decision we make is a result of how we are feeling about ourselves in that particular moment. When we're behaving kindly and compassionately towards those around us, it's because we're feeling good about ourselves. When we're spikey, cold, judgemental or derogatory, it's usually because we're feeling bad about ourselves.

You cannot love another until you first love yourself, and you cannot love yourself until you first accept yourself. Therefore, the degree to which we can accept, forgive and love ourselves is in direct correlation to that with which we can extend to others (and make no mistake, this is often a difficult and lengthy process). This doesn't mean we don't maintain appropriate boundaries or that we 'let people walk all over us'. It means that we remember that we're not perfect, either.

Our primary job, then, is to make accepting and forgiving our own mistakes our priority. This starts with doing a detailed inventory of our past errors, which can be a painful and some-what gruelling process. However, it's essential to the cultivating of our sense of self-worth and ensuring the success of our future relationships. When we're clear about what we've done wrong in the past and set the intention to forgive ourselves with the aid of our Higher Power, we will no longer need to feel shackled with the shame and remorse which we then, in turn, project on to others. Once we've committed to our own self-forgiveness, we can then look at who else in our lives we need to forgive.

You may have been holding on to a lot of past resentments from your childhood, previous relationships or other situations without even knowing it, and this will keep you feeling stuck and negative. The Forgiving Others exercise below will guide you to release and heal the wounds from your past so that you're free to create positive new experiences for yourself in the future.

EXERCISES

Forgiving Yourself

1) In your journal, write a list of the major mistakes that you have made in your life. This may be short or long, depending on your own personal experiences, so just write down whatever comes up for you. It may be helpful to structure and organise the list into five-or-ten year increments, or into specific periods of your life.

2) When you have finished the list, listen to the following meditation, with the intention of forgiving yourself.

Forgiveness Meditation

1) Go to www.theinnerfix.com/meditation

2) Sit upright with your legs crossed and palms on your lap facing upwards, and breathe slowly in and out – as you breathe in, your stomach expands; as you breathe out, your stomach contracts. The recorded meditation will guide you to focus your attention inwards.

3) When you have finished, feel free to write down any thoughts or feelings that come up for you in your journal.

Forgiving Others

1) Now, refer back to the table you made in chapter 5, Resentment, and fill out the final column, titling it: 'My Part'. Here, we want you to identify *your* part in the situation – however small it might have been. For example, if you wrote down that you resented your friends for arranging a weekend trip away and not inviting you, you might realise that you've made very little effort with them lately since starting your new romantic relationship.

2) When you've finished the final column, re-listen to the above meditation, this time with the intention of forgiving those people that have hurt you in the past.

Write a Letter

Another very powerful practice is to write a letter to any of the people above who have hurt you particularly badly, and who you're struggling to forgive. Tell them why you were hurt, and own up to your part in the situation, as explored in the final column of the chapter 5 table. Finish the letter(s) off by telling that person that you forgive them, and are willing to let your resentment go now.

Do not send the letter; this exercise is designed to help you release your personal resentments, and it's better to leave the other person out of it for the time being. There may well be an opportunity for direct communication with this person further down the line, but for now, keep the focus on yourself.

Sharing with a Trusted Friend

Once you've finished the two lists and letters, you may like to read them out to a trusted friend, if you feel comfortable doing so. Sharing in this way is a really powerful experience and a signal to yourself and your Higher Power that you're ready to let go of your grievances and make space for the new and the healthy.

Daily Forgiveness Practice

Forgiveness is a muscle; it needs to be exercised regularly and consistently in order to grow. You can't just do one big round of forgiveness and be done with it – you've got to keep 'working out' daily to continue experiencing the benefits, in the same way that you go to the gym to maintain your physique.

Therefore, we recommend that you do the following exercise every evening for the next month. You may find this challenging, but all you need to do is show a willingness to forgive the things you note down and, once again, ask your Higher Power to help you let go of these resentments. This particular practice is just for you – you don't need to share it with anyone else.

If you commit to this practice for the whole month, you'll no doubt see a massive positive shift in all of your relationships, because remember: *the degree to which we can accept, forgive and love ourselves is in direct correlation to that with which we can extend to others.*

Evening 'Quiet Time' Practice

1) In your journal, write down three things that you are going to choose to forgive yourself for today. These might be big things, or they might be little things.

Examples might include:

- Not going to the gym when you said you would.
- Being passive-aggressive towards a colleague who irritates you.
- Drinking one glass of wine too many.
- Spending too much money on clothes.

2) Then, write down three things you forgive others for today. Again, they can be big or small, depending on where you feel you've been wronged.

Examples may include:

- The person you're dating for not texting you back.
- Your housemate for finishing all your peanut butter.
- The bus driver for not stopping when he saw you running to catch the bus.

CHAPTER 10

GRATEFUL

Persia

'Some people grumble that roses have thorns;
I am grateful that thorns have roses.'

A Tour Round My Garden, Alphonse Karr

'm sat in Starbucks waiting to have coffee and a catch-up with Bella. My phone vibrates on the small table in front, and I see that an email has come through from the company I've been using to obtain my O-1 visa that will enable me to work in the States. I haven't heard from them for nearly a year now – not since I parted with my entire savings to get the visa processed through them. Now that Tiger and I are no longer together, I'm significantly more interested to see whether the visa has arrived yet – after all, other than Joey, there's not all that much keeping me in London anymore.

The email is short and to the point. It turns out that the visa company has gone into liquidation, and I'm not going to be seeing an O-1 (or a single penny of that money) any time soon, if ever.

Bloody. Hell.

About thirty seconds after I get the bad news, Bella glides through the door, looking effortlessly radiant in a pale-blue cashmere jumper and skinny jeans.

'Darling, what's wrong?!' she says, instantly aware of my panicked expression. I fill her in on the visa situation – and my rapidly growing fear that I'm now down to my last £100. In. The. World.

'Oh sweetheart, I'm so sorry to hear that. Just remember, you can't see the whole picture right now; maybe this is just another storm to clear the way for something better – like your break-up with Tiger.'

'But, why do the storms always have to happen all at once?!' I moan.

'Just the way it goes sometimes darling. No point in wasting your energy trying to understand why.'

'I just really don't know what I'm going to do with my life now; I always thought acting was it. I really did.'

'I know you did. Just keep asking your Higher Power for clarity and guidance Persia. You never know, one day you might be grateful that the visa fell through. Sometimes the worst things that happen to us lead to the best things.'

A few days later, I get a call from Salena's dad, known to all our friends as 'Uncle Joe'. He and his wife Lynne were like surrogate parents to me when I was growing up. Uncle Joe has always been hugely supportive of my career – he's been to pretty much every show I've ever done, and has always told me I'd make a success of myself, whatever I chose to do.

He asks if I happen to be free next Saturday, as he has a spare ticket to a one-day seminar for entrepreneurs. When he thought of who he could give the ticket to, I instantly popped into his mind – which is strange, considering I've never shown any interest in business whatsoever.

However, what I *do* have now is a lot of free time, and I need to do something productive to take my mind off the visa situation – and Tiger's new relationship status.

Although my father's a born entrepreneur and has built his property portfolio from scratch, it never occurred to me that I may have inherited some of those genes. I thought I was simply a creative, doomed to live out my tortured artistic existence hand to mouth (particularly now that Hollywood's a no-go). This event, therefore, is the last thing I'd have ever imagined myself enjoying, and yet, here I am . . . enjoying it.

Daniel Priestley, the founder and host of the seminar, uses a particularly powerful metaphor demonstrating how many entrepreneurs overlook their value. He says that this loss of perspective is akin to climbing to the top of a mountain and looking out across at all the other peaks in the distance; in that moment you think that, in order to feel worthy, you need to summit those other mountains in the distance. What you fail to realise, however, is that you're already standing on top of an incredible peak yourself – and other people on those distant mountains are thinking exactly the same thing about where you're standing! Likewise, when it comes to building a business or becoming an entrepreneur, we often fail to register that we're already standing on a mountain of value: all those passions, gifts, talents, skills and life experience that we possess provide the perfect training for us to go out and serve the world in a way that only we can.

On the bus home, I think back to my trip to Thailand with my dad in early 2011. While there, I'd had an emotional clearing session with a young Australian lady who was an intuitive healer. At the end of the hour, she'd told me that I was here to help people overcome their false beliefs about themselves, and that I'd write a book in the next five years guiding them to do this. They'd be moved and inspired by my inner life – and, in particular, my voice.

At the time, it all sounded too good to be true. Only six months before the Thailand trip, I'd been snorting drugs with millionaires in a strip club and up to God only knows what else; who would ever take me seriously or want to solicit advice from someone like me? But, then I was sent the relationship with Tiger. It was exactly what I needed to smack me awake and break me open enough to change those destructive patterns that were keeping me stuck. Now, I actually *know* a little about recovering from having next to no self-worth, because I've had to learn it from scratch.

As I remember the healer's words, an intense wave of energy and excitement surges through me – so much so that my entire body starts to buzz.

Follow this feeling, I keep hearing. *Follow this feeling.*

The next week, Joey and I meet for brunch. I tell her about the seminar, and how something in me feels absolutely certain that she and I are meant to find a way to share the spiritual journey and lessons we've learned together over the last year.

'I've been thinking the same,' she replies, smiling.

We spend the next few hours making lists, notes and sketches about what this 'movement' of ours would look like, and how to get started. A blog with YouTube videos on it with tips and tools to help girls our age in all areas of life seems like the most obvious point of entry – especially as our drama school training means that we're reasonably comfortable in front of a camera.

We decide to call our new project Addictive Daughter – on account of the fact we both have addictive personalities, and are both daughters – as is every female, whatever her age. Also, 'daughter' feels more apt than 'woman' to us, because it alludes to the personal contexts and history that have shaped each of us. 'It always comes back to childhood and the family,' my therapist once told me.

With the concept of Addictive Daughter fresh in my mind, I venture off to the north of England for the church week away – or 'God Camp' as Joey and I jokingly refer to it. Although I'm very susceptible to being cringed out by the whole Christian culture scene, I vow to show up this week with an open heart and mind.

On the first night, around 5,000 people gather in a huge blue tent (the kind I raved in at many a festival with Tiger) and lift their hands to sing to God in gratitude and praise.

This communal union through singing has always had a very powerful effect on me. I feel at my core we were all designed to sing together like this. After all, singing as a collective is something humans have been doing for thousands of years. It's a tribal activity that brings us together, elevates our mood and connects us to something greater than ourselves. It also relieves stress: much like meditation and chanting, it gives us a single focus, and takes us out of our heads and all our insignificant day-to-day problems.

But, best of all, it makes me feel really high – without the nasty comedown afterwards. During each of the worship sessions throughout the week, I find that my breathing deepens, my body tingles and fizzes, my head goes all swimmy, and at times, I swear, I'm even gurning a little. I wanted a transcendental experience, and here I am having one – without any substance intake whatsoever.

When I look around me at the other people singing here, I realise I'm not alone in my ecstatic state – most other people seem to be in on it, too – in fact, we could almost be at a normal secular music festival. I think we're all just after the same thing at the end of the day: to experience the feelings of love and joy. We're just taking different routes to get there.

I continue to get signs and affirmation that Joey and I are on the right track with Addictive Daughter while I'm here. The majority of the people I'm drawn to at this place are recovering addicts (naturally). One of them, a film director called Luke, is interested in potentially collaborating with Addictive Daughter. I call Joey to tell her, and we both share how grateful we're feeling to have found something we're so passionate about, and that we believe could really help people one day.

Towards the end of the week, I find myself talking to Charlie Mackesy – the artist that gave the Nativity sermon at the carol service Tiger took me to last Christmas. I tell him about Addictive Daughter and my own personal journey of running away from God and the church, because I felt so ashamed of my behaviour and who I'd become.

'Churches are hospitals, Persia, not members' clubs where we should all just pretend to be on our best behaviour. If you look in the Bible, God's always using broken vessels to carry out His work.'

He then takes out his phone and shows me a photo of one of his paintings. It's of a father holding a young girl in his arms. The accompanying text reads:

> This is the story of the Prodigal Daughter – it should really be called the father who waited every day for his girl to come home – the daughter who had rejected him so badly – but when he saw her from a long way off – he ran to her and hugged her and kissed her.

Joey

'We can only be said to be alive in those moments
when our hearts are conscious of our treasures.'
Thornton Wilder

'I ahsk zee sree of you to stay for coffee et patisserie wis me,'
invites the artist, whose studio we've just stumbled into on our
quest to find *une toilette*.

Immanuel, a lithe French, sun-weathered bohemian man of
fifty-five, with piercing-black eyes and greying hair, stands
before us awaiting a response. There is a depth to him that I'm
instantly drawn towards. A silver fox, if ever I saw one.

'We'd LOVE to!' Persia replies.

Myself, my gay best friend Louis and Persia are currently on
holiday at my family's villa in south-west France, and after a
sweltering bus journey, we've arrived in the beautiful Provençal
town of Pézenas.

'Pleese, com inside and I will sho you zis work uff mine.
Aurélie?' He bellows into the vast studio space before us, which
is separated by a complexity of fabric hangings and divider
walls. A young woman appears from nowhere.

'*Oui?*'

Aurélie is tiny and toned, with short, curly hair, freckles across
the bridge of her button nose, and a doe-eyed innocence.

'*Va chercher des petits gâteaux et fais du café,*' Immanuel orders.

She nods and promptly disappears from sight to prepare
coffee and cake for us.

Immanuel's art studio is otherworldly. It's crammed full with
huge canvases of broken souls, women and angels – the essence

of vulnerability captured by brush. The atmosphere's rustic and magical, the scent of coffee mixed with fresh paint lingers in the air and, at every turn, I'm met by huge candles that have previously cried waxy tears and now stand hardened without flame.

Immanuel works with angels. He tells us that he prays before he begins to create, and believes that angels guide him while he works. He does not acknowledge himself as creator of the magnificent work that surrounds us, insisting instead that he's simply the vessel, channelling it from a higher source. He explains he's been given the gift of creativity, and since gifts are always given, that for him is proof of the existence of something greater. He tells me that his name, of Hebrew descent, means 'God with us'. I see and feel connectedness in action all around Immanuel. I'm fascinated by his work and the way he talks about otherworldliness. As it turns out, he becomes equally as fascinated by me.

As much as the saner part of me feels thankful that Josh has not once been in touch, three months on I'd be lying if I said that his silence hasn't been a blow to the ego. Particularly since Tiger has contacted Persia, without fail, on the first day of every month since their split (they have a thing about the first of the month, as it's when they got together). Nonetheless, it's been good for me to be so completely alone these past few months. Receiving not an iota of romantic validation from anyone, I feel as if I'm learning how to generate those feelings of love from within.

Over the course of the afternoon, I begin to feel as if we've been dropped into a Woody Allen film, as the four of us converse over fresh oysters, while Immanuel falls further in lust with me. He makes little effort to conceal this from the others – much to Persia's irritation; she's accustomed to the focus being very much on her in social situations. Up until now, I've always taken the supporting role in our friendship, and this is the first time that the dynamic has been reversed. It's funny how easy it is to fall into playing a particular role within friendships, and how clunky it can feel, for both parties, to step outside the mould we create for ourselves. She later apologises for any hurt caused by the green-eyed monster getting the better of her.

I find Immanuel's attention both overwhelming and resuscitating in equal measure. I have been fixing, forcing and chasing romance for so long that I've forgotten how it feels to be adored for just being me. As it turns out, nothing at all happens with Immanuel. I remain completely single – without so much as a kiss – for eight whole months following Josh. Yet, his passion serves as a gentle awakening of how requited and emotionally available affection feels, and it shows up at the perfect time.

Halfway through the holiday, Louis returns to England, leaving Persia and I alone together at the villa for the remainder of the trip. Having only very recently come back into each other's lives, we're appreciative of this time to reconnect. Although we don't know it yet, we'll forever refer back to this period as our 'self-made summer rehab'.

My parents dreamt of having a provincial holiday home for years, and worked hard to make it a reality. We've had some wonderful family holidays here, and more recently the villa has served as a heartbreak sanctuary for me. It's not luxurious by any means, but it has a simple and practical homeliness and, best of all, it's a short walk from the ocean. There's nothing like the ocean to put things into perspective.

I think back to where I was just two years ago, during my divine storm of 2010. That summer, I travelled out here alone – post break-up with Rory – and spent all week lying on a rug indoors, staring at the ceiling, surviving on a diet of rosé, raw peppers and music. The week before, in London, I'd picked up a compilation album called *Lost and Found* in Oxfam for 99p.

I'd been drawn to the sketch on the cover (a linear drawing of tangled string that depicted a winding road leading up to a large house) and lay on the floor, listening to it on repeat for the entire week. One of my favourite songs on the album was called 'Give Up and Let It Go'. The lyrics really spoke to me:

> *It wasn't until much later I find my whole life down*
> *Storming round the town with insecurity in my pocket*
> *And worries in my bed*
> *I was forced to see the doctor and the good doctor said;*
> *Give up and let it go*
> *Give up and let your life flow*
> *Give up and let it go*
> *Give up and let your life flow*
> *Give up and let it go*

Back then, I wasn't quite ready to act on the message, preferring to wallow in the melancholy, the 'poor me' state of being with which I was much better acquainted. At the week's end, I returned to England more miserable and quite probably paler than when I left (if that's possible).

Sitting beside Persia on the sofa now, I look down at that same rug on the floor, where I once lay desolate. Outwardly, my circumstances haven't changed all that much – I have, after all, recently been dumped, and once again find myself single. Yet, I'm struck by how different things are this time; the *inner* experience, I mean. I'm out here with my friend, taking gentle care of myself, sober, accepting, processing and taking all the lessons I can from my time with Josh. I don't feel bitter or angry – I'm choosing to believe that there was a reason he was brought into my life, and also a reason he's been removed from it.

Persia, having called me in from outside to join her, is sitting holding a small book in her hands. She looks apprehensive.

'Now. I want to read you something, it's from the Bible – I know, I know, it's really *cringe* – but just hear me out, because I think you'll like it.'

I sit, cross-legged and attentive on the sofa beside her and glance at the open page to read the title, 'The Parable of The Lost Son'.

She slows down for dramatic effect as she nears the end of the passage:

> The older brother became angry and refused to go in. So his father went out and pleaded with him. But he answered his father, 'Look! All these years I've been slaving for you and never disobeyed your orders. Yet you never gave me even a young goat so I could celebrate with my friends. But when this son of yours who has squandered your property with prostitutes comes home, you kill the fattened calf for him!'
>
> 'My son,' the father said, 'you are always with me, and everything I have is yours. But we had to celebrate and be glad, because this brother of yours was dead and is alive again; he was lost and is found.'

Persia closes the book between her palms and tries to read my face for signs of a response. As coincidences would have it, the story ends on the name of the album I'd been listening to on repeat two summers earlier: *Lost and Found*. It confirms something that I'd been hoping about my understanding of God: that He's ready to meet me *exactly* where I am.

On the flight back to London at the end of our trip, I feel a profound sense that I'm being guided. Experience is showing me that some people are angels, brought on to our path to guide us along our way. I feel grateful for everything that's gone before, the good and the bad, because it's brought me to where I am right now. We touch down in Luton and a message pops up on my phone from Immanuel:

Au revoir ma chérie. Je prie pour toi et je demande à mes anges de te mettre sous leur protection. Mes anges sont très puissants, tu peux compter sur eux, ils veilleront sur toi nuit et jour.
Ton Ange,
Immanuel

Goodbye, my darling. I pray for you and ask my angels to protect you. My angels are very powerful, you can rely on them to watch over you day and night.
Your angel,
Immanuel

You

'Gratitude is not only the greatest of virtues,
but the parent of all others.'
Marcus Tullius Cicero

In our darkest hour, we are often plagued by what seems to be missing from our life. Our experience of pain is so inextricably linked with what we are attached to, that when we lose something important to us – the job, the relationship, the money – we lose our sense of perspective along with it. We're so focused on that one thing we don't have, we're blind to everything that we do.

For many of us, we have a lot to be thankful for. The problem is, when it comes to measuring ourselves and our lives against others, more often than not we look to those that have more, and so feel like we're constantly falling short.

We quantify our own self-worth not in accordance with *who we are*, but with *what we have* in relation to those around us. Once, this was limited to celebrities that we didn't know, but now through the emergence of social media it includes every single person we've ever come into contact with (as well as their entire personal network). And, the thing is, we're not even comparing ourselves to other people's actual *reality*, we're comparing ourselves and our lives to a carefully curated depiction of the 'best bits' or 'highlights reel' of someone's life.

In many ways, it would seem that the more we gain, the less happy we become. We've developed an appetite so insatiable that we never feel fully satisfied – at least, not for any extended period of time. We lose ten pounds, and immediately set ourselves a new goal of dropping five more. We fall in love, and three months in the grass is already looking greener elsewhere. We get the latest iPhone, but soon there's a better model available.

Our dependency on these instant hits of joy and gratification – whether it's through sex, drugs, alcohol or shopping – now dominates our societal consciousness to an extreme degree. We've become so consumed by the search for more that life's been reduced to one long trawl around the metaphorical supermarket, as we seek to tick our way through a shopping list that has no end point.

Perhaps it's time to press pause and appreciate what's already in our trolley, because, contrary to what our social landscape fools us into believing, it's gratitude for what we have, not the acquisition of that which we don't, that makes life more pleasurable.

It's worth mentioning that gratitude for what we have is not limited to material possessions – or even positive experiences in our life, but the painful ones, too. Those very things that have caused us suffering in the past can, in fact, increase our capacity to experience love, if we choose to look for the silver lining in all our trials and tribulations.

If you look back on your life with an open mind, you will likely see that some of the worst things that ever happened to you turned out to be blessings in disguise. Having your heart broken may have given you the opportunity to learn to be content on your own. Being made redundant could have been the push you needed to get clear and focused on what you really want to do with your life. Breaking your leg might have shown you the importance of slowing down and taking good care of yourself.

Remember, when we're in the midst of a storm we cannot see the whole picture. As Marilyn Monroe is thought to have said, 'Good things fall apart so better things can fall together.' During those difficult transitions, it helps to remember to be grateful for all the other good things in our life, because even when everything appears to be going wrong, there is still much to be thankful for. It's this feeling of gratitude that makes the hard times all the more bearable, and helps us navigate the turbulent waves until calm has been restored.

In this respect, gratitude acts as a soothing balm that not only serves to heal our wounds, but connects us directly to our Higher Power. The closer we are to our Higher Power – that loving energy that's gently guiding us towards our highest good – the more we'll experience a sense of flow in our lives, because we're working in collaboration with life, not trying to resist it. After all, it's the resistance that causes us pain, and resistance is generated by striving for things beyond our reach, rather than appreciating what lies within.

What's important to remember here is that gratitude is an *experience* – a tangible, physical sensation, not just an idea. Therefore, in order to actually *feel* grateful, it's necessary to discover ways of accessing that experience that work for you as an individual – and commit to practising them daily, as the exercises below will guide you to do.

EXERCISES

Count Your Blessings

1) In your journal, write a list of every single thing in your life that could be described as an 'asset'. Go back to basics here: is your health generally good for the most part? Do you have someone in your life who cares about you and shows you consistent love and support?

2) You can then get more specific and note down the skills you have learned and education you've had access to, as well as all the little privileges you enjoy. For example:

- A laptop.

- Access to a garden or some green space.

    Being able to afford the odd meal out.

3) Now think of certain aspects of your life that, on first appear-ances, may seem more like problems or liabilities, and see how you can shift your perspective on them. For example:

- If you've recently come out of a relationship, instead of seeing this as negative, you could choose to see this as an opportunity to travel, take up new hobbies and meet new people.

- If you're not happy in your job, use your frustration as impetus to discover what it is you would really love to be doing.

Daily Gratitude Practice

You may like to add the practices below to the Quiet Time you've been carving out for yourself every day.

Gratitude Meditation

1) Go to www.theinnerfix.com/meditation

2) Sit upright with your legs crossed and palms on your lap facing upwards, and breathe slowly in and out – as you breathe in, your stomach expands; as you breathe out, your stomach contracts. The recorded meditation will guide you to focus your attention inwards.

3) When you've finished the meditation, feel free to write down any thoughts or feelings that come up for you in your journal.

Evening Gratitude Practice

Write down in your journal three things that you're grateful for today. They can be as small as receiving a smile from a stranger, or as large as getting promoted. What's important here is developing your gratitude muscles; the more you work them, the stronger they'll become.

Gratitude Group

You may also like to set up a small 'gratitude' group of friends over email or text to share your gratitude with. Not only will you experience the positive effects of your own gratitude, you'll feel the benefit of theirs, too.

PART THREE

THE
FUTURE

Having been introduced to a more spiritual approach to living in part two, it's now time to put these concepts into practice. Happiness, as we've already mentioned, really is an *inside* job. Part three provides a practical guide to incorporating a spiritually aligned existence into major life areas. The core of Addictive Daughter's message is: 'If you focus on the insides, the outsides will take care of themselves', and that's precisely what you'll learn: how to live your life from the *inside-out.*

Those who identify with having an 'addictive personality' may have experienced some of the more negative repercussions of it in the past – in chasing the highs of *more, more, more,* you'll be familiar with the lows, too. And, let's be honest, the things we pursue in our quest for *more* tend to be outside of ourselves and very much material: possessions, substances, romantic partners, social media popularity, and so on.

Though the term 'addiction' has strong associations with destructiveness and being out of control, this isn't actually its definitive meaning. The word 'addict' originates from the Latin *addictus,* which was used more positively to describe attachment, devotion and dedication. With this interpretation in mind, what would happen, then, if our addictive energy could be channelled into a force for good? If we became enthusiastic devotees of all things positive? This is the very question we asked ourselves only a few years ago, and acting on it not only rapidly changed the direction of the paths we were heading down, but also led to the creation of Addictive Daughter. In getting addicted to more negative pursuits, we found ourselves gradually spiralling further downwards, but getting addicted to the *good* stuff had the opposite effect.

Many creative, successful and charismatic people who are doing great things in the world today have battled on some level with an addictive personality or inner conflict of their own. The ones who've turned a corner and come out on top seem to be those who are open to change. By being receptive to growth and learning, they've been able to channel their energy in a more skilful way, drawing strength from their experiences, rather than staying a slave to their struggles.

There's little doubt that the health and wellness boom over recent years has encouraged many of us to take better care of ourselves. If we're not careful, though, it can also lead us to relate to the whole concept of spirituality in a rather superficial way. An interest in spirulina and sun salutations can quickly become more about following a 'trend' and posting attractive workout selfies than a genuine desire to nourish the mind, body and soul.

The lifestyle bloggers we follow are there to inspire us, but for many, the gap between their perfect posts and our reality often feels so wide – and overwhelmingly unattainable – that it drives us to sabotage all the more. The endless images on our newsfeeds of sculptured bodies poised on yoga mats sometimes leaves us feeling *worse* than before we opted to get 'spiritual' and healthy; compare and despair at its most insidious.

Perfectionism and our obsession with attaining it is one of the most damaging things we're doing to ourselves today, and the fashion industry, celebrity culture and our own carefully curated lives on social media don't always help matters. With the bar set so high, many of us are left constantly feeling less-than about where we are – and find that we're wholly unforgiving of ourselves when we do slip up.

It's *so* easy to forget the importance of being able to accept and forgive the times when we veer off course. Whether it be shovelling down cookies at midnight after a treat-free week, or texting an ex in a moment of loneliness, *everyone* falls off the wagon once in a while. Having a spiritual toolset to turn to helps us to get right back on track, and the more we use it, the quicker we bounce back.

This final section of the book, despite focusing on the external topics of body, work, money, friendship and love, isn't about achieving outward perfection in any of these areas. You are simply encouraged to approach each one armed with self-love, and a connection to your inner guidance, in order to take gentle steps in the direction you desire to be heading.

By now, you'll have established that parts of our own stories are messy. While our lives may be less extreme today, things still go wrong, and of course both of us still fall short at times. Often, progress means two steps forward and one back, and that's OK; growth isn't always linear.

When we talk about 'getting addicted to the good stuff', we don't mean having the perfect diet or never having a hangover again – although those things may well become part of life as a by-product of this journey. It's about getting honest with yourself about where you currently are, and what is right for *you*. For some, that may mean abstinence from a particular substance, food type or behaviour, while for others, it may be far less black and white. When you pay attention, you might find that your experiences will have been communicating with you for quite some time, telling you what it is you need to be moving *towards* and moving *away* from, in order to become the highest version of yourself.

From our own experience, having a punishing and rigid approach to self-improvement doesn't work long term: self-love and acceptance needs to come first which, in turn, positively affects the choices you go on to make. The trick isn't to aim to be perfect, but, instead, to commit to speaking to and treating yourself as you would a friend you love.

Once you feel good on the inside, you're in a far better position to start creating the outer life that you've been hoping and wishing for. Most of us have experienced, at some stage, a clear vision for what our future could be – and the excitement that vision brought us. But life happens, and, as we encounter struggles, rejections and disappointments, our self-worth slowly begins to dwindle, as do our dreams.

Part three is an opportunity to reignite that vision you hold for the years ahead, and find out what it is you want to build towards for your future.

CHAPTER 11

BODY

Persia

'Bodies have their own light which they consume to
live: they burn, they are not lit from the outside.'

Egon Schiele

It's 6.30 a.m. in September 2013. I'm watching the sunrise with Jess from the balcony of a house set in the foothills of Andalucía in Spain. Although we'd barely seen each other since LA in 2011, we were recently drawn back into each other's lives following her own experience with heartbreak. Over a year into running Addictive Daughter with Joey, I'm glad that I'm now in a far healthier headspace to be the friend that Jess has needed. As a thank you for my support, she's generously brought me to a week-long yoga and meditation retreat here.

I now find myself about ten months into a relationship with Sam, a guy I met at the church I've been attending for over a year now – the same church Tiger took me to at Christmas time a few years ago. A thirty-one-year-old criminal lawyer originally from Beirut, Sam is very different from any boy I've ever been with.

Although we've had our challenges, I feel very secure in our relationship, and have successfully managed to maintain a life outside of it: I've made a concerted effort to put time and energy towards my spiritual practice and my friendships, which is why I've been able to really be here for Jess over the last few months.

Sitting on this balcony at sunrise reminds me of that conversation with my dad on the balcony in Thailand at the very start of my spiritual journey. Back then, I had *a lot* of work to do on my relationship with my body. In the months preceding the Thailand trip, it had become all too clear that my inner chaos had started to manifest into outer ailments: I'd been taking drugs far too often, which led to regular anxiety and panic attacks, and I felt like my body was constantly on rent to men who couldn't care less that every bone in me ached with sadness.

I'd also put on two stone in two months during my time acting in Shanghai, as a result of drinking far too much beer and eating a ton of what can only be described as 'mystery meat'.

Having been relatively slim for the majority of my life, these extra pounds were really painful for me to carry. I'd stand in the changing rooms of Topshop, pinching my love handles and sobbing as dress after ill-fitting dress was chucked to the floor unceremoniously.

For months, I resigned myself to wearing only leggings and loose tops that covered my ever-expanding bingo wings. My new style (or lack thereof) didn't go unnoticed. While I could conceal the drug-taking and promiscuity from my family, this rapid weight gain was less easy to disguise – not just because I was no longer flaunting my curves in skimpy outfits, but because I was visibly uncomfortable in my own skin.

Although I wasn't living at home at this time, my parents – who were themselves experts in the art of concealing self-destructive tendencies – soon cottoned on that not all was as well as I was pretending it to be.

In addition to their struggles with substance addiction, my parents have also undergone their own battles around body image. When my mum was in rehab, she went down to about six-and-a-half stone. It's apparently not all that uncommon for addicts to develop an eating disorder when being treated for drug abuse – it's the only thing left for them to control, I suppose. I remember going in to see Mum and hugging her for the first time to find that she'd practically disappeared. While she thought she looked 'fabulous', it wasn't an easy sight for a twelve-year-old to take in.

My dad, on the other hand, has the opposite problem. A self-confessed 'Fridge Farmer', he loves to eat – as in *really* loves to eat. Like me, he can't leave a plate of food unfinished, it's *all* got to go.

But, like Mum, Dad's found ways of managing his relationship with food and his body. An adrenalin junkie through and through, he takes himself off for weeks at a time completing treks and climbing excursions all over the world – even getting to Camp One on Mount Everest. The mountains are where he most connects to his own Higher Power, and it's really evident by the way he looks when he returns: sun-kissed, slender and satisfied.

So, after witnessing how hastily I'd ballooned in size post-Shanghai, Dad booked us to go out to his annual yoga detox retreat in Thailand for the first few weeks of January 2011. Although he had no idea of the impact he was about to have on my life, those words Dad spoke to me on the balcony that morning – 'Focus on your insides, and the outsides will take care of themselves' – were to completely revolutionise my entire relationship with my body.

While I was learning all about the effects of growing up surrounded by active addiction via Robin Norwood's book, I was taking daily yoga and meditation classes, and going on a twelve-day detox fast, as well as drinking five cups of volcanic clay mixed with psyllium husk every day to stave off hunger and draw out all the rubbish from my heavily intoxicated body.

To enhance the detox process, I also had a colonic irrigation session each day, which taught me a very important lesson about myself: whenever something is not right for me, I know it in my gut – and I mean that quite literally.

The day after the awful experience with the American man and two hostesses at the Soho strip club in 2010, I was on the bus heading into town for my second shift when a sudden shot of pain surged through my abdomen. It felt as though someone was doing a Chinese burn on my intestines.

The pain kept coming in waves, each one worse than the last. As I hobbled past the Curzon Cinema on Shaftesbury Avenue, however, it started to become unbearable.

I took out my phone and called Joey – who I was about to move in with. I described my worsening symptoms to her, and as I approached the club, the pain became so intense that I collapsed on the pavement outside, clutching my stomach.

Hearing my groans, Joey demanded that I get a taxi back to my flat and call my parents, which I did – the first sensible choice I'd made in a long time. They picked me up and took me straight to A & E, where I waited for two agonising hours, before being taken through for an X-ray of my abdomen.

Half an hour later, the doctor returned with my diagnosis.

'What is it?' I asked, bracing myself.

Food Poisoning? Appendicitis? *Bowel Cancer?*

'Um, well . . . it would appear that you have . . . severe faecal impaction.'

Come again?

'So . . . you're quite literally full of shit then,' my mum chuckled.

I'd been living to such excess that my insides had actually started to *dry out*. Having been given some heavy-duty laxatives by the doctor, I spent the next two days on the toilet, sensing that perhaps my blocked gut had been a blessing in disguise. I didn't end up going back to the strip club again after that night.

However, once I'd fully recovered from the faecal impaction, I found myself slipping back into my toxic lifestyle habits, and so my ever-faithful gut continued to try and halt my spiral into self-annihilation.

While in LA with Jess at the start of 2011, I caught an untimely stomach bug on the night of the Oscars. This resulted in me shitting myself at the Chateau Marmont (or 'Shateau' to my friends), while stood next to some of Hollywood's most influential celebrities – an unpleasant signal that this city maybe wasn't for me, after all. I also experienced a similar stomach malady the night I learned that Tiger had cheated on me (which was mirrored by his dog shitting all around his bed the following morning).

The point is, my gut *knows*. Since that retreat in Thailand, my diet and lifestyle choices have been far from perfect, but what has happened is that I've stopped ignoring the warning signs.

Today, I do what I can to treat my body with the respect it deserves for managing to keep me alive, despite what seemed like my best efforts to destroy it. I eat my greens. I consume minimal gluten, dairy and sugar, because they really bloat me. If I'm drinking, I always try and match each alcoholic drink with the equivalent amount of water. I make every effort to practise yoga for around half an hour most days, because it makes me feel good physically, mentally and spiritually.

But more importantly than all the above, I make it a daily

habit to let myself off the hook when I *do* eat a whole bar of chocolate, drink a bit too much red wine or watch TV for hours instead of going for a run in the sunshine. I know I'm never going to look like Kate Moss, but I do what I can to feel and look my best on any given day, and after that, I try to let it go.

Joey

'The miracle of self-healing occurs when the
inner patient yields to the inner physician.'
Vernon Howard

The alarm goes off on my iPhone across the room.

'Oh, hell,' I mumble, pushing my face into the pillow and pulling the duvet over my head.

Persia's lying next to me. She stayed over last night and is accompanying me to hospital (which is just up the road from my house) in a few hours' time.

I have never been a fan of smear tests – to the point that I get faint and panicky. I'm not sure that anyone really *enjoys* having a cold, metal rod thrust in and opened up inside them, but from the reactions of the nurses I've had, my aversion to them is more severe than most.

Today is no ordinary smear test, though. Ever since a set of results flagged up 'borderline changes' to the cells on my cervix in my early twenties, I've been called in for regular six-monthly check-ups. After seemingly endless letters over the years referencing 'further examinations' and 'follow-up visits', the most recent one to arrive through the post, after having a colposcopy (close examination of my cervix), states:

The results following your recent visit to the colposcopy clinic are below:

Punch Biopsy   CIN2

The HPV virus test result is High Risk HPV Detected (Positive)

The results show that treatment is necessary and can be easily treated with simple loop excision procedure.

I research it online, and CIN2 means moderately abnormal pre-cancerous cells. On top of that, I've been diagnosed with HPV (human papilloma virus) of the 'high risk' variety – apparently this increases the risk of the potentially cancerous cells being aggravated.

I'm slightly reassured to learn that around 80 per cent of women will contract some form of HPV during their lifetime, so I'm not alone. I ring the doctor's surgery and enquire as to how I can treat the HPV virus, but I'm told there's no definitive cure, although sometimes the body can heal itself. So, it seems I'm powerless over HPV.

Having embraced a healthy lifestyle overhaul just over a year ago now (which has subsequently led to embarking on the creation of Addictive Daughter), this whole scenario comes as a bit of a blow. Typical that I should receive news like this the moment I start to look after myself properly.

On closer Google inspection, the 'simple loop excision procedure' seems a lot more intimidating than the letter's description.

Persia sits with me on the edge of the bed.

'Joey, if it helps, I have a spare anti-anxiety tablet that Sam lent me for a flight recently. It'll take the edge off it a little?'

Sam, Persia's endearingly odd boyfriend, is a workaholic and frequently uses prescription meds to relax into a decent night's sleep. I'd much rather decline, but I'm so terrified that I accept. After all, what can one tiny anti-anxiety pill do? With the gift of hindsight, for someone who's been sober for over a year – from alcohol and every other mind-altering substance – the answer is: *quite a lot.*

I pop the pill, we throw on our clothes, and are soon on the bus heading up the hill towards the hospital. I find myself holding on to the yellow loop dangling above my head more and more tightly as everything starts to feel woolly and softens into a delightful haze.

Inside the hospital room, with legs akimbo in stirrups, two nurses stare down at my vagina then back up at my face, apprehensively.

'What has she taken?' one of the nurses asks Persia, who's growing paler by the minute in the corner of the operating room.

'Seriously guys, I'm fine. I've ta'en a relaxer to relax me. I'm verrry relaxed,' I slur.

'I'm not sure that we can operate on her like this,' the other nurse mutters.

Next thing I know, I come to hours later back at home in bed, Persia having tucked me in. I turn to her.

'Did they do it?'

Her nod confirms that they did.

I read in a book recently that abnormal cells or cervical cancer is associated with the 'rape archetype' – referring to women who've been taken advantage of, or who feel sexually disempowered. Medically speaking, it's true that the disease is generally a result of unprotected intercourse with men – it almost never appears in women who've had little or no intercourse (or lesbians for that matter).

I know that much of my behaviour over the years has come from not feeling too great about myself, even if I've tried to convince myself otherwise at the time. After breaking up with Rory a few years back, reaching for quick-fix distractions felt like the only way to make it through. One of these distractions was Liam, an old friend of my housemate. Liam was a highly sexed plumber from Portsmouth. I was aware from day one that we were in no way compatible, and over a period of five months or so, I began distancing myself from him.

On one particularly lonely weekend, though, I caved in and invited him over. Lying there in bed, I turned to him, curious. 'How many girls have you slept with since we last saw each other?'

The lesson to follow here: don't ask a direct question unless you're ready for a direct answer. He thought for a second.

'Five.'

'*Five?* Did you use protection?'

Without hesitation or a hint of remorse, he shook his head. 'No.'

I was *furious*.

'Get out of my room,' I said blankly.

He jumped off the bed, grabbed his stuff and left to find my housemate downstairs. I sat there stewing. How *dare* he put the Great Me at risk like that? I could have any disease under the sun right now! But, it quickly dawned on me that, in the same period of time, I hadn't behaved so much better myself. And besides, it hadn't even crossed my mind to ask him to use protection.

Following this, I was struck down with cystitis, a bladder infection that I've been plagued with repeatedly over the years – usually a consequence of alcohol and intercourse combined. Having gone away for a few days with my friend Kitty, she spent the majority of the trip sourcing cranberry juice and bringing me pints of water as I lay in agony on the sofa.

I remember turning to her solemnly towards the end of our trip, echoing, almost exactly, my mum's words about John Smith many years earlier.

'Kits, *never* let me see that boy again.'

Though it wasn't really the *plumber* who'd caused it, he was just a symptom of a much wider issue: the decisions I was making. Author Dr Christiane Northrup says that, 'If your soul needs to talk to you, it'll often come through your body'. Looking back, I can see that my soul was doing a lot of communicating; it just took time for me to pay attention.

On the acting course that Josh recommended prior to the creation of Addictive Daughter, the words of our movement teacher, Donna, left a real dent on my heart. Donna was a dancer and choreographer in her late-thirties from Los Angeles. She was magnificent: tanned, radiant, with a dazzling smile and a killer body. She was a mother of two, and it was clear she really had her shit together. More than any of that, she was also kind, grounded and had the ability to really speak from her heart. After one of her movement sessions, exhausted and depleted, we all sat on the floor around her.

'*Wow.*' She whispered. 'Wow, wow, wow,' she said, as she glanced around the room at our red faces, still perspiring from the intensity of her session.

'Each and every one of you has these *incredibly precious* bodies – look at them! The most amazing bodies that you've each been gifted. And they are so special, you know? Look after your bodies. Be careful who you show them to and who gets to enjoy them. Your body is sacred. Honour it and it will honour you.'

Being Brits, we sat gormlessly, feeling awkward in the face of such sincerity. Inside, however, something shifted for me: it was exactly what I needed to hear.

It amazes me, looking at myself and my friends, just how

abusive we can be to our bodies before any cracks begin to show on the outside. Having always had a speedy metabolism, my lifestyle choices had little impact on my weight – and if you can't see the damage, it's quite easy to persuade yourself it isn't there.

Today, I don't profess to be 'perfect'. I may not drink alcohol, but my compulsive behaviour can come out in other ways, often around food. I've been known to eat a full plate and go in for seconds, regardless of how hungry I actually feel. This isn't ideal and, while I'm aware of it, I also believe we address things as and when we're ready to. Right now, I'm OK with a little overindulgence once in a while. When I do find myself putting away a hefty portion of (generally very nutritious) food, I try to balance it out with exercise.

On reflection, I can look back and acknowledge that 95 per cent of the negative experiences in my life occurred as a result of being under the influence of alcohol. I've never been good at – or seen the point in – having just 'the one'. I've tried to limit myself enough times to know this.

For a long time, though, I questioned whether I actually had a dysfunctional relationship with alcohol because I was never a daily drinker. I've since learned that it isn't about how *often* you drink, but what *happens* when you do. For me, being black and white about substance use has proved easier than teetering around in the grey area, trying to control it.

In the early days of sobriety, the perks of waking up without the 'morning dread' or a hangover, and being told I looked well, kept me going. Further down the line, while I'm still grateful for these things, what's more profound is how my journey of sobriety has gone hand in hand with my journey of spirituality. Not having the option to escape or 'take the edge off' reality with a few drinks has been both a strengthening and spiritual experience. Feeling everything so fully has, without a doubt, drawn me closer into a relationship with my Higher Power. I've gained a huge amount through attending the Twelve Step meetings, which have taught me how to evolve my thinking and remain on good form, spiritually.

Over time, I'm learning more deeply how to treat my mind and body with gentleness and respect. I very rarely suffer with bad skin these days, and when I do it's always a clear sign that I'm not resting or looking after myself as well as I could be. I even ran the London marathon earlier this year, which (just ask my old PE teacher) is a miracle in itself.

Several months after my follow-up appointment, I receive another letter through my front door:

> **The results following your recent visit to the colposcopy clinic are below:**
>
> **Your cytology test result is**   **Normal**
>
> **The HPV virus test result is**   **All Clear**

You

'The mind has great influence over the body, and
maladies often have their origin there.'
Jean-Baptiste Molière

You may initially be surprised to discover that, in this chapter, we aren't going to tell you specifically what to eat, ways to exercise, or provide a precise set of instructions that will prevent self-sabotage and destructive pursuits. In reality, all of us know what we *ought* to be doing to look and feel our best – we're just not doing it. With a wealth of knowledge and resources at our fingertips, if self-will isn't working then perhaps it's time for a radically different approach.

The truth is, we spend a fortune on expensive clothes, when the majority of our wardrobes will only last us a few years at most. Yet, when it comes to our body, it's easy to forget that we get just the *one* to last us a lifetime. We would never dream of abusing our clothes in the way we so often abuse what lies beneath them.

Charities are doing fantastic work to fight against the diseases that threaten our health (cancer, strokes and heart disease being the three biggest killers). However, if you look on the websites of many of these charities, you learn that the major causes of these diseases are attributed to excessive lifestyle choices like smoking, alcohol, diet and obesity. We may look to the medical profession to treat the *symptoms* of disease, but how many of us are taking responsibility to tackle the *causes*? Are we proactively nurturing our health on a daily basis in order to reduce the manifestation of disease further down the line?

When the mind and body fall out of balance, in order to alert us that something is wrong it often manifests within us as sickness. It's as if our soul has had to resort to more extreme measures, since its previous cries for attention have fallen upon deaf ears.

Once we hear the call of our body, we have a choice: we can either continue to ignore it and do the minimum, treating our sickness as an inconvenience. Or we can respond to it as the cry for help that it is, showing it the love and respect it requires in order to heal.

As we begin to develop a spiritual connection, the gaping void within us that we previously stuffed with quick fixes starts to fill up with the substance of spirit instead. Or where, beforehand, we punished our bodies with obsessive exercise or disordered eating, we are now discovering a gentler way.

Taking a 'healthy lifestyle' to extremes – either by being overly militant or restrictive – can end up impacting us just as negatively as more obviously 'destructive' lifestyle pursuits. Though we may start out with the innocent intention of healthy eating, some of us find that this develops into a rigid set of rules dictating exactly *what* and *how much* we should be consuming. Any deviation from these rules can lead to us beating ourselves up and, longer term, to negative implications on our social lives, relationships and, somewhat ironically, our health. A good question to check in with our relationship to health and wellbeing, therefore, is: am I demonstrating a *loving* or *punishing* attitude towards myself right now?

Although this chapter seems action based, the work it entails requires us to remain spiritually fit in tandem with it. The punishing ways of our past may have provided a temporary fix, but now a spiritual connection is needed to readdress the balance and achieve a longer-term lifestyle change. If we're hoping to feel motivated and energised, the work here relies just as much on our *minds* as it does on the strength and stamina of our physical bodies.

In modern culture, the instant gratification of things like coffee, fast food and mind-altering substances – aside from not being great for our health – also train us towards a reliance on immediate solutions. The guidance in this chapter is the antithesis to a quick fix, and, when worked properly, stands to offer far more sustainable results.

In order to make changes from the inside-out, you need to first accept *exactly where you are* in this moment. That doesn't mean you have to stay here for long, but it's important to acknowledge your current situation and make peace with it, as a starting point.

There may be a fitness goal to reach or a negative vice to banish, but condemning your current flaws and failings doesn't help you to heal them. Instead, it tends to invite further self-sabotage along for the ride. This work requires a gentle approach and an awareness of the way in which you talk to yourself.

Before taking any outward action, begin gently asking the Higher Power you may be starting to build a relationship with for the *willingness* to make the lifestyle changes you desire: a prayer in the morning to ask for guidance to remove your temptation to smoke, closing your eyes to channel motivation as you put your trainers on for a run, or asking for strength when you feel yourself caving into a late-night rendezvous with someone you know really isn't all that into you.

During this section of the book, your sole focus needs to be on only what you *are* able to do, and carrying that out to the best of your ability, one day at a time. Some days, you'll struggle more than others, and on those days you are encouraged to go even more gently, giving yourself the support you need. If you slip up or make a mistake, that's OK too – forgive yourself and get back on track as soon as you're able to. There's no rush. Soon enough, by taking it one day at a time, a stretch of days will rack up behind you, and your small steps will have yielded noticeable results.

There are a million diet and nutrition resources already in existence, and our intention isn't to add to the pile. Our aim is to guide you to look inside and get clear about what living well means for *you*. Eating and exercise habits are simply another form of self-love. How you decide to treat and fuel your body impacts the way you feel, and that'll look slightly different for each one of us. A specific one-plan-fits-all approach rarely sticks, when we're all at different stages of our wellness journeys. Instead, it's useful to look to our *own* experience and ask:

when I'm feeling at my best, what does my eating and exercise regime tend to look like?

The more you practise loving and respecting your body through meditation, prioritising sleep and fuelling your body with nutritious food and exercise, the better you'll feel about it, and the faster it will reach its healthiest potential. Remembering to be gentle with yourself and to keep tuning into your inner guidance is key. When you turn your attention to developing new habits, instead of battling against old ones, the things that don't serve you will sooner or later fall away of their own accord. As you continue to practise these new behaviours, you learn to *listen* to your body, to what it does and does not respond positively to.

Making the decision to cut out either a food, substance or behaviour that's proving harmful to you is often a gradual process. You may initially opt for an easier, softer way by attempting to use the vice in question in moderation. Over time and through experience, however, there are those of us who come to realise that it may be necessary to abstain from certain things altogether. It's important to remember that, although the thoughts and feedback of others can be useful, no one can make this decision for you; it's up to you to be honest with yourself about what you might need to let go of.

Whether we're conscious of it or not, in intimately sharing our body with another person, a connection on a soul level takes place. Responses to the question of when to sleep with a romantic partner can vary anywhere from 'the minute I set eyes on them' to 'not until I'm wed'. There's no definitive time frame, and we're not going to try and define one – it's a very personal choice. However, the following questions may be helpful to consider as guidelines before doing so:

1. Do I feel respected by this person?
2. Am I of sound mind when I make this decision?
3. What is my expectation with this person further down the line?

In our often casual (and increasingly normalised) sexually promiscuous culture, the majority of us will have directly or indirectly experienced some of the more negative consequences of this already: the agonising emotional fallout after a break-up, gaining an unfavourable 'reputation', an STD or an unwanted pregnancy. We know what can happen when we treat our body with disrespect, and neglect the protection of our health and hearts. Like everything else in this book, it's about becoming mindful of what is right for *you*. In honestly assessing what feels constructive and what feels destructive to your wellbeing, you will develop your own personal boundaries around intimacy.

As well as considering what you may need to eliminate or moderate, it's also worth asking yourself what you'd like *more* of in your life. When considering what to increase, look to the things you get the most amount of pleasure from. Surrounding yourself with your preferences of the 'good stuff' will encourage you to keep coming back for more. What exercise feels most fun for you? Which nutritious foods do you most enjoy eating? How many hours' sleep do you need to function at your best?

So often, the irritable restlessness we feel that can trigger sabotaging behaviours can simply be dealt with by a good sleep. Rest is the last thing that occurs to us when our self-care routine goes out the window, but it's usually the one thing we need most to bring us back into balance. Sleep helps to heal our bodies and keeps our minds focused and strong.

EXERCISES

Identify Your Vices

In your journal, write down what external comforts you turn to in order to change the way you're feeling and why you think you rely on them. Make an honest note of the benefit you think each vice provides you with.

Examples might include:

- I tend to smoke cigarettes socially. It relieves any anxiety I feel and makes me feel more confident.

- I always make sure there's a love interest in my life. Having someone there makes me feel secure. Without it, I get lonely and life feels empty.

- I'm obsessive about calorie consumption and eating clean. It makes me feel more in control, particularly when other areas of my life get stressful.

Daily Gratitude for Your Physical Body

In the morning, perhaps, as you're sitting in front of the mirror getting ready, take a few moments to focus on the things that please you about your physical body. You can also recall compliments that other people may have given you in the past as well as quirky things about yourself that you might once have seen as negative, but are now growing to love. Look into the eyes of your reflection and say, out loud, 'thank you' for three positive attributes about your physical appearance. Try to make these different every day.

Your Body Goals

1) Consider any body-related areas that you'd like to make positive adjustments to. This could be a fitness or weight-loss related goal, the intention to give up a habit that doesn't serve you, or setting yourself a boundary around a behaviour that no longer feels empowering.

2) In your journal, write down the desires and intentions that come to mind, and a realistic time frame, if applicable.

Make Your Goals Enjoyable

1) In your journal, draw out two columns. List all the healthy foods and exercise activities that have worked for you in the past, as well as any new ones that you'd like to introduce into your routine. Avoid listing anything that feels like a chore or punishment to eat or do!

HEALTHY FOODS I MOST ENJOY EATING	MOST ENJOYABLE FORMS OF EXERCISE

2) Exercise doesn't tend to happen without prior scheduling. Open your diary and block out time for it on a weekly basis (it's up to you to decide the frequency). Be realistic – it's often best to start small and increase as you go. You may also find it beneficial to decide on a day to do the weekly food shop.

Write a Love Letter to Your Body

1) Note down all the ways that you've neglected your body in the past. Once you've detailed the ways in which you've abused it, take a moment to read over your words.

2) When you feel ready, continue to write, this time asking for your bodies forgiveness.

3) Then, write down all the reasons you're grateful for it – after all, it's done a lot for you.

4) Conclude the letter by noting down how you plan to love and nourish your body every day/week with little acts of love (that you actually *enjoy* – no punishing here!).

CHAPTER 12

WORK

Joey

'There's never been a map. Only a compass whose
dial always knows where it's pointing.'

A Waterside Year, Fennel Hudson

An aggressively capitalised eight-word email appears on the screen of my iPhone:

ARE YOU AN ACTRESS OR AREN'T YOU JOANNE?

It's a fair question. I'm seconds away from leaving for a violin exam with Daisy, the eight-year-old girl I'm currently looking after, and, typically, my acting agent has popped up with a last-minute TV drama audition. I haven't heard from her in over six weeks, but she needs me on the other side of London . . . *now*. I'd love to go, but there's no way I'm able to duck out of my nannying responsibilities at the eleventh hour.

My phone pings; another email from my agent:

> If this is another casting missed Joanne it is going to be a tragedy –
> can't you sort something out.

Thirty seconds later, a third:

> This is really becoming impossible Joanne you have missed more
> apts than I have had hot dinners. I cannot run a career and a
> business like this!

She is absolutely right. As an actress, I'm expected to drop everything at a moment's notice for an audition. However, I'm four years out of drama school now, and the prospect of cancelling important fixtures in my day to attend what usually turns out to be a casting for KFC has long lost its appeal.

I am currently working three days a week as a nanny for a family near my home in north London, and on the other days I get as much as I possibly can done for Addictive Daughter; which is becoming more and more of a full-time fixture in my living. What began just a couple of years ago as a brutally honest blog about our problems and discovering a more positive way of living, is beginning to gain momentum. Alongside our weekly output of 'Life Nugget' videos and blog posts, we're now undertaking life-coach training, as well as creating talks and workshops around our message.

While I'm managing to juggle Addictive Daughter and my nannying job with ease, things aren't flowing quite so well when my acting career gets thrown into the mix.

Persia mentioned a while ago now that she doesn't believe she's destined to become an actress anymore, and, while I respect that, I don't want to give up on my own dream just yet. After getting dropped by my first acting agent two years after graduation, I've worked hard to sign with a new one, and I'm aiming to keep my toe dipped in the acting pool if I can. But the truth is, the jobs my new agent has been able to get me seen for are wholly underwhelming.

On my wall, I had a piece of paper stuck beside my bed for years, affirming my top three choices for acting representation. A while ago, I took this down and filed it away, as looking at it was making me feel delusional. I've had a niggling feeling for some time that, if it's meant for me, acting will be something I'll step into more comfortably in the years ahead. Feeling conflicted over this, I've been putting it out to the universe, quietly praying that I be used – at this point in my twenties – in the way I can be of most service to the world.

Strangely enough, a clear pattern is beginning to emerge. While, pretty consistently, every acting door has been abruptly shut in my face, Addictive Daughter is completely in flow. Where I have fought, forced and lost opportunities in acting, they are coming freely, unexpectedly and in abundance with Addictive Daughter. Maybe this is my answer? I recently read a quote on social media that got my attention:

> God has three answers to our prayers:
> Yes
> Not yet
> I have something better in mind.

I like that. Persia and I have been encouraged by the amount of emails we've been receiving from girls in a similar place to where we were, thanking us for our honesty and relatable advice. This is helping me to trust in what we're doing and I'm hoping that things will become clearer in time. It's actually beginning to dawn on me how many of the skills acquired through my drama school training and part-time jobs over the years are coming in handy with the running of our venture. *All* my jobs have, in some way, added to my skill set and taught me the importance of feeling fulfilled on a day-to-day basis. I'm not sure that I'd feel as driven to pursue my vision for Addictive Daughter if I hadn't had a taste of what life looks like without a sense of purpose, along the way.

In my friendship group growing up, I was always the advice-giver (usually, whether it was asked for or not). This advice tended to be dispensed on a 'do as I say, not as I do' basis, my own life being far from the shining example at the time. A while ago now, a mentor of mine told me that whatever you find yourself whiling away hours talking about at a dinner party with good friends, whatever that thing is that you're endlessly fascinated by, *that* is where your soul's calling lies. For me, that would definitely be relationships and supporting people through challenges.

I am discovering that pursuing this vision for Addictive Daughter requires me to be in top mental, physical and, most importantly, *spiritual* condition. Experience is showing me that if I maintain my spiritual fitness, I feel balanced, and the other two come along for the ride anyway. When I'm spiritually fit, I want to exercise, eat well and take care of my body. When I'm spiritually fit, I'm mentally calm, I'm kinder and my life feels more manageable.

This is a far cry from my darker days as a jobbing actress, when I'd reach for a glass of wine before an audition to take the edge off my nerves. When I did land an acting role, I developed a tendency to drink my body weight in cocktails at the wrap party, mainly out of a social anxiety and a melancholic fear that I'd never work again.

I attended a church service with Persia recently, and the sermon was about using your gifts to serve the world. A woman there prayed over me, and whispered, 'Mother heart.'

Mother heart.

Those words resonated with me profoundly. At my core, I am a nurturer and comforter. I've spent much of my life trying to fix those around me, but mainly those who haven't *actually* asked for my help. Ironically, I've come to realise that I can be of no real service to anyone else unless I focus first on sorting myself out, and continue making that a priority. Just as the tarot card reader described the image of a fairy with a broken wand, in fixing my wand I'm in a much stronger position to support others in doing the same.

Months after the audition clash drama with my acting agent, I come across a heap of rejection letters from the many acting agents I'd written to back in the day. I pick up the top letter on the pile: it's from United Agents – one of my 'top three' I'd had firmly pinned to my bedroom wall. As with all the others, the answer had been a 'no'.

My heart does a little flip, as I suddenly realise that I've got *exactly* what I wanted, but in a form I'd never expected. Persia and I recently signed a contract with a literary agent . . . at United Agents. After spending years chasing after them as an actress, they ended up approaching us about representing the literary side of Addictive Daughter.

I'm learning that, sometimes, it isn't that God says 'no'. It's simply a 'not yet', or that there really is something better waiting for you.

Persia

'If God gives you something you can do, why
in God's name wouldn't you do it?'
Stephen King

After an Al-Anon meeting in early 2014, my new sponsee, Sasha, invites me over to her place around the corner for a cup of tea and a catch-up. Sasha is like me in every way; same chaotic upbringing, same self-sabotaging patterns and, now that she's in Al-Anon, the same deep desire to heal and move forwards in her life.

Girls like Sasha have appeared in my life consistently since starting Addictive Daughter a year and a half ago; they're like homing pigeons. They keep me remembering why I'm doing this, why I've *got* to do this. In helping them heal, I continue to heal myself. In watching their painful journeys unfold, I'm reminded how important it is I do all that I can to stay on track – for my sake, as much as theirs.

Walking into Sasha's kitchen, I see a cobalt-blue guitar leaning up against a wall and am magnetically pulled towards it.

'No way,' I whisper.

'What's up?' Sasha responds, looking over her shoulder as she makes us tea.

'My butterflies,' I reply, gesturing towards the guitar, where three butterfly stickers are stuck to the outer edge, pointing in the direction of the strings.

Gabrielle Bernstein, an American self-help guru, talks a lot about the idea of 'signs' as a form of divine guidance whenever you need support or clarity over a particular issue.

For quite a while now, I've had a weird obsession with dinosaurs and butterflies – dinosaurs, because *Jurassic Park* is my
favourite film of all time, and butterflies because of that email
Tiger wrote when we broke up about me being like a butterfly,
and him being my chrysalis (I've always loved a good metaphor). Joey has the same thing with birdcages – she's loved
them since she was a little girl.

Dinosaurs, butterflies and birdcages have shown up everywhere for Joey and I since starting AD – on stages we've spoken
on, on cards or in books that friends have bought us, on street
art we walk past, and in so many other unexpected ways.

Although most people I try and explain the whole 'sign'
philosophy to think it's absolute rubbish – that you only see
your 'sign' because you're looking out for it, I think that's kind
of the whole point: you're paying attention; aware trumps
unaware, in my opinion. I'd rather look out for evidence that
I'm being supported, than for evidence that I'm not.

Signs have also helped me to make some little, and not so
little, decisions over recent months. The first time I met with
Sasha to discuss being her sponsor, she turned up on her
two-year-old son's scooter which had a dinosaur head as the
handlebar. When we went back to her flat, there were two dinosaur teddies on the table and her son was wearing a dinosaur
jumper. Not only that, but when she opened the Kinder egg
she'd just bought him, the toy inside was a DIY dinosaur. That's
one hell of a lot of dinosaurs in the space of an hour, and I took
that as a little nudge from the universe that sponsoring Sasha
would be a good idea.

So, seeing these butterflies on her guitar like this makes me
sit up and pay attention – especially since I asked for some
really clear guidance around buying a new guitar this very
morning.

I used to play a lot – back when I was with Tiger. I wasn't great, but I was good enough to write my own songs and play the odd gig. If I'm honest, though, the reason I was so committed to my practice was because Tiger told me he'd fallen in love with me when he saw me play and sing. Also, because he couldn't play, anything I came out with was impressive (even if it was just D-G-C chords on repeat).

However, since I've been with Sam my guitar playing and songwriting have gone out of the window. Sam once played guitar for a famous singer, and is a thousand times better than I'll ever be.

Although I've never been one to favour hiding in someone else's creative shadow, when Sam recently asked me to sing backing vocals for him at a little church in west London I happily agreed. Singing has always been relatively easy for me – playing the guitar and writing songs, however, not so much; they require far more discipline and self-confidence.

My old guitar's been sitting in its case next to my radiator for nearly a year and a half now. As a result, it's become damaged and useless, and the longer I've refrained from practising, the more afraid I've become of creating songs in the free and effortless way I'd done when I was with Tiger.

I've always been a chronic perfectionist; a lot of creative people are, I think. Perfectionism does have its upsides though: it got me high grades and higher standards when it came to my acting and other artistic pursuits. It also gave me vision and laser-focused drive, and I have my parents to thank for that. After they both got sober, they channelled all the addictive energy they'd once used so destructively into creating houses so beautiful that they're almost like works of art in themselves.

Yet, as my parents know more than anyone else, perfectionism comes at a price – that price being, nothing you do or create ever feels good enough. This is never a nice feeling, especially when you've poured your heart and soul into a creation.

Tiger once told me that, if you hear the same 'thing' mentioned three times or more – whether it's a book, a travel spot or a person – you should take that as a sign from the universe that you're meant to pursue or investigate that thing.

Following his advice, I recently found myself reading the book *The Artist's Way* by Julia Cameron. A twelve-week spiritual programme of sorts for creatives, *The Artist's Way* encourages you to recover from all manner of artistic blocks – including fear, self-sabotage and limiting beliefs.

I've heard about this book far more than just three times, but I wasn't quite ready to face my creative demons until a few weeks ago, when I picked my mother's copy off of the book-shelf in our study.

Throughout the book, the reader is encouraged to tackle their issues around a vast range of typical artistic dilemmas, including our response to criticism, our relationship with our own self-worth and our blocks around earning money from our art.

As soon as I started reading the chapter on perfectionism, my mind was immediately taken back to the songwriting that I'd abandoned when Sam and I got together. I realised that I hadn't stopped writing and playing because I didn't want to, but because I didn't feel good enough; if I wasn't going to be *the best* and make a proper success out of my creative pursuits, then there was no point in trying at all.

Sasha observes my strange fixation with the butterfly stickers on her guitar.

'You know I've got a butterfly tattoo, don't you Pers,' she says, turning around and lifting up her top to reveal a beautiful pattern swirling from the nape of her neck to the middle of her back, with two butterflies flying upwards.

She grabs the butterfly-adorned guitar, and begins playing me one of her new songs. It's like looking in a mirror: we have a very similar vocal tone and songwriting style.

Watching her play, a thought drops in: *I don't need to be good, I just need to be willing.* I don't need to be concerned with the outcome of starting to write songs again – of where it will or won't lead, or if I'll ever make any kind of living from singing. I just need to start, to write for myself – simply because I love doing it.

'Don't die with your music still inside you,' said the late Dr Wayne Dyer. 'Listen to your intuitive inner voice and find what passion stirs your soul.'

Creation for creation's sake, only.

I go home, and order the best acoustic guitar I can afford online. When it arrives, I write my first song in over two years:

The Little Door

Nothing can be changed until it's faced,
No one can be set free without grace,
The ice around this heart will melt away in time.

Your love unlocked a door, I came undone,
Consumed by shame I turned to other ones,
But nothing satisfies a void that's shaped for more than earthly lies.

I let go of all this broken heart has clung to,
Bind the pieces, lift the stone,
I cannot carry this alone,
With you, I don't have to.

Through darkness diamonds spread their richest light,
Resolved I'll walk by faith, not by sight,
And if it brings me to my knees
Now I know that's right where I should be.

You're there in every mess that I make,
You're there in every bend, every break,
And though my heart was cracked in two,
I know the wound is where your light got through.

You

'Make your work to be in keeping with your purpose.'
Leonardo da Vinci

Work is not only a means of economic survival, but one of the most powerful ways we experience spiritual growth and fulfilment. When we're engaged in work we love, we feel inspired, excited and enjoy a sense of flow. Life becomes instantly more compelling, and hours slide by at work without us even realising it. By consistently practising our skills, talents and passions (whether in a job or career in a traditional sense, through volunteering, or by applying ourselves wholeheartedly to our hobbies or studies), we feel more than just joyful, we feel useful.

In the world of self-help, this idea of finding your 'calling' (work that you're 'destined' to do) is a popular one. However, while this concept can be a powerful motivator for many people, it can leave others feeling anxious and confused: *What if I never find my calling? What if I find my calling, but I can't make it work for me financially?* In fact, we can often become so overwhelmed with the pursuit and attainment of this elusive idea of finding our calling, that we become even more stressed out and miserable than we were before we started searching for it.

Therefore, we've found it helpful to lessen the pressure by thinking of your calling as simply work that you're good at, that you enjoy doing and that serves the world in some way. If the work (or hobby) you're doing now fulfils even *one* of these three aspects (and it's very likely that it does), then you're already actively participating in your calling.

The key thing to remember is that true fulfilment and satisfaction in work goes hand in hand with a service-orientated mentality. When you approach your work from the standpoint of what you can *give* rather than what you can *get*, you undergo a mental shift that completely transforms your personal experience of work.

In a culture that has become increasingly preoccupied with the gratification and success of the individual alone, this is a somewhat radical perspective. But, as we've learned from our own experience, a service mentality does not prohibit the joy, wealth and success we gain from our job, it enhances it.

There are as many ways to serve the world as there are people in it. It doesn't matter whether you're a jewellery designer, artist, accountant, grave digger, teacher, doctor, librarian, marriage counsellor or beautician, what sets the service-driven person apart is a matter of attitude and intention. If you're making coffee for a living, then you can transform someone's day simply by serving it with a smile. If you work as a personal assistant, you have the opportunity to make someone else's workload so much more manageable and pleasurable by being a calming presence and having excellent attention to detail. Even if you don't love the work you're currently doing and it's just a way of making ends meet, you can still choose to approach it positively, because, if nothing else, it'll make for a more pleasant experience for you.

Many of us often believe our gifts can only be used and directed effectively to one very specific end: we must be an actor, a banker, a painter, a doctor or a fashion designer, and if we don't 'make it' as that thing, then we feel like a failure. However, if you stop for a moment to think outside of the box – to consider what the raw essence and intention of your gift or vocation is, a whole other range of opportunities suddenly become available to you.

A friend of ours had always wanted to perform on stage in order to inspire, move and entertain people. Tired of waiting around for his agent to call, he took initiative and set up his own theatre company, delivering educational productions to schools and universities that help young people learn about different topics in a unique and interesting way. This took a lot of hard work, but eventually it really paid off. Today, not only is his company thriving financially, he's able to inspire, move and entertain people just as he always wanted to do – but on his own terms, and in ways he'd never imagined back at drama school.

Let's be real for a moment: *most* industries are incredibly saturated; there are too few jobs in proportion to people who want them. As a result, there are a lot of talented people out there who are extremely frustrated, because they aren't getting to do the work they really love.

One solution to this dilemma is to follow in our friend's footsteps and work out how to successfully generate a living by using your unique gifts and skills, and to combine that with a genuine desire to help or serve other people in a way that's meaningful to you. This could mean using your talents in a slightly different way than you might have set out to do. But, as our friend learned, it's very possible that you'll end up enjoying this alternative career path even more than the original.

When you start to actively 'connect the dots' of your life – as we'll guide you to do in the exercises at the end of this chapter – you'll probably find yourself quite surprised by how all the different aspects of your experiences fit together to illuminate a whole host of value that you've been sitting on without even realising it. This includes what you learned from all those jobs you may have hated doing at the time.

Remember, your calling is not 'out there somewhere' – you're already doing it, you maybe don't realise this because *you might not be doing all of it at the same time* just yet. However, as you start to become more aware and focused, chances are you'll find yourself attracting a wide variety of opportunities, coincidences and synchronicities related to your desired vocation. These may come in all manner of forms: an unexpected call from an old colleague telling you about a new position opening up at their work that would be perfect for you. An article in the paper looking for volunteers to go and help a charitable foundation – something you've always wanted to do, but never taken the time to properly research. Sitting next to someone on a flight or a park bench who happens to work in the industry you want to cross over to – the possibilities are endless.

The exercises below will not only help you to become more grateful for all aspects of your current work situation, they'll also help you get really clear on your unique skills, talents and passions, too.

EXERCISES

Gratitude for Your Current Work Situation

In your journal, write a list of all the positive aspects of your current work situation. Even if you really don't enjoy your job, there will always be elements of it that are beneficial or that have taught you something of value. For example: does it pay well? Have you made good friends at work? Has it taught you a useful skill? Is it flexible? The more grateful you are for where you are, the faster you'll get to where you want to go.

Connect the Dots

1) In your journal, write a list of all the hobbies, studies or other pursuits throughout your life that you most enjoyed or excelled in. Why did you enjoy these particular activities so much?

2) Then, note down the main skills you've acquired from the above. For example, proficient writer, computer literate or good at organisation. Also include skills that are more personal and that other people have praised you for in the past – such as good listener, eloquent speaker, detail orientated, etc.

3) Now, list all the major life experiences that you've had in the past that have had the most profound effect on you. This could be anything from your parents' divorce when you were ten, to living abroad, to having your heart broken.

4) Finally, spend some time trying to connect the dots between these experiences. Can you see any common themes? What stands out to you?

Celebrate Your Jealousy

Feeling jealous of someone else's career and success often reveals a lot about what it is we want for ourselves. Therefore, instead of feeling bad about being jealous, we can instead use this as fuel for motivation.

In your journal:

1) Write a list of the people who most trigger a jealous response from you concerning work.

2) Now, look for the patterns. What job do these people do? What qualities do they have? What is their lifestyle like?

Discovering Your Calling

With the following questions, write the first thing that pops into your head. Write quickly and without editing – 'free-writing' like this will help you connect to your most authentic answers.

1) What things make you smile (events, people, projects, hobbies, etc.)?

2) What activities make you lose track of time?

3) Who inspires you most (people you know or don't know)? Which qualities inspire you in each?

4) What do people usually ask you for help in?

5) If you had to teach something, what would it be?

6) What would you regret not fully having, doing or being in your life?

7) What are your most important values (loyalty, fun, innovation, etc.)?

8) How could you use the above values, talents and passions to help or serve (people, causes, the planet, etc.)?

CHAPTER 13

MONEY

Persia

'There can be no freedom or beauty
about a home life that depends
on borrowing and debt.'

A Doll's House, Henrik Ibsen

It's April 2014, and I'm sat in my bedroom at my parents' house, unpacking the two large suitcases of clothes that have been at Sam's flat for the last year and a half.
Last night, we broke up.

Over dinner, he finally admitted what I've been so afraid of hearing for the last six months:

We want different things.

Having worked so hard on my behaviour and commitment issues in romantic relationships, I now know that I one day want to get married and have kids. Sam, it turns out, does not – at least, not with me.

Five years my senior, he married in his early twenties and, sadly, it didn't work out. A staunchly independent lover of freedom, he realised it wasn't fair to stay in a relationship he knew was never going to progress.

Although I'm obviously devastated, I know I'm going to be OK. I trust that this is the right thing, that there's someone out there who *will* want the same things I do – we're maybe just not quite ready for each other yet. I think I've got a little more growing to do (and a few more stories to tell) before I meet my 'one'.

What this break-up has done, though, is cast some light on my living situation. I'm twenty-eight now, and feeling a little embarrassed that I'm *still* living with my parents – especially as I spent the early part of my twenties travelling and living on my own.

Staying at my parents' was supposed to be a three-month stopgap and money saver between living with Joey in north London, and moving to LA. But then I fell in love with Tiger and put the whole visa-acquiring process on hold for a year while I lived like a nomad between home and the warehouse.

Since I started going out with Sam at the end of 2012, I've been spending half my weeks at his west London flat. I didn't see the point in wasting money on rent unnecessarily, when I was putting so much time, money and energy into getting Addictive Daughter off the ground with Joey.

The thing is, people who don't know the details of my life think I have money, because I've always been very good at making it seem like I do. 'Champagne tastes, lemonade pockets,' a friend used to say.

When I was about nine and my parents were in the height of their drug addiction, I remember lying to Salena about having my own horse – Clementine – up in Scotland. I was incredibly jealous that Salena could have her pick of horses, seeing as her parents owned the stables. I knew that my family would never be able to afford a horse, so I made up a fictional one as a way of feeling better about myself. I think Salena always knew I was lying, but she never called me out on it. In fact, her parents were so good to me that they gave me Salena's old pony, Sprocket, on loan at a reduced rate. Seeing how happy horses made me, my dad gladly accepted Uncle Joe's gesture, despite the fact that it was still another costly outgoing my family really didn't need at the time.

Much like his drinking and drug-taking, my father's generosity was progressive – especially after he got sober and felt the full impact of what his and Mum's addiction had cost our family. Although I did various temp jobs for a bit of pocket money throughout my late teens and early twenties, Dad took care of all of the big stuff, and so I remained fully dependent on him for my survival. I never equated working hard with earning my own money, but simply with achieving something that looked good on paper – straight As at school, a degree and travelling the world acting (on a minimal wage).

I was never a big spender, but when it came to making money I very much stayed within my personal comfort zone. My bank balance always hovered around the same amount, give or take a few hundred pounds.

I was caught in a vicious cycle of overachieving and under-earning, because subconsciously that's what I thought would win me love in the eyes of a man. As I saw it, their job was to look after me financially, and my job was to be as fabulous as my mother so that they'd do so willingly. Not the most feminist perspective, I know.

Although my mum had started her own small massage therapy business after rehab, she still relied on my dad to keep her in the comfortable lifestyle she'd become accustomed to as his property development work had grown more lucrative over the years.

Like any couple, my parents both have their roles to play in the running of the household: Dad takes care of the bills and business negotiations, and Mum tirelessly manages and juggles all other aspects of family life.

However, while Dad has always said that he'd never have been able to achieve his level of success without her support and incredible eye for interior design, Mum's often noted that she feels guilty and undeserving when spending any of the profit from their property business, even though she played a pivotal role in creating it.

It's no wonder that I soon attracted a relationship that mirrored that of my parents' – in a financial sense, anyway. Despite the fact I'd always gone out with struggling artistic types (who I often ended up paying for on dates with my limited funds), by the time I met Sam I'd done enough work on my self-worth to feel deserving of being treated to the odd slap-up dinner. What I wasn't expecting was to be treated quite so often. On the one hand, this felt great, but on the other, it brought back all those shameful feelings around not being able to pay my own way.

Having been on the receiving end of many of my fear-filled money rants, about six months ago Joey bought me a book called *Money: A Love Story* by an American author called Kate Northrup. It dealt specifically with women and their relationship with their finances, and now I finally felt ready to look at my own.

I made the decision to fully commit to the exercises and tools it set out, in the same way I'd worked on my relationships, and the results were beyond anything I could've imagined. Within four months I was out of the overdraft I'd been stuck in for over a decade. Six months on, I'd doubled my monthly earnings – even managing to save some money too.

Most importantly, however, my entire relationship with money has changed. I once read somewhere that people only ever want money for one of three reasons: power, status or freedom. I've never been that bothered about being able to afford designer clothes or an expensive car. Instead, I've always spent my money on having great *experiences* – whether that's in the form of a holiday, a nice meal or going to the theatre.

What I realised I most want to feel around my finances is *free*: free to be generous with the money I earn. In the past, I always felt so tight and in fear around giving to friends and family because I was worried I wasn't going to have enough left over to take care of myself. But what I've learnt is that the more you give away, the more you tend to receive – not just materialistically speaking, but through the joy-filled experiences you get to share with the people you love.

Taking heed of the idea that being generous is a process that becomes habitual the more it's practised, I created a 'giving' account. Now, every time I'm paid, I put 10 per cent of my earnings into this account, and use this to treat my friends and family to the occasional dinner or coffee, as well as making small contributions to my church and various charities. The amount may be modest, but if I don't give now when I have a little, I won't be comfortable giving when I have more further down the line.

Considering the huge progress I've made in the past few months around my money 'stuff', perhaps I need to start being a little more grateful and humble with regard to my living situation. Many people in this world would kill to have a roof over their head like I do. Being at home has not only enabled me to experience the childhood I never had growing up, it's also allowed me to follow my passions with Addictive Daughter, and I can't put a price on how happy that's made me.

I don't need to have my entire future figured out today. Like with everything else in the last few years, I trust that my living situation will be taken care of when the time is right.

Joey

'How wrong is it for a woman to expect the man to build
the world she wants, rather than to create it herself?'
Anaïs Nin

'You know, you wouldn't have to work *and* raise a family,' he
said, lying on his side, hand propping up the side of his face.

'Meaning?' I inquired.

'Well, if you wanted to stay at home and have that side of
things covered in the first few years of starting a family, I'm in
a position to support the both of us – for a while, at least.'

It's a Wednesday morning in late April 2014 and I'm lying in
a lavish Soho hotel room with the man I'm going to marry –
after he got down on one knee in an empty, candlelit church
and popped the question yesterday afternoon. If I'd been told
this was going to happen – even just a year ago – I'd never have
believed it.

I've had some notable realisations about my relationship
with money of late. Although I can clearly recall the moment,
in the months following drama school graduation, that my
bank balance read £78.24 – the lowest it had ever been – the
truth is, I've never been in the red. Since moving to London at
the age of eighteen, I've been fortunate enough to be able to
borrow money from my parents on the occasions I've needed
to, and I've always known, if things got *really* bad, that I could
move back home, up north again. I am incredibly fortunate –
of that I'm well aware. Additionally, having deliberately opted
out of any kind of overdraft option on my bank account, I've
never given myself the flexibility to drop below the line.

By nature, I'm a grafter. I spent years doing minimum-wage work and juggling five or six different part-time jobs at a time. They were character-forming experiences and I look back proudly on them; I was no princess when it came to earning my keep.

During my divine storm of 2010, Persia forwarded me an email about a 'hostess' job where the requirement was simply to look pretty and flirt with successful entrepreneurs for an evening – all for the attractive fee of £120. Together, we turned up at a central London hotel where we were to don the little black dresses handed to us, before being plied with free booze. While we sat with around fifty other hostesses in a side room waiting to be briefed, a girl leaned over to us and whispered, 'Apparently they used to use *actual* hookers for this job'.

Now, this male-only event was for the richest and most significant businessmen from a variety of industries. Among them were many celebrities, all of them dressed in dinner suits and sitting on large tables in a ridiculously ornate ballroom.

After we finished 'working' at midnight, we were free to leave or continue to socialise as we wished to. Persia and I, along with a few other girls, had been invited out with several of the men to a private members' club in Mayfair. One thing led to another, and soon enough we found ourselves at a drug-fuelled after-party in a swanky hotel suite nearby. I have little memory of the night apart from losing Persia fairly early on – it turns out she left for a hotel on the opposite side of the city with a man who later confessed to being married with two children.

After returning to the after-party hotel and blagging her way past reception in the late hours of the next morning, Persia found me out for the count surrounded by several (thankfully fully dressed) snoring strangers. She woke me up and we got out of there pretty sharpish, uncertain of how the night had got so out of hand.

Three years on from that evening, after some deliberation, I decided to do it again – the event, that is. This time round, I was nine months sober and Addictive Daughter was half a year young, with a very modest following. My decision to work was purely down to earning an easy £120, as I was spending more and more time working on our passion project but not earning a penny from it.

I felt OK about working the event, I simply had to be affable towards the London male elite and then I could duck out at midnight – easy work for an actress. In reality, though, the experience of being there was uncomfortable, and stone-cold sober there was no denying the seediness of it all. The table to which I was assigned belonged to one of the leading media companies in the UK, and I got chatting with Roy who, as it turned out, held a very senior position there. He didn't attempt, like several of his colleagues, to slip a sneaky hand around my waist. In fact, he seemed genuinely interested in holding a conversation with me. Just as I was thinking how different Roy was to the others, he pipped me to the post: 'You aren't like the others here, Joanne, you've got your head screwed on. What is it you do?'

I joked that if he'd met me at this very event a few years earlier, he might not be saying that. I briefly described the journey that had led to the very recent birth of the lifestyle movement Addictive Daughter that I'd set up with a friend.

Before I headed off at midnight, Roy pushed his business card into my hand. 'If you ever need any help, give me a shout.'

Six months later, I decided to take Roy up on his offer and dug out his details. Fast forward a few weeks, and that chance encounter with him resulted in Addictive Daughter being offered a regular online magazine column, a feature in one of the UK's top gossip magazines and, on top of that, a TV appearance.

Several years apart, despite it being the very same event, the two evenings had dramatically different outcomes. Often, it's our intention within a situation (and not the situation itself) that matters most. The universe has a habit of bringing gifts in disguise in all manner of scenarios – we just need to remain open to receiving them.

One particular gift on offer (in the form of a lesson I needed to learn) was the reoccurring pattern in my life between money and romantic partners. From the very first date with someone new, I was in the habit of insisting I pick up my half of the bill, since I've always felt an illogical pressure that I owed the other person something (sexually) if they paid for me.

This went down quite well with many of the guys I chose to date, as the majority of them were financially unstable. I suppose in being attracted to destructive and unmanageable types that was hardly surprising.

Financially speaking, being the more 'sorted' one in a relationship gave me some sense of security and even superiority. On a subliminal level, perhaps I hoped it might persuade the guy in question to stick around. I told myself I didn't mind almost continually dating broke men – after all, it motivated me to work hard and remain independent. I'd rather it be that way round than the reverse: of relying on someone else entirely.

I've grown up witnessing my mum's strong work ethic, often earning more than my dad in recent years when her consultancy business really took off. In turn, she'd been driven to be financially independent after witnessing how reliant her own mum was on the weekly housekeeping allowance that my granddad would hand to her. Historically speaking, women really haven't had their own money for very long at all. In fact, we're pretty much still in the teething stages of evolution in this respect.

However, the *desire,* at least, to be self-sufficient has been passed down from Mum to me, and this is something I'm thankful for.

I look across at my fiancé, lying beside me on the hotel bed. Before starting this relationship, I'd sat down with a pen and paper and written out a list of the qualities that felt most important for a future partner. One of the top points on my list read:

Generous (in all respects), financially stable, wealth a bonus.

In spite of this, I've not been actively seeking a man who is able to take care of me, and yet, quite unexpectedly, here he is.

Yet, a patriarchal, more traditional set-up doesn't sit well at all. If someone's controlling your money, they're effectively controlling your freedom – and for me, a lack of freedom isn't an attractive proposition. As I've learned to value myself more, self-sufficiency has become increasingly important to me. I need to know that, regardless of what goes right or wrong in my romantic life, I can take care of myself.

You

'People are always blaming their circumstances for what they are.
I don't believe in circumstances. The people who get on in this
world are the people who get up and look for the circumstances
they want, and if they can't find them, make them.'
Mrs. Warren's Profession, George Bernard Shaw

The majority of us have issues around money, and yet it's possibly one of the most taboo and under-discussed subjects in our society today. However, whether we like it or not, money is an unavoidable part of our world. Like air and like water, we cannot survive without it. Although most of us don't associate it with spirituality or self-love, a lack of financial independence can make us feel worse about ourselves than any other area of our lives.

When it comes to our personal finances, we have only two choices: we can keep burying our head in the sand, because the idea of confronting our money issues is just too over-whelming. Or, we can choose to be brave and commit to healing our complex relationship with money, in the same way that we've been working on every other aspect of our lives in this book – through a gentle, loving approach, and with a lot of self-compassion.

Many of us use money in the same way we use drink, drugs, sex or eating – to temporarily change the way we feel. It doesn't matter if we earn a lot or a little, the behaviour's the same. Although many of us struggling to make ends meet tell ourselves that 'everything would be all right if only we had X amount in the bank', this isn't entirely true. You just need to look to those people who inherit fortunes and then fritter it all away in next to no time, to see that simply earning more money is not the answer, because if our relationship with money is an unhealthy one, we won't be able to keep it (and even if we do, we might be surprised to find that it doesn't actually make us as happy as we thought it might).

For example: if you're used to being broke, and are given a few hundred pounds for a big birthday or as some inheritance, what's the first thing you might do? You could find yourself spending that money as fast as you received it, because subcon-sciously you're more comfortable with not having money than you are with having it.

As with every other area of our lives, our beliefs around money are shaped by the manner in which it was presented to us in our childhood. The way that our family behaved around money – particularly our parents – will have shaped our relationship with it far more than we may realise. If we grew up hearing that 'money doesn't grow on trees' or that 'there's never enough money' or 'we can't afford that', then we'll have no doubt developed a lack mentality; no matter how much we make, it will still feel like we're coming up short. On the other hand, if we were given everything as a child but never taught the real value of those things, we might have a poor understanding of the cost of living. Rather than setting about getting ourselves educated in this area, our fear leads us to sidestep our financial concerns altogether. The worse things get, the more afraid we become, and so denial and ignorance often seem like the preferable way to approach our situation.

Our attitudes to money are also hugely influenced by the messages we're fed by society. A dominant thought system in our culture is that earning lots of money is 'bad' and people who do so are 'dishonest', 'greedy' or 'lazy'. When we internalise this sort of thinking, our subconscious will ensure that we stay poor or 'comfortable', so that we can remain 'good' and 'honest'. Even if we tell ourselves we want more money, our subconscious will do everything in its power to make sure we never get it (or if we do, we don't keep it), because, why would we want to have something that people will judge and condemn us for?

Women in particular are also subtly coerced into believing that earning more money might damage their relationships with men. We're told all too often that men are intimidated by strong, successful women, which might make increasing our finances that bit less appealing. So instead, we may rely on a 'prince' to come and rescue us and take care of all our money problems, leaving us feeling totally powerless and fearful around our finances.

Considering that for the majority of history men have been in charge of the finances of the women in their life, hoping that a Prince Charming will come and fix our money problems is not all that unusual. After all, having financial independence is a relatively new concept and practice for women. Although we may appear to have access to a similar lifestyle to men, various studies have shown that women are much less likely to expect or request a promotion or a pay rise, whereas men tend to feel far more comfortable and confident doing so. Over time we're sure this will change, but in the meantime we'd benefit from being more compassionate towards our money struggles.

There's also a widespread social belief that you can either make money doing something you don't enjoy or be broke doing what you love. In actuality, there are many, many people in the world who get to have the best of both worlds, but once again we tend not to focus on them. If we *do* happen to, they often leave us feeling somewhat suspicious because they don't fit into our belief system, as well as jealous that they're achieving what we don't believe is possible for ourselves.

The first step in healing our relationship with our finances is to understand that, in reality, money is neither good nor bad – and neither are the people who make it; it's the *meaning* that we attach to money and money-makers that shapes our relationship to it.

What we've come to learn over the past few years is that, in many ways, what money really represents is our level of self-worth. We don't mean that people with more feel better about themselves and people with less feel worse (in fact, the opposite can often be true). What we mean is that the extent to which we pay attention to and nurture our financial lives is directly proportional to how much we value ourselves.

In the same way that our diet and exercise habits reflect our level of self-care, so too do our earning and spending habits. By

choosing to ignore our finances, we're unconsciously reinforcing the belief that we're not all that valuable. After all, closing
our eyes to an area of our life that troubles us does not make
the problem go away, it causes it to grow worse. Not only that,
but our biggest fears around money usually stem from the fact
that, because we're too scared to look at our finances, we have
no idea what's actually going on with them.

If you've made it to this point in the book, we'd hazard a
guess that valuing yourself is important to you, and you've
hopefully gone some way in committing to some of the daily
self-care habits we've already suggested. Please trust us when we
say that working on your finances is not only an essential
element of becoming the happiest version of you, it's also one
of the most transformative and powerful.

The most important element we want you to take away from this
chapter is that money is *not* unspiritual – far from it. Money is a key
component of our happiness and wellbeing, and we all deserve to
feel good about our finances. If we are to believe that there is a
divine force operating in our lives – whether we call 'It' God/the
universe/our Higher Power – then surely that force wants what's
best for us: to feel abundant, free and generous, not to struggle
and stay broke – that doesn't serve ourselves, or the world.

The healthier our relationship with money becomes, the
more we're able to show up and be fully present in other areas
of our lives, too. When we slowly and gently take little action
steps and develop habits that nurture our finances, we feel
good about ourselves, because we're making progress. We find
we have more space and energy to give to our loved ones, and
more freedom to pursue the work we feel called to do.

As we begin to see our efforts pay off – whether that's successfully getting out of debt, growing confident enough to ask for a
pay rise, or witnessing our savings account increase every

month, we're far more likely to want to share what we have with those that need it – even if this is a very small amount.

Our intention with the following exercises is to help you get clear and honest with yourself about where you currently are in your financial life, and then lovingly guide you to take the practical steps necessary to work towards your financial goals.

EXERCISES

Money History

Work through the following questions in your journal.

1) What was your parents' attitude to money? What sort of things did you hear them say about it?

2) Describe your lifestyle growing up: did you have anything you wanted, or did you always feel short-changed?

3) What are your positive and negative experiences of earning money in the past? How did you feel about the work you were doing and the money you were earning?

4) What's been your reoccurring negative pattern and frustration around money? (For example, are you always maxing out your credit card, getting hit by fines after going overdrawn, or do you find people expect you to pick-up the bill, aware that you're financially better-off than them?)

5) What does more money most represent to you: more power, more status or more freedom? To help you answer this, note down exactly how you would spend £10,000 if you were given it right now. For example, luxury items might suggest status or power is important to you, and travelling or paying off debts could mean freedom is what you value most.

Prayer

Read the following prayer out loud before your next meditation:

Please help me to be grateful for all the abundance I have – both in my finances and every other aspect of my life. Please help me to release my fears around money. Help me to forgive my financial history, and let go of any resentment I have towards myself or anyone else around money – including my parents. Help me to welcome a new, loving experience of money.

Abundance Affirmations

We're always affirming things to ourselves, but most of the time they're negative and unconscious. The thoughts we hold about our financial situation affect how we feel about it, and that in turn influences the actions we go on to take. By choosing positive and empowering thoughts, we slowly begin to rewire our brain to produce more 'feel-good' hormones, which over time transform our long-held habitual thinking patterns into something more productive and beneficial to us.

Like with physical exercise, consistency is needed in order to see results. Read the following affirmations out loud after your morning meditation every day for the next month – better still, create your own that are specific and relevant to your own situation. This will help reprogramme your mind so that instead of experiencing feelings of lack and fear around money, you will start to train yourself to feel grateful and abundant instead.

I have all the money I need today.
My bank balance is increasing every month.
I can afford to be generous.
Money flows freely into my life.
My attitude towards wealth and money is always positive.

Now that you've become clearer on your financial history and negative beliefs around money – it's time to start making some changes to your behaviour around money.

Expenses Tracking

1) For one whole month, note down EVERY single earning and expense.

2) At the end of the month, go through these expenses and highlight any that make you feel anxious or guilty. When you have finished, look over the highlighted items and look for any patterns.

3) It doesn't matter if you spend a lot on going out if you can afford to and going out is really important to you – the same with shoes, haircuts, gifts or anything else. We only tend to feel guilty if we're unconsciously spending on things we don't really value.

Profit and Loss Spreadsheet

At the end of the month, plot all of your expenses and earnings into a Profit and Loss spreadsheet (you can download one of these at www.theinnerfix.com). Feel free to amend the spreadsheet so that it works for you.

We can almost guarantee that if you continue to do this daily expense tracking and monthly spreadsheet for six months (or beyond), your fears around your finances will decrease dramatically, because you'll know exactly where your money is going. You'll also likely find that your money starts to grow, simply because you're placing your attention on it, and, according to Oprah Winfrey (one of the richest women in the world), 'What you focus on expands'.

Different Accounts

Another helpful tool is to set up a few savings accounts with your bank (they will guide you through the process) to help you manage your money more effectively. These accounts will be in addition to your 'Essentials' main bank account, which will pay for things like your rent, travel, food and other basic necessities.

The amount that you put into the other accounts listed below is totally up to you. The goal is to start to develop the habit of budgeting and saving.

The main accounts we'd recommend creating are:

Investment Account

Every month, place 10 per cent (or another chosen amount) of your earnings into this account. It's never to be spent, just invested. This will help you feel more stable in your financial life because you know you are taking steps to invest in your future.

Giving Account

Every month, place an amount of your choosing into this account and give it away to any charitable causes that you like. You may also like to use this account to buy gifts, coffees, etc., for friends and family. The more you practise giving, the more generous and free around money you will feel, and the more you'll attract.

Fun Account

Every month, place 10 per cent (or an amount of your choosing) of earnings into this account to be spent on anything that makes you feel abundant. Just be sure to spend all of the money in this account each month to experience the benefits of abundance!

You may also like to place 10 per cent of monthly earnings into the following (or make up your own!)

- Holiday account

- Self-development and education account

- Tax Account (whatever the appropriate percentage is for you)

Five-Year Financial Vision

1) Write down what you would like your financial life to look like five years from now. Where would you live? What would you be earning? What job would you be doing to earn it?

2) Now, write down three simple action steps you could take to work towards these goals. They may start really small and simple, such as:

- Spend a morning updating my CV and contacting recruitment firms.

- Save £100 a month towards going travelling next year.

- Babysit twice a week and put that money aside to help get me out of my overdraft.

CHAPTER 14

FRIENDSHIP

Joey

'Anybody can sympathise with the sufferings
of a friend, but it requires a very fine nature
to sympathise with a friend's success.'

Oscar Wilde

Wading through my stuff, I'm rapidly developing a ruthlessness in choosing what stays:

Have I used it in the past year?

Is it visually pleasing to me?

Does it emanate good vibes?

If none are a 'yes': into the bin liner it goes. So far, there are eight bin bags full, and I'm just getting started. I'm currently in a season of clearing out the old, in order to make space for the new – I mean this both materially and energetically. Inspired by various books on the subject, I've finally managed to carve out two days in my schedule to declutter my living space.

The TV's on in the next room and my ears prick up at the sound of a familiar voice. I wander through to see whose face is on the screen and realise it's Olivia's, guest-appearing on a popular chat show.

Over the last few years, we've spoken less and less. After no contact in months, I sent her a message a week or so ago and for the first time I haven't heard back. The last time we saw each other properly was in a coffee shop in Soho almost two years ago now – not long after breaking up with Josh – when Addictive Daughter was just a tiny mad seed of an idea.

That day, we chatted in detail about many things, but not until recently have I realised how *completely* unable I was to call out the elephant in the room: I didn't once broach her career. I didn't ask her how life was changing, how she was dealing with it, or even acknowledge everything she'd achieved since we'd left drama school. Pride had a hold of me yet.

I think back to when I shared a flat in north London with Olivia after leaving drama school, at the beginning of my divine storm and her star rising. Years on, the ridiculousness of one particular memory feels so vivid, it's as if it were yesterday.

It was the summer of 2010, and I was cooped up in my bedroom, having not washed or left the house in days. Olivia's dad and brother had come over to dismantle furniture and box up her belongings, as she was moving out. Persia was to take over her room.

Truth be told, this was a relief, as Persia wasn't in a great place either and I felt I could be myself around her. Persia and Olivia, although close friends of mine, had never been great friends with each other. Both extroverts, there'd been unspoken rivalry between them during our final year at drama school, ever since I'd struck up an unexpected friendship with Persia on a group trip to New York.

I opened my bedroom door to catch a glimpse of Olivia's relatives kneeled down packing up her things, before shutting it again. I'd slept in until late (as usual), and with growing anxiety that I'd now made my presence known – that they might come knocking on my bedroom door for a chat – I began to calculate my escape. Peering through a crack in my door, I could see them bent down with their backs turned, and so I seized my moment. Bounding straight past them, wrapped inside my duvet (for disguise), I sailed down the stairs, through the front door, out of the garden gate and on to the street. I didn't care that I was in public enveloped in a bright red duvet, the peephole just large enough to navigate my way along the pavement.

I looked back moments later to see Olivia's dad stepping out through the gate, taking a box to the car, and swiftly turned the corner out of sight. Now in the local park, I flopped down on the grass in my duvet cocoon, as the blazing sun attempted to penetrate my dark hiding place.

I'd barely spoken with Olivia since the night a small group of us had celebrated the news of her acting role, in a bar in Islington several weeks earlier. She'd been staying at her family home – probably not wanting to make a fuss around the flat as her life shifted up ten gears – and I was relieved by her absence.

At that point, I couldn't possibly get over myself and express happiness for her – I felt too low after the recent blow of being dumped by Rory. I've never before considered myself to have a particularly competitive or envious streak, but, as uncomfortable as it is to admit even now, I was jealous of Olivia. I knew my own career was unlikely ever to reach the pinnacle that hers had so early on.

Much more recently, after I got engaged, I found myself in a similar situation with Persia. My happy news came during a challenging period in her life and I could *feel* (energy is such a strong communicator) how difficult it was for her. Being on the receiving end of this didn't feel good; I felt like I was being punished for finding 'my one'. Although you expect those who care about you to celebrate in your triumphs wholeheartedly, it's not always easy for them when you get the very thing they've been hoping for. The feelings I experienced around Olivia's big break helped me to understand this. It took time, but I tried my best to stand in Persia's shoes: it wasn't that she didn't want to celebrate my situation – she did try to – she was just in the process of grieving her own.

After watching the TV chat show for a few minutes, I return to my room to continue the declutter. Quite unexpectedly, I happen across several sweetly worded cards and gifts Olivia gave me. It reminds me how thoughtful she was, at a time when I was unable to mirror the same back to her. Hearing her voice trailing in from the next room, I suddenly feel incredibly far from the friendship we once shared. It's as if she's in a different world now, and much harder to reach.

Pride, and my tendency to become *separate from* in place of *sharing with*, is something I've always struggled with. It's my hamartia, or fatal flaw. There've been many instances of this playing out in my friendships over the years: my reluctance in admitting that I feel insecure; of confessing that, actually, I *don't* know everything . . . and in having to say those excruciating words 'I'm sorry'. I know that my friendship with Persia would've been left in tatters long ago if neither of us had been able to swallow our pride and face the slightly less desirable facets of ourselves.

Like with lovers, I've had a habit of neglecting the reliable and loyal friends in my life. Instead I've tended to turn my attention towards the more unpredictable ones – somehow feeling I need to work harder to keep hold of them.

Unfortunately, the choices we make can lead to consequences that aren't always easily reversed.

While it still hurts, losing my friendship with Olivia is something that, today, I choose to feel grateful for. It's prompted me to identify the important friendships currently in my life and ensure that I'm taking the time to nurture them. I've been known to prioritise my relationships over friendships (as many of us do). Experiencing it all go wrong and having to crawl back to my friends, with my tail between my legs, has happened one too many times. My childhood friend Kitty is someone who gives a lot, despite a lack of delivery on my part in the past. Fortunately, she's still in my life and these days I try hard to acknowledge and reciprocate all that she brings to our dynamic.

When I made the decision to give up drinking and embrace a different lifestyle several years back, I worried it'd mean losing some people who were in my life. To a degree, things did change. However, the transition was much more subtle than I'd expected. It wasn't a case of cutting anyone out (or being cut out for that matter), but more a gradual distancing from those I no longer had as much in common with. It wasn't that anyone was 'right' or 'wrong', just that we were choosing different experiences.

When certain acquaintances drifted away, there was a period where my social life felt quieter. At the time, I read an analogy that likened a new life phase to a field. When crops are harvested from a field, the soil needs to be left fallow before new seeds can be planted. This time is necessary, as the land needs to regain its balance and nutrients before it can begin a new growth cycle. Applying this idea to my social circles (and after a romantic relationship came to an end too) helped me to be patient and trust in the transition process. Soon enough, a whole influx of new friends entered my social sphere – people who shared my interests and supported the person I was becoming.

It wasn't just new friends, either. After a five-year hiatus, Elle (my wild-child school friend) and I gravitated back together – something that neither of us anticipated would happen. Sometimes, although you can drift so far from someone that reconciliation seems impossible, in time, even people on entirely different trajectories end up crossing paths again.

Maybe the same will happen with Olivia, maybe it won't. All I can do today is surrender to the situation and trust that if we're meant to be brought back into each other's lives, we will be.

Persia

'A friend is someone who knows all about you and still loves you.'
Elbert Hubbard

The torrential rain beats heavily against Sophie's car as we make our way back from Wilderness Festival in Oxfordshire, sodden, exhausted, but still euphoric after an incredible weekend together.

After months of conflict over my relationship with Tiger, Sophie and I eventually made up with each other. We were having drinks at a mutual friend's house on the evening of Christmas Day in 2011, and sensing how uncomfortable mine and Tiger's presence was making her, I finally plucked up the courage to apologise to Sophie out in the garden. After a bit of a verbal scrap, to my surprise she accepted my apology, acknowledging that we'd both done some very questionable things as a result of being in love with Tiger; he seemed to have that effect on girls.

Since that night, we've slowly developed the kind of friendship where you don't see each other very often, and yet you hold a certain fondness for one another that always draws you spontaneously back into each other's lives.

I seem to possess an extraordinary ability to become friends with girls who, by all intents and purposes, should hate my guts (and usually do, for a period of time). I have been extended grace by such girls more times than I can remember, and the only explanation I can conjure up is that I'm good at making sincere and authentic amends when I know I've done something wrong.

At a time when most of what we see of female relationships stems from the back-stabbing, bitchiness and jealousy portrayed on reality shows, I have a lot of gratitude for these unexpected friendships I've a habit of collecting. They remind me how powerful and pleasurable the bond between women can be when we stop trying to tear each other down all the time.

I can see this with my friendship with Salena, too. We grew up as sisters, essentially, and until recently I never really stopped to consider how intrusive my constant presence – in her school, her home, her parents' stables – may have been for her. I literally gatecrashed her life.

We were in ceaseless competition with each other at all times, and it was gruelling for the both of us. Though it did encourage us to up our game in our singing, horse-riding and revision for exams, it also made us extremely insecure and nasty to each other much of the time, and I don't know if our little successes were ever really worth the stress.

Recently, Jess found her diary from when she was sixteen. In it, she'd written:

My friend Persia has given me the best relationship advice EVER. She said that you shouldn't see your boyfriend as the foundations in your life, but as the cherry on top.

This was clearly advice I had yet to put into practice myself. However, since primary school, I'd always been the one that girl-friends would come to for guidance. The fact that my own life was a reckless shambles most of the time didn't seem to deter them for some reason, perhaps because I had such an energy of authority – misplaced or otherwise – when I imparted my nuggets of wisdom.

What I now realise is that I was always a strong champion of my friends' romantic, academic or creative pursuits – when I was in the right headspace to be so. I was only able to properly be a good friend to both Jess and Salena in those moments when I stopped competing with them as an actress or singer, and stepped into my natural ability as an encourager. When I focused on watering the grass on my own side of the fence, instead of coveting the grass on *their* side, I felt good about supporting them, because I was feeling good about myself.

Well into my twenties, I always felt most alive when I was philosophising about life, or passionately declaring how fantas-tic my friends were over several bottles of wine. I may have been drunk, but I meant every word of what I said. I was always far more at home and confident doing this than when I was pretending to be someone else on stage.

Yet, I could only really be a consistent friend and support to these girls when I learned how to bestow the same level of faith, acceptance and love on myself – and it took me a whole lot of soul-ache to humble me enough to start that process.

Today, the girls I get along best with are the ones I refer to as my true 'soul sisters', mainly because they, like me, have one foot planted in the spiritual realm, and the other very much in the secular one.

We all share a mutual affection for seemingly contradictory lifestyle choices: we love raving and meditating, red wine and green juice, yoga and fashion magazines, a juicy ribeye and quinoa, partying and praying. The two extremes may appear to be paradoxical, but they don't feel like it.

My life doesn't work so well when I try and make black or white choices about *every single thing*. I tend to find that I need *both*: I need the divine and the worldly, the discipline and the freedom, the pain and the pleasure, in order to make it all feel worth it. I'm equally happy journaling on the balcony at sunset on a yoga retreat in Spain alongside Jess, or dancing with our friends in a field at a festival, glugging back warm cider and having the odd puff of a cigarette. Both are spiritual experiences in my opinion, because both are celebrations of what it is to be alive. The combination of the two in my life feels exciting and liberating.

While I know that moderation isn't for everyone, I'm currently exploring what works for *me*, personally.

Today, the only two vices from my past that I've absolutely sworn off as out of bounds under *all* circumstances are cocaine and cheating, because both took me and those I love to a dark, dark place that I do not wish to return to; it's just not worth it.

When it comes to alcohol, while I no longer rely on it as a solution, I do allow myself to enjoy it as a pleasure sometimes. However, I've pledged to (try and remember to) always ask myself the following questions before having a few drinks:

1 What are my genuine intentions for wanting to do this? Am I doing it to escape how I'm feeling, or to celebrate something?
2 Am I with people that I trust and do I feel safe?
3 Am I willing to *happily* accept the consequences of this action?

I'm not saying that I'll always get it right (being human and all), but these questions at least give me some guidelines to help me stay within safe boundaries. They stop my life from feeling limited, because they keep me focused on how I want to feel (which is *good*), and enable me to adjust my choices accordingly.

I believe that every person on earth should get to decide what combination of lifestyle choices works for them (so long as they don't hurt other people), without feeling judged by others who may not share their preferences.

My friendship with Joey has only managed to survive as long as it has because of our commitment to accepting each other's differences. The irony is, we had first become friends because we bonded in New York over our mutual predisposition to unhealthy men and alcohol. When we started working on ourselves individually, these crutches were no longer the linchpin of our friendship and, truth be told, that caused us some problems. What it made us realise is that we are, underneath all that old reckless behaviour, very, very different girls with very, very different outlooks on life. This has been both the key to our success with Addictive Daughter, and the reason we can often come to blows.

While Joey excels at being loyal and consistent, and I at being spontaneous and a risk-taker, we are also both wounded in different places. My biggest fears are being controlled or judged, so if I've done something 'bad' my instinct is to lie to get out of it. Joey's are being lied to or abandoned, and if she feels like this is happening her instinct is to control and reprimand. And thus, we have the ingredients for a perfect storm of emotional triggering, because my teeth fit her wounds, and vice versa.

When our backs are up against the wall, we'll both act out of these wounded places within us. Whatever the circumstances, it's usually the same pattern: Joey on the attack, I on the defensive.

Back before we started on this spiritual path, it was sometimes easier just to avoid the friendship altogether, and we often wouldn't speak for months at a time. This was always very painful, because, despite our differences, we have a love and a bond that's hard to put down in words; like Salena, I see Joey as my sister.

Now that we're running Addictive Daughter together, which promotes forgiveness, acceptance and *letting go of resentments*, Joey and I have really, *really* had to practise what we preach. Therefore, what we've come to realise, is that we are each other's greatest teacher.

You

> 'A true friend never gets in your way unless
> you happen to be going down.'
> Arnold H. Glasow

We can't choose our family, but we can choose our friends. Close platonic friendships make our experience of life all the more joyful and pleasurable. Nothing can make us laugh like reminiscing over times gone by with old friends. Few things can make us feel more comforted and loved on a dark day than a long phone call or catch-up with someone we've known for years.

Like with romantic relationships, our choices about who to be friends with tend to reflect what we think and feel about ourselves. Often, we're drawn to people who possess the character attributes that we think are important and admirable, or who have a similar outlook on life as us. Sometimes, we find ourselves wanting to be friends with those who live a lifestyle that we aspire to. Maybe they're high achievers or very outgoing. Or, perhaps they prioritise their health and general sense of wellbeing, and so by hanging out with them, some of their 'togetherness' might rub off on us. As author and motivational speaker Jim Rohn said, 'you are the average of the five people you spend the most time with'.

But, just as friendships can inspire us to become higher, better versions of ourselves, they can also trigger us profoundly. This is particularly true of those friends who've known us a long time and so are aware of our personal weaknesses and where we often fall short. These close friendships hold a mirror up to us and show us everything that we don't like about ourselves. They can be a breeding ground where all our neuroses and character defects are taken to their most extreme, because when we become close and intimate with someone, we also become vulnerable and exposed. Just like with a lover, when we allow ourselves to be fully seen by a friend, we open up the possibility that they might reject us.

This fear of rejection or abandonment can cause us to act out in all manner of ways in a bid to try and protect ourselves. If we feel our friend has betrayed us or acted in a hurtful way, we immediately get on the defensive and retaliate, trying to 'win' back the power. Sometimes, we'll play the victim to make them feel guilty for their behaviour. Other times, we'll shut them out and go cold and silent on them so that *they* can feel the same rejection or pain that they've caused us to feel. Others of us who are perhaps more confrontational might interrogate the friend they feel has wronged them as a way of coercing them into an apology. But, all of these approaches tend to push the other person further away and increase the conflict, rather than resolving the situation.

In this way, we can sometimes find ourselves losing friendships that are extremely important to us. This might just be for

245

a few months, or, depending on the intensity of the fallout, can go on indefinitely. A major reason for this comes down to our pride. Much of the time, we'd much rather be right than happy. But, no conflict is completely one-sided. No matter how small our own mistakes in the situation, it's our job to take full responsibility for them. In owning our own faults, we make it a whole lot easier for our friend to feel safe enough to own up to theirs.

We can only experience healthy, happy relationships to the degree that we can accept others for who they are (not who we'd like them to be), and forgive them when they mess up. We're all flawed because we're all human. While some faults may be easier to forgive than others, we must remember that forgiving someone for their shortcomings is not about saying that what they did was OK, but that our peace of mind is more important than their fault.

All of us are wounded in different places. Ironically, we tend to attract the people who are more likely to trigger these wounds because, although they will likely cause us pain, it's a pain we're familiar with.

In the self-help world, such relationships are sometimes referred to as 'life assignments'. We all have these types of people in our lives – the ones we love more than anyone else, but who can also get underneath our skin in a way no one else can. We often have the best and worst experiences with our life assignments; they're our saviour and our torturer in equal parts.

The good news is that these people offer us the opportunity to heal the very wounds they trigger. But it's our job to first get clear on what behaviours aggravate us and why. After all, just because we're particularly sensitive to being told off or criticised as we experienced that often as a child, we can't expect our friend to understand that unless they've been through the same thing themselves. Likewise, if their issue is being lied to because of being repeatedly betrayed in the past, they might be extremely sensitive to the smallest hint of rejection or disloyalty on our part.

Setting clear boundaries about what we can and cannot tolerate in our friendships will, for the most part, prevent extreme conflicts from occurring, because it leaves no confusion as to where the line is. If it gets crossed, our friend will know it and expect consequences.

So many of the struggles that we encounter in our friendships and relationships are a result of not being clear and direct about what our boundaries are or when they've been crossed. This leads us to silently stew in resentment, while our friend often has no idea that there's even a problem – until we eventually explode.

The thing is, we often don't assert or make clear our issues, because we feel that they are silly and that a friend might reject us for them. We're too afraid and vulnerable to say, 'When you do X, I feel rejected, abandoned, disrespected, upset, etc.' But if we don't say it, how can we expect them to know? It's actually *our* lack of security in owning our truth – *not* their boundary-crashing or mistake – that's the problem here. Our friends don't *want* us to feel bad – not if they're good ones, anyway. It's our responsibility to make their job easier by being clear and honest about where our biggest fears and insecurities are, so that they can do their best to be sensitive to them.

Apart from helping to prevent fallouts in the future and giving them permission to share their own insecurities, sharing our truth with those closest to us in this way will also serve to deepen the friendship, because vulnerability is what connects and bonds us with one another. It's also worth noting that not all need be lost in a friendship just because we have a fight; sometimes fights can be very healing, as they force us to confront our own issues more deeply.

Certain behaviours or mistakes on the part of a friend may lead us to conclude that we no longer want them in our life – for the time being, anyway. But, even so, we can still convey this information in a calm, kind and respectful way.

The more healing we do around our own personal wounding, the less we tend to find ourselves gravitating towards those who'll trigger us. Instead, we become more drawn to people who reflect and affirm our growing sense of self-worth.

The exercises below will guide you to get clear on which friendships are the most important to you and why, as well as helping you to hone in on the values and attributes that make you a good friend. You may be surprised by how much you learn about yourself, as well as the degree to which your friendships and other relationships improve as a result.

EXERCISES

Friendship Qualities

1) Take a page in your journal and draw a line down the middle of the page.

2) Label the left-hand column 'Attributes', and list three qualities you have that make you a good friend. For each, write one action that you do regularly that you think helps contribute to the attribute you've written down.

3) Label the right-hand column 'Areas for Growth', and list three traits that friends or partners have most often criticised you for in the past. Write down one action that you can take this week (and ideally on a regular basis) to help you make progress in this area. For example:

ATTRIBUTES	AREAS FOR GROWTH
1. *WISE – I read lots of self-help books and friends always come to me for advice.*	*SELFISH – volunteer at a homeless shelter.*
2.	

Social Circles

1) Take a full page in your journal and draw a circle in the middle and label it 'Core'. List the most important people in your life (likely your immediate family, best friend and boyfriend/girlfriend).

2) Draw a bigger circle around the 'Core' circle and label it 'Inner', listing the people in your inner social circle.

3) Around the 'Inner' circle, draw another circle and label that 'Outer', listing all the people you would consider in your outer friendship group.

4) Finally, draw one more circle entitled 'Acquaintances' and list those, too.

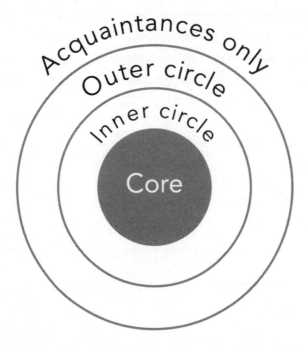

Sometimes when doing this exercise, you realise that your time is not being dispersed in the way you would like it to; ideally, your core group should get the most of your time and energy, and, as the circles get bigger, that time and energy will decrease.

Use these circles as a reminder of who you want to take priority in your life. Don't be afraid if the names in the circles change over time – that's normal.

Close Friendships

1) Take a full page in your journal and, turning the page to 'landscape', divide it into five columns.

2) In the first, note down who your closest friendships are with.

3) In the next column, note down what you love about each person.

4) In the third, note down what qualities you don't like so much in that person.

5) In the next, write down what your arguments tend to be about, how often they occur and the typical consequences. Do you stop speaking for months, or do you get over them pretty quickly?

6) In the final column, note down one or two actions that *you* could take to improve the friendship.

For example:

FRIEND	QUALITIES I LOVE	QUALITIES I STRUGGLE WITH	ARGUMENTS AND CONSEQUENCES	HOW I COULD IMPROVE FRIENDSHIP
1. *Anna*	*Fun, confident, good listener.*	*Can be unreliable at times.*	*I get annoyed that she's always late and she thinks I'm too controlling. This happens about once a month, but we usually just brush it off and get on with it – so it keeps happening!*	*Have an honest chat with her and apologise for coming across as controlling, but tell her I would be really grateful if she'd give me a bit more warning if she's going to be late/needs to cancel our meet.*

Cultivate New, Healthy Friendships

Some people have shared with us that they have lots of acquaintances, but no real close, solid friends who like to do the same stuff as them. The key to developing healthy friendships is to find some common ground with an individual (or a group) that you can bond over. If you'd like to explore creating new, healthy friendships, the following exercise will set you on the right track:

1) Take a page in your journal and write a list of all your favourite hobbies or pastimes (e.g. reading, swimming, hiking, etc.).

2) Research the social activities in your area, and try and find one or two groups that you like the look of that meet regularly.

3) Commit to trying these groups out for at least three weeks so that you give each a fair chance; sometimes it takes a little bit of time to settle in to a group dynamic.

Don't expect to make/worry about making close friendships straight away. Instead, enjoy the activity itself while keeping yourself open to any new friendships that might be formed.

CHAPTER 15

LOVE

Persia

'I love you not only for what you are, but
for what I am when I am with you.'

Elizabeth Barrett Browning

Rex kisses me one last time, then turns away and walks towards Green Park tube station, leaving me standing alone at the bus stop clutching the green dinosaur teddy he bought me from Disneyland Tokyo. Our two-month courtship is officially over.

In many ways, it's been the healthiest dating experience I've ever had. A twenty-seven-year-old banker, Rex is good-looking, intelligent and chivalrous. Since we met at the end of January 2015, he's taken me out for lots of nice meals and talked about all the holidays he can't wait to take me on. We've had great chemistry from the get-go, and Joey even invited him to her wedding next month.

If I'm really honest, though, Joey's impending nuptials are probably the main reason why I wanted it to work out with Rex so badly. Unfortunately, the one thing that hasn't been so synchronistic timing-wise between Joey and I is our romantic lives – not since our mutual dumpings in 2012 anyway. When I was at my happiest with Sam, Joey was really struggling in her relationship with a guy called Ollie. As she started falling in love with her now fiancé, my relationship with Sam was slowly deteriorating. Two weeks after our break-up, Joey got engaged.

Their engagement was a real test of our friendship in many ways – not because I wasn't happy for Joey, of course I was over the moon for her. But because I'd honestly thought that I'd marry Sam one day. Having been so afraid of commitment all my life, this was a big deal for me, and it hurt a lot when my desire for a future wasn't shared.

I think I was also mourning the fact that Joey and I would never experience our friendship in quite the same way as we had that summer of 2012 when we were both single. When your best friend goes through a big life transition it changes the nature of your relationship – not necessarily for better or worse – but it does change things. And it takes time to adjust.

As well as all this, I'd just turned twenty-nine when I met Rex, and despite all of the work I'd done on myself to feel content and fulfilled being single, I wasn't exempt from the pressures of being asked by various family members when I was 'planning on settling down'. Although I knew my worth didn't come from having a boyfriend, the onslaught of engagement rings, wedding snaps and baby bumps on my social media feeds did occasionally incite pangs of jealousy and fear that maybe I wouldn't ever meet someone. So, when Rex showed up in my life, there was quite a lot riding on my hope that *this might be it*.

Hence why I was so disappointed when he told me he'd accidentally double-booked himself for Joey's wedding weekend – disappointed, but not all that surprised. From the moment Joey had invited him, I just knew he wasn't going to be there on the day.

Although I've really enjoyed dating Rex, having been single for nearly a year before I met him (the longest time I've ever been without a boyfriend), I've had an underlying sense of anxiety bubbling under the surface the entire time.

On paper, Rex is everything I *thought* I wanted, yet something was undeniably missing between us.

'He's lovely Pers, he's just not very . . . *you*,' Jess had said the day after meeting him at a friend's gig.

She was right; he wasn't. I knew this because it didn't feel effortless to be my real self around him, which it always does when someone is right for you. Sometimes, no matter how much you want something to work, the answer is just 'no'.

What I *do* know is that I'm meant to attend Joey's wedding on my own, and actually I'm really happy about that. After all we've been through together over the last six years, it's my chance to be 100 per cent present for her on the most important day of her life. I couldn't do that if Rex was at the wedding with me.

I really don't want to fall into the trap of wishing away my time being single. You don't get this time back. As I learned during mine and Joey's 'summer of self-love' three years ago, being on your own is an amazing opportunity to deepen your bond with your close friends, and develop a full, rich life outside of your romantic one – which gives you the best chance of having a healthy, happy relationship further down the line.

Being single is also the best time to reflect on your past relationships. I remember reading about the different forms of romantic love in *Women Who Love Too Much* back in Thailand four years ago. What I'd learned then, was that the majority of my previous relationships were based solely around what the ancient Greeks called *eros* – a love that's born out of lust, passion and desire. My entire relationship with Tiger was built on this kind of love. While this was undeniably exciting, it soon burned itself (and me) out under the weight of its own intensity.

With Sam, on the other hand, I'd had the experience of *agape* – a love that's founded on friendship, loyalty and commitment. Despite his 'bad boy' reputation at church (an oxymoron if ever I heard one), his offensively inappropriate sense of humour and prescription pill abuse, Sam was still a big step forwards in my journey towards choosing a healthy suitor – as Tiger had once been on account of his sobriety and meditation practice.

Through the early stages of setting up Addictive Daughter with Joey, Sam had been my rock. Ever dependable and supportive, he was always telling me how brave he thought I was for following my heart and passions when there were no guarantees they'd amount to anything. We had our problems, but they paled in comparison to what I'd gone through in previous relationships. Sam knew my history with cheating; 'Please don't shit on my heart,' he'd joked when he asked me to be his girl-friend. And, I didn't. I didn't cheat on him once – again progress for me.

However, while Sam had taught me how to have a steady and relatively healthy relationship, our connection ultimately lacked the passion, excitement and spontaneity that I craved. I sense that, had I continued on with Rex, I may well have experienced the same thing I'd gone through with Sam – not because of who they are, but because we just weren't quite right for each other.

Even though my thirtieth birthday is drawing closer, I choose not to fall into a relationship with someone for the wrong reasons again – to temporarily relieve my loneliness and fear of being single forever, or to have a plus-one for weddings I'm being invited to. I won't settle for anything less than a relationship that inspires and challenges me – with someone who gives me butterflies. He doesn't need to be perfect, but he does need to be more than just a *safe bet*. Now I know *what* I want, the who and the how will take care of themselves when the time is right, I have no doubt.

Speaking of butterflies, I've been seeing even more of them lately. The week before Joey's wedding, I meet with an old friend who tells me that butterflies are a symbol for the 'twin flame' relationship, and that mine may well be on its way to me in the not too distant future.

I remember Bella telling me about twin flames back when Tiger was away on the Camino. A twin flame is a spiritual concept describing a special soul connection between two people. The idea dates back to the ancient Egyptians and Greek philosopher Plato, who said that 'when one of them meets with his other half . . . the pair are lost in an amazement of love and friendship and intimacy, and one will not be out of the other's sight . . . even for a moment.'

There are several characteristics associated with the twin flame relationship, most notably linked to the first point of meeting. There is a sense of instant recognition – a powerful bond or feeling of 'love at first sight'. These two souls also find they know exactly what the other is thinking, often finishing each other's sentences, as well as experiencing a very open and fluid style of communication with each other.

Now, it must be said, this is potentially very dangerous territory for an idealistic Codependent like me. What I worry about is that this type of connection sounds a little too close to what I experienced with Tiger, and I never want to be consumed by love like that again.

When I research the topic a little further, however, I discover that a crucial non-negotiable facet of the twin flame union is that you are both complete and whole people *before* meeting, and are each willing to continue to commit to your own personal and spiritual development first and foremost, to ensure the relationship doesn't burn itself out. In the words of one of my favourite old-school poets Kahlil Gibran:

> Love one another but make not a bond of love:
> Let it rather be a moving sea between the shores of your souls.
> Fill each other's cup but drink not from one cup.

I do think there's something in this twin flame business and, whatever it is, I'm not going to beat around the bush: *I want it.* I want to one day be in a relationship in which both individuals inspire and encourage one another to become the most loving, generous, compassionate and successful versions of themselves in all areas of their lives. I want passion and intimacy, adventure and stability, romance and friendship, Eros *and* Agape. It's a tall order, I know, but I believe it's possible, because I think Joey's about to marry her own twin flame.

Joey

> 'Your task is not to seek for love, but merely to seek and find all the barriers within yourself that you have built against it.'
> Rumi

The backs of the heads of one hundred of those who love us most sit in neat rows ahead of me. It's 2.15 p.m. on 22 May

2015. Butterflies of excitement flutter in my stomach.

'Ready?' the reverend asks, his eyes twinkling.

I turn to look at the four girls behind me: my sister, my Texan cousin Natty, Persia and my oldest friend Kitty, all dressed in dusky rose, their bouquets intertwined with gold fern and feathers.

'I love you,' Persia mouths.

'I love you,' I mouth back.

And with that, I link my dad's right arm and, with the reverend before us, we begin our descent down the aisle.

My soul knew I was to marry my husband before I did. Persia had dragged me along to the 'God Camp' she went on the previous summer, with the promise that it'd been the best week of her life. Despite having established a very personal relationship with a Higher Power of my understanding, I didn't identify with Christianity – believing that all of us are children of one benevolent power and not separated by religious semantics. However, I was feeling hugely conflicted at the time over my almost year-long relationship with a guy called Ollie, and resorted to going along with Persia in the hope of seeking some solace.

Ollie and I met online, on match.com. My profile stated that I was a non-drinker, looking for another non-drinker (or at least someone with a healthy respect for alcohol), and he answered the call. On a soul level, I cared for him deeply. He was rugged, creative and independent – with a few distinguishing freckles dotted over his cheeks and nose, and dark tousled hair. Yet day-to-day our relationship was strained. Ollie was on the run from his past, and although he was now sober (doctor's orders – the result of alcohol induced health issues), he'd never processed the reasons behind his previously destructive relationship with drink. Eradicating the crutch used to fill the void did not solve the fact that the void itself was very much still there.

Ollie and I had shared some magical times, but I was slowly realising that, while I was in a place of no longer wanting to sit in the shit, he seemed quite comfortable staying there. Addictive Daughter was just over a year old at the point of meeting him, and I understood enough about codependency and fixing people to know that forcing the hand of help where it wasn't wanted, and trying to change a person (an old favourite of mine), was no longer an option. It'd never worked before and it wasn't going to now.

Yet this situation was tough. Ollie was convinced at times that he *did* want to change, and every time things came to a head between us a renewed desire to do so would persuade me to stay with the relationship a little longer. The darker days, when he isolated from me completely, were followed with such deep and intense reunions that the soul-tie between us was growing ever stronger, making it harder for me to give up on it.

I cared for Ollie, and desperately wanted to work through the depression with him. But it was proving to be slow progress, and I was struggling to align myself with Addictive Daughter's message when one area of my life felt so draining.

'I think you're ready for a higher relationship,' Persia said to me during a meeting over coffee one afternoon.

Although it was quite painful to hear, I knew she was right. I'd come a long way in my own life, and was ready to meet someone I could share that with, someone who lifted me up and challenged me, not pulled me backwards.

It had been a testing few days at God Camp, where I felt like an outsider amidst intense talk of 'The Lord' and 'Jesus' all around. One morning, myself, Persia and the six other girls we were sharing a caravan with had made a group fry-up, rationing the portions so that we could all eat. Now, I have a big appetite, and our plates were depressingly sparse. Suddenly, one of them that was balanced precariously on the counter fell off and landed face down on the floor.

'God's will!' one of the women shouted joyously.

F*ck this, I thought, *I'm hungry.*

I disappeared off to call Ollie, and through tears told him how alienated I felt. I was totally OK with the idea of a Higher Power, but I had to draw the line at a God who apparently wanted us all to have less breakfast.

That afternoon, I finally satisfied my hunger at a barbecue near our caravan when, upon overhearing a conversation about Addictive Daughter, a guy sitting several metres away piped up and joined in. Weirdly, the group of ten or so people who were sitting around dispersed, one by one, leaving the two of us alone.

Luke, as it turns out he was called, was a recovered addict who'd found a relationship with God through the Twelve Step recovery. He had a colourful past and was now thirty-four, sober, happy and successfully running his own film production company. Persia had called me from God Camp and mentioned his interest in collaborating with Addictive Daughter the previous summer.

I wasn't head over heels in lust, but I felt instantly at ease with Luke. He seemed like a straightforward and rational kind of guy who exuded an attractively calm energy. Suddenly feeling conscious that we'd been sitting alone for a while, he headed off to find the others while I returned to the caravan.

I stood at the sink, washing up the plates from breakfast and mulling over the situation with Ollie in my mind. Out of nowhere – and very calmly – a thought about Luke dropped in:

That's the man you're going to marry.

Uncharacteristically for me, I parked it and continued to wash the dishes.

A month on, and still no closer to finding any clarity around my relationship with Ollie, I was taken on holiday by my ninety-year-old grandma. Coming towards the end of her life, and wanting to treat us with the remaining savings she had, she'd invited my parents, my sister and I to join her on a Mediterranean cruise.

Before leaving for the trip, although I hated doing it, I saw no option but to give Ollie an ultimatum: either he sought professional help or we'd have to part ways. Mutually agreeing to no contact during our time apart, we hugged goodbye and, unprompted, he assured me that he'd get his therapy sessions underway while I was gone.

One sweltering afternoon, as I sat with my grandma in a shady café in Rome, our conversation turned to the topic of my late grandfather and the long marriage they'd shared.

'You know, I've always said you can tell when you've met the person you're to marry, because each of you feel you've got the best of the bargain.'

My heart sank; I wasn't sure that either Ollie or I could say we felt confident of that.

Later that night, standing alone at the back of the ship in the middle of the ocean, I was overcome with a strong sense that Ollie wasn't going to follow through on the therapy, and, aware of the boundary I'd laid down this time, panic rose up in my chest. With nobody watching, I flung my arms outwards (*very* like Kate Winslet in *Titanic*) and spoke out loud to my Higher Power.

'HP, I pray that whatever happens will be for both of our

greater good. I trust that whatever decision Ollie makes is exactly as it needs to be. Please guide me, I trust you and hand this situation over completely to your care.'

Almost immediately I felt calmer and, aware that I looked a little eccentric, put my arms down before anyone saw.

Several days later, after sitting in a Twelve Step meeting on the boat, I was getting up to leave when a lady in her sixties from Alabama approached me with her hand extended, ready for shaking.

'I'm Patti, wanna go grab a cup of coffee?'

I knew I had to say yes.

Minutes later, we were sitting together on the lido deck, mugs in hand, as she listened intently to my dilemma. After taking it all in, she paused for a moment before saying with conviction: 'Bless him, change me.'

Change me? This was laughable advice. *I'm the one in a good place, it's him who needs to change.* I told her so.

'Bless *him*, change *me*. He's got his own issues, sure, but honey, you're *choosing* to stay with him when it's making you unhappy. You have to bless him – send him off with love – and change yourself. The only person who can do anything about this situation is *you*.'

There was little point in protesting any further.

On my return to England a week later, I was met with the outcome I'd hoped wouldn't be so – Ollie had not taken any action. I knew what I had to do, and although it felt painful and very sad, I began to embark on life without him.

At first I felt angry; it was as if he'd been brought into my life to test my weakest spot. In him, I'd been sent someone who I shared a deep connection with, who was actually quite *keen* for me to play the role of fixer to him, and yet I knew I needed to walk away. If it's true that people are brought to us as spiritual assignments, then Ollie was possibly my most important one to date: teaching me how to take my hands off and, instead, accept what was no longer working for either of us.

Several months later, I was attending church with Persia in South Kensington and, as we sat there on the floor, I opened a Bible that was lying beside me. A piece of paper that was resting inside the front cover fell out on to my lap, and I saw that it had a verse from the Gospel of Luke scrawled on it. I picked it up and, with a cheeky grin, passed it across to Persia (who knew of my odd premonition about marrying Luke from God Camp).

Leaving church with Persia thirty minutes later, and the paper bookmark tucked into my bag, she squeezed me tightly as she spotted who was standing outside, just a few metres away on the pavement. Having had no contact at all since our initial meeting, Luke was now in my line of vision and heading towards us.

Over a series of dinners and coffee dates that followed, it transpired that we'd both been in relationships earlier that summer, and with no knowledge of each other's situation had decided to walk away from the people we were with.

From the minute Luke entered my life, he was *all in*, making it abundantly clear that he wasn't going anywhere. While, in theory, this should have been the dream, I quickly found myself withdrawing from him. I knew how to deal with people leaving, but feeling sure they were going to stay? This was new territory for me.

One evening, he arrived at my front door with a bunch of flowers, and upon seeing them, my face dropped.

'I just want him to play hard to get. He's so perfect, but he's SO keen P, it's *really* freaking me out,' I whined to Persia on the phone later that night.

'But isn't this what you said you wanted – someone who's

actually available, who *wants* a relationship, too?'

'Yeah, but I . . .'

'What are you not sure about with him?'

'Oh, he's amazing – I just wish he'd stop returning my calls or hook up with someone else, just so there was a bit of a chase, you know?'

We both fell silent.

'Oh God,' I said.

In that moment, I knew that, if my time with Luke was to go any further, I needed to learn to be able to hold the space for what he was offering me – real commitment.

It took a few weeks of it feeling a little clunky and overwhelming, but I managed to readjust my relationship sails, and suddenly something clicked into place. After that, it wasn't too long until my grandma's words rang true and we realised, that for the first time, *both* of us felt we'd got the best of the bargain.

You

'Love must be as much a light, as it is a flame.'
Henry David Thoreau

You may have heard it said that the best time to work on a relationship is before you enter one. There's something extraordinary about being single through the healing and self-discovery process, since it's so often when alone that you're at your most receptive. Time focused inwards can provide a much-needed opportunity to heal old wounds and release the baggage accumulated from past heartbreaks, if you choose to embrace it as such. That said, there's no 'perfect time' to begin recovery of the heart. It really doesn't matter if you're single, married or other, as long as you're willing. All relationships that you've chosen to enter, stay in or break free from are gifts, brought to assist your soul's growth and guide you forwards.

We're one of the first generations to experience a multitude of relationships during our lifetime – and a multitude of relationship breakdowns, too. Whether you're pining for the steady and less complex romantic relationships that people seemed to have in the 'olden days', hugely grateful for the freedom bestowed upon Western women today, or somewhere in between, it's worth acknowledging that, while romantic freedom can be a lot of fun, alongside the highs comes a rollercoaster of disappointment and heartache.

Many of us will have been hurt in romance at some point, resulting in a reluctance to let ourselves be completely open and vulnerable again. A closed heart acts as a barrier to love; it attracts in more of what you don't want, since the universe tends to reflect back to you what it is you believe. When you shut off your heart and decide that the world's full of dangerous people who'll screw you over, your frequency will tune into exactly *that*, and you'll attract those who affirm this belief for you. At the end of the day, very few decent, emotionally healthy romantic mates are going to be drawn towards someone with a hardened heart, because like attracts like. By staying stuck in fear and cynicism when it comes to romance, you sabotage any chance of experiencing (or even recognising) someone with more promise.

Any pain you feel when it comes to love and intimacy is necessary – in fact, it's a blessing. Emotional discomfort shows you what you no longer want to be burdened with, and encourages you to do something about it. Even those who have caused you hurt can be seen in a positive light: as spiritual assignments, providing an opportunity to understand yourself more deeply. All lessons, no matter how painful, can be used to elevate you to new heights, the very minute you choose to perceive your experience through the lens of love, forgiveness and gratitude. When you turn away from spiritual assignments, they tend to come round again in the form of different people and situations, until you're ready to take on board what it is you need to learn.

In many cases, we try to recreate scenarios that echo the battles from our past, in a subconscious effort to 'win' them in the present. For example, if you had a father who raged, and a mother who was passive and unable to stand up for herself, you may find yourself drawn towards partners with a short temper, while feeling just as powerless as you remember your mother being.

When it comes to seeking out a new relationship, we can be easily sidetracked by the wildly attractive *exterior* of a lover, only to realise, much further down the road, that their *interior* may leave a lot to be desired. When making a 'future partner checklist' in our minds, the focus tends to be on the externals: what height, eye colour, teeth straightness, occupation or car we'd like them to have.

We forget to put our attention on what inner qualities are most desirable and compatible with our own. Are you looking for reliability? Passion? Loyalty? Generosity? Honesty? A good sense of humour? Do you want to feel respected? Is it important to share similar ideals and goals for the future? By shifting your focus on to a *soul* connection over a *superficial* one, you begin to hone in on what really matters and endures.

It's useful and interesting to look at what you *say* you want romantically, and what, in reality, you're giving your energy to – and being able to discern whether the two match up. How many of us have declared that we're waiting for a stable, kind-hearted, ready-to-commit soulmate, yet expend most of our energy on chasing emotionally shut down and unreliable commitment-phobes? It may not always feel like it, but who you choose to give your heart to is a *choice* you get to make. Your job is to get clear on what it is you want, and then to work on staying emotionally healthy, so that you're able to recognise it when it crosses your path.

If steadiness and consistency are what you're seeking, there's little point in investing in someone who blows hot and cold on a regular basis. If you're looking for a summer fling, it's probably best to avoid the person who is unapologetically searching for their 'one'. If you're keen to settle down and start a family, then becoming enmeshed with someone who holds marriage and children at the very bottom of their priority list is asking for trouble. Likewise, if you're hoping to be treated like a princess and enjoy an extravagant lifestyle, it makes little sense to pursue a partner who's financially unmanageable and permanently broke.

When it comes to what is of personal importance to you, your choices undoubtedly take you either towards or away from attaining your desires. In the Twelve Step community, there is a well-known phrase: 'Don't go to the butcher's for bread.' Yet, so often we do, and we leave feeling disappointed, having not got what we were hoping for. Of course, you don't need to be overly rigid, either. While you may be unwilling to compromise on certain non-negotiable qualities, there's also room to remain open-minded. The right person is frequently brought to you in a form you don't expect, and therefore some flexibility when it comes to the finer details often goes a long way.

While we may long to find the 'one', many of us find ourselves unprepared when that person finally arrives in our life, and we do everything we can to sabotage our long-awaited happy ending. We may desire to feel loved, but do we actually believe we're worthy of it? We may moan about the unavailability of our love interests, but what'd happen if someone were to fully commit to us – are we *really* ready for that?

Those who are drawn to you are a reflection of where you're at, personally. It stands to reason, then, that if you aspire to attract in a different type of partner to the ones currently on your radar, you must look inwards, and work on becoming the best version of yourself. Only then will those who reflect your new frequency be drawn in.

A huge part of this inner work is down to developing a solid sense of self-worth. Through nurturing a spiritual connection, you gradually discover that you're able to adopt a loving attitude towards yourself. As your self-esteem increases, you'll find your whole outlook on dating and relationships transforms. Instead of obsessing over thoughts of, 'Does she like me?' or 'Is he going to ask me out again?' you begin to ask yourself, 'Do *I* like her?' or 'Do I *want* to see him again?'

However, no matter how clear or sure you might be about someone, it's important to be honest with yourself about how *interested in* and *available* they are to you. You may have found *your* idea of the perfect fit, but if the object of your affections doesn't feel the same, you're barking up a very pointless and potentially pain-inducing tree. Being able to recognise a non-starter and gracefully removing yourself from the equation is something you'll only ever thank yourself for further down the line.

Whether you're currently in a relationship or you're single, it's important to remember that a romantic partner cannot be expected to fulfil *all* roles, nor provide for your every need – that's an unhealthy amount of pressure for one person to deal with. Similarly to how you go to different friends and family members for different things, you can't expect a romantic mate to be your *everything* . . . and yet, so often we do. It's amazing that we hold such expectation towards a loved one, when most of us are unable to provide that level of loving consistency even for ourselves!

The beauty of a relationship with a Higher Power is that you gradually become less dependent on the people in your life and grow more *self*-reliant instead. By strengthening your spiritual connection, you become free to focus simply on loving yourself first, knowing that once that's in place, the rest will unfold exactly as it needs to.

EXERCISES

Taking Stock of Your Past Relationships

1) Write a list of all your past (serious) relationships. For each one, write the following:

The good qualities each partner possessed.

The bad qualities each partner possessed.

The positive aspects of the relationship.

The negative aspects of the relationship.

The big mistakes you made in the relationship.

The reason for it ending.

2) Note down the main patterns and similarities emerging throughout the relationships. For example: did you always seem to go out with a 'bad boy'? Did you always cheat? Did those you dated always have money struggles?

3) What are the similarities and differences between your own relationship patterns and that of your parents?

Prayer

Read the following prayer out loud before your next morning meditation:

Please remove any barriers I have put up around my heart. Please take from me the games I play to deny myself the joy of love. Help me to hand over my deepest fears and insecurities around romance to you. Thank you for healing my wounds from past relationships, so that I am open to love freely, in a totally new way.

Future Partner Values List

In your journal, write a list of your romantic partner non-negotiables. List the qualities and attributes that you'd like your next partner to have, putting a star next to the most important ones.

This is an opportunity to get clear about what you've learned from your previous relationships, and where your values lie for your romantic future.

Of course, this list can evolve as time goes on. You may meet someone and find that, actually, you're happy to compromise a little. However, if you don't get clear on where you'd like to end up, you could end up anywhere. So be specific and write down what it is you desire.

Take Yourself Out On a Date

Get dressed up, decide on a plan that excites you and take yourself out.

The good news is that you get to choose every bit of this experience. If you're expecting someone else to enjoy a date with you in time to come, you need to learn how to enjoy your own company first.

Whether you're in a relationship or single, getting into the habit of wooing yourself on a regular basis will attract in the positive experience of love that you desire.

CONCLUSION

'You are here to enrich the world.'

Woodrow Wilson

While we'd love to tell you that by putting everything in this book into practice your life will forever run smoothly from this point, it wouldn't be true. The journey ahead may bring unexpected, and sometimes unpleasant, twists – and no amount of meditation or prayer can guarantee otherwise.

We are a delicate generation. We panic when things go wrong, have a tendency to lose perspective and are easily offended. Our culture has bought into the belief that life is about being happy *all* the time – which is why many of us are so quick to anaesthetise painful feelings the moment they come up.

But, perhaps life isn't about being in a permanent state of elation. As William Blake observed, 'without contraries is no progression'. In other words, we grow through contrast: discovering and appreciating what's of value and what's pleasing to us by experiencing, also, what is not. We often neglect to recognise that the negative and painful encounters are spiritual too, and that from times of despair come our most significant periods of soul-growth.

Every single one of us has a story: a series of events that have marked out our journey so far. As you've worked through this book, your own story will no doubt have begun to emerge more clearly. For those of you who've been replaying the same page of your life over and over, we hope it's given you the nudge you might need to turn to a new chapter. That's really what a spiritual path offers: a choice – the choice to embrace the pain we feel, with love – instead of running from it, in fear. By learning to breathe into our pain when it hits, we find that the low periods inject even more joy into the positive ones, as we begin embracing life on life's terms.

To help you continue on, keep practising daily meditation, as well as the tools and exercises that created the biggest shifts for you. Take what worked and keep working on it. Creating a routine will support you in staying spiritually fit and enable you to keep connecting with your inner guidance.

You aren't alone; there are many, many like-minded people on a similar path. We *are* the people we hang around with, so surround yourself with those who encourage and inspire you. Get involved with communities who share your passions, and events or support groups that speak to you. You'll find some recommended resources at the back of this book, if you need a place to start.

As we acknowledged in the introduction, 'The Parable of The Lost Son' echoes the experience many of us go through of losing our way, and then slowly coming back to ourselves. However, the story doesn't have to end with just one person's return home. Through your own journey of healing, a desire may have ignited within you to reach those who are still out in the wilderness. Even if, for the moment, that's just sharing one thing you've discovered through reading this book, your words may be the hope and strength another is seeking to find their way back too.

RESOURCES

Join Our List

Sign up at www.addictivedaughter.com to receive our weekly newsletter and updates about our latest events and workshops.

Connect With Us Online

www.addictivedaughter.com
www.facebook.com/AddictiveDaughter
Instagram @addictivedaughter
Twitter @AddictiveDau
www.youtube.com/user/addictivedaughter

Quiet-Time Practice Inspiration

Every morning or evening, we recommend setting aside some time for your daily spiritual practice. You could include two to three of the below ideas, and feel free to mix them up or change them whenever you feel like it:

Yoga
Running/other exercise

Walking in nature
Meditation
Affirmations
Gratitude list
Journaling
Listening to uplifting music
Playing an instrument
Drawing, painting or other creative pursuit

Our Life-Coaching Programmes

Work with us one-on-one – visit www.addictivedaughter.com to find out more about our life-coaching programmes.

www.heart-rehab.com – a twenty-one-day online programme which guides you to heal your heartbreak and find 'The One'.

Books We Recommend

Thrive – Arianna Huffington
Daring Greatly– Brené Brown
Women Who Run with the Wolves – Clarissa Pinkola Estés
The Seven Spiritual Laws of Success – Deepak Chopra
The Power of Now – Eckhart Tolle
Committed – Elizabeth Gilbert
The Celestine Prophecy – James Redfield
The Artist's Way – Julia Cameron
Money: A Love Story – Kate Northrup
The Road Less Travelled – M. Scott Peck
A Return to Love – Marianne Williamson
Conversations with God – Neale Donald Walsche
Eleven Minutes – Paulo Coelho

Light Is the New Black – Rebecca Campbell
Women Who Love Too Much – Robin Norwood
The Monk Who Sold his Ferrari – Robin Sharma

Music To Inspire You

Head to www.theinnerfix.com to check out our playlist (which includes all of the music referenced in the book).

ACKNOWLEDGEMENTS

There are lots of people who've contributed to the creation of this book in so many different ways:

Our literary agent – Ariella Feiner at United Agents, our editor Liz Caraffi and marketing and PR girls Caitriona Horne and Rebecca Mundy at Hodder & Stoughton – it's been *so* much fun working with you all.

Our friend, Sandy Newbigging, who came up with the title for the book in a moment of divine inspiration!

Those who helped us to create *The Inner Fix*'s brilliant trailer; Frogspawn Film, Michael J. McEvoy and actress Hannah Warren-Green – you guys rock.

Amy Leighton, our amazing assistant (quite possibly the most organised and productive person we know – we're so lucky to have someone like you on our team).

Our wonderful group of freelance and professional friends who've so generously gifted their time and skills to help us develop Addictive Daughter over the years (especially when dreams were big but funds were small!) – this book and AD would quite literally not exist without you.

Those friends and family members who've helped us with the editing process for *The Inner Fix* – your insights have been invaluable.

All the incredible women we've life-coached one-on-one so far – it's been an honour to have been a small part of your journey and we continue to feel inspired by your growth and progress. Many of you now feel more like sisters after working so closely together.

All of those who attend our workshops, events and watch our YouTube videos. You probably have no idea how encouraging it's been for us to receive your own stories and kind words of thanks over the years.

Our sponsors and fellowship friends for all your support, and the incredible wisdom and perspective we've gained from sitting in Twelve Step meetings.

Marianne Williamson, Marie Forleo, Gabrielle Bernstein, Neale Donald Walshe, Paulo Coehlo, Danielle La Porte, HTB and St Dionis Church, as well as all the brilliant friends and mentors we've made in the wellness world – you've all challenged and inspired us so much in our own spiritual journeys.

Charlie Mackesy for creating art work that moves us to tears every time we look at it (especially The Prodigal Daughter.)

Our extended families and close friends – some of whom are mentioned in this book, and many who aren't – thanks for the love you've given us both over the years, and for your reassurances during the more emotional moments of writing *The Inner Fix*.

Uncle Joe for being the catalyst behind us starting Addictive Daughter. From day one, when many people (understandably) thought we were crazy, your unwavering enthusiasm and belief encouraged us to pursue our vision until it became a reality.

Persia would personally like to thank her housemate Noo for being such a supportive and generous friend over the last few years, as well as her boyfriend 'Joey Wilderness' (who she met whilst writing *The Inner Fix*) – you're the most open-minded, fun and spontaneous twin flame I could've hoped for.

She'd also like to acknowledge her family's late dog, Elizabeth T, who lay at her feet everyday whilst she was writing this book, and her (surrogate) sister Salena, brother Toby and sister Evie for being such great siblings. Huge thanks to Joey for being the most loyal of wing-women – Addictive Daughter has been an incredible adventure with you.

Most importantly, she'd like to thank her parents, Mark and Jane, whose own story and commitment to healing not only transformed their family's lives, but was also a huge inspiration behind *The Inner Fix*.

Joey would like to thank her husband Luke, who patiently endured six whole months of book writing from the moment they touched back down in the UK, post honeymoon. Thank you, Bear, for the deep chats and helping me keep perspective during this often emotional writing process!

She'd also like to acknowledge her beautiful sister, Dani – whose fleeting mention in the book in *no way* reflects her importance and the love Joey has for her. Gratitude to Persia, for the exhilarating journey together so far and for being the risk-taker of their dynamic duo.

And finally, the biggest thank you and 'I love you' of all, is owed to her parents – for whom this book certainly wasn't an easy read. She'd like to thank them for their continued love, belief, support and generosity over the years – you could not have done more.

Continue your journey to being stronger, happier and braver with

THE INNER FIX
app